Collaborate Now!

Those who seek change in civic life have much in common: they each bring valuable expertise to the table and need to strategize with others about what to do. That's why new collaborative relationships between diverse thinkers are essential. Yet they're difficult to form. *Collaborate Now!* presents a new argument about why that is, along with tools to foster them anew. As with any form of voluntary civic engagement, these relationships require time and motivation. Yet on top of that, collaborators often start off as strangers, and are uncertain about relationality: whether they'll relate to each other in ways that are meaningful and brimming with interaction. Using case studies, field experiments, interviews, and observational data, this book provides a rich understanding of the collaborative relationships needed to tackle civic challenges, how uncertainty about relationality can produce an unmet desire for them, and actionable tools to surface and meet this desire.

Adam Seth Levine is SNF Agora Associate Professor of Health Policy and Management at Johns Hopkins University. He conducts research on how people with diverse forms of expertise collaborate to tackle problems. He is also President of research4impact, a nonprofit that creates powerful collaborative relationships among researchers, practitioners, and policymakers.

T0384778

Collaborate Now!

How Expertise Becomes Useful in Civic Life

ADAM SETH LEVINE
Johns Hopkins University

CAMBRIDGE
UNIVERSITY PRESS

Shaftesbury Road, Cambridge CB2 8EA, United Kingdom

One Liberty Plaza, 20th Floor, New York, NY 10006, USA

477 Williamstown Road, Port Melbourne, VIC 3207, Australia

314–321, 3rd Floor, Plot 3, Splendor Forum, Jasola District Centre,
New Delhi – 110025, India

103 Penang Road, #05–06/07, Visioncrest Commercial, Singapore 238467

Cambridge University Press is part of Cambridge University Press & Assessment,
a department of the University of Cambridge.

We share the University's mission to contribute to society through the pursuit of
education, learning and research at the highest international levels of excellence.

www.cambridge.org
Information on this title: www.cambridge.org/9781009411905

DOI: 10.1017/9781009411882

First published 2024

A catalogue record for this publication is available from the British Library

Library of Congress Cataloging-in-Publication Data
NAMES: Levine, Adam Seth, 1981– author.
TITLE: Collaborate now! : how expertise becomes useful in civic life / Adam
Seth Levine.
DESCRIPTION: Cambridge, United Kingdom ; New York, NY : Cambridge
University Press, 2024. | Includes bibliographical references and index.
IDENTIFIERS: LCCN 2023039712 | ISBN 9781009411905 (hardback) |
ISBN 9781009411882 (ebook)
SUBJECTS: LCSH: Policy sciences – United States. | Expertise – Political
aspects – United States. | Cooperation – United States. | Public
administration – United States – Citizen participation. | Civic
improvement – United States. | Community organization – United States.
CLASSIFICATION: LCC H97.L49 2024 | DDC 307.1/20973–DC23/eng/20231128
LC record available at https://lccn.loc.gov/2023039712

ISBN 978-1-009-41190-5 Hardback
ISBN 978-1-009-41187-5 Paperback

Contents

Figures

Tables

Acknowledgments

The origin of this book is somewhat unusual. In 2017, I was involved with starting a nonprofit organization to enable people with diverse forms of expertise to build new collaborative relationships. My cofounders and I thought it would work, yet it didn't. The research that I conducted for this book grew out of a desire to understand why it failed and what we needed to do instead. It also grew out of something much broader – a recognition that what we were observing raised deeper questions about civic life and civic engagement that could only be answered by embarking on new research.

The name of the nonprofit is research4impact. In 2017, Don Green, Jake Bowers, and I started it, and the initial version (research4impact 1.0, so to speak) was a LinkedIn-style online platform in which researchers and practitioners could build profiles and then reach out to each other to form new collaborative relationships. We knew that great things could happen – valuable new knowledge exchange to inform strategic decision-making, and impactful new projects – when people from these different sectors engaged with each other around issues facing communities they care about.

Yet the problem we observed was that, while hundreds of people built profiles on the online platform, very few actually reached out to anyone else. This outcome was disappointing, but it also motivated us to try to understand what went wrong. So, I reached out to several people to learn about their experiences and, importantly, their hesitations. Over time my thinking broadened, as I realized that this experience was just the tip of the iceberg. While the initial research4impact experience was specifically about connecting researchers and practitioners, what we were observing was one example of something more fundamental about civic life: the fact that valuable new collaborative relationships between people with diverse forms of expertise do not always arise on their own.

The upshot was that I started the research in this book initially with a particular use in mind – to figure out how a revised research4impact could work better – yet along the way I realized that there was much to learn about the science of collaboration and its role in civic life more broadly. The result is an example of what the political scientist Donald Stokes has called *use-inspired basic research*.

All of this is to say: Writing this book has been an amazing journey, and it would not have happened without the support, thought partnership, and inspiration from so many important people along the way.

First, I want to thank Don Green and Jake Bowers, my research4impact co-founders. The three of us have worked closely from the very beginning, and they were incredibly supportive and encouraging as I took the lead on several new organizational initiatives (and were the ones who initially suggested that I should be president of the organization). They have always been open and eager to strategize and offer ideas for what to do next, and great friendships have emerged from our work together.

I am also extremely thankful for the opportunity to work with many others who have joined the research4impact team and poured their ideas and energy into growing its reach and impact, including Betsy Brunner, Logan Casey, Sarah Gollust, Malliga Och, Beatriz Rey, and Madison Shumway.

Speaking of research4impact, profound thanks go to Elizabeth Christopherson, President of the Rita Allen Foundation. She has been one of the biggest champions of research4impact since the early days, along with the need for research on the science of collaboration more generally. And on top of that, she's a dedicated community builder, and I've greatly enjoyed the opportunity to become part of the thriving civic science community thanks to her.

Within the civic science community, I am especially grateful for the insightful conversations about the content of this book with Peter Levine (who also read and offered terrific feedback on parts of it!), Karen Andrade, Mariette DiChristina-Gerosa, Blake McGhghy, Holly Rhodes, Dietram Scheufele, and Tiffany Taylor.

My endless and deepest thanks go to Hahrie Han, for many reasons. As research4impact pivoted from the online platform in 2017 ("research4impact 1.0") to a more successful hands-on matchmaking model in 2018 ("research4impact 2.0"), she was the first person to suggest that I should write about our experiences and what we were learning, and she also encouraged me to explore the deeper questions about civic life that our experiences were raising. Since then, as the broader research agenda on the science of collaboration has taken shape, Hahrie has always been one of my biggest champions, and I am so incredibly grateful for her support, ideas, feedback, encouragement, and, above all, friendship.

I also owe profound thanks to several Johns Hopkins colleagues in addition to Hahrie who offered great feedback on various aspects of the book, and more generally have been great mentors, friends, and colleagues as I got settled at JHU: Keshia Pollack Porter and Beth McGinty (my two faculty mentors who truly went above and beyond to make me feel welcome as a new faculty member in the public health school), Colleen Barry, Vadim Dukhanin, Henry Farrell, Shannon Frattaroli, Shelley Hearne, Jill Marsteller, Stephen Ruckman, Kristina Weeks, Christine Weston, and Albert Wu.

I would also like to thank several incredible coauthors who I have had the great fortune to work with on projects related to the science of collaboration (many of which are discussed in this book), including Lomax Boyd, David Broockman, Elizabeth Day, Jeff Kahn, Josh Kalla, Lia Kelinsky-Jones, and Debra Mathews.

I owe great thanks to several people who share a deep passion for creating new collaborative relationships in civic life, and who generously shared details about their work with me that I discuss in the book: Angela Bednarek, Max Crowley, Nina Hall, Zeyneb Magavi, Ivvet Modinou, Danielle Mulligan, Justin Rolfe-Redding, Taylor Scott, John Tracey, Kelsa Trom, David Yokum, and Jack Zhou.

For insightful conversations about the content in this book (and many related topics), I offer immense thanks to several colleagues across academia, government, philanthropy, and the nonprofit sectors: Carina Barnett-Loro, Arlene Bierman, Dan Butler, Ali Cirone, Cynthia Coburn, Jamie Druckman, Diana Epstein, Shana Gadarian, Elisabeth Gerber, Kristin Goss, Jennifer Grodsky, Danny Hayes, Eitan Hersh, Geoff Hunt, Sabrina Karim, Judith Kelley, Skip Lupia, Mike Manville, Mary McGrath, Jamila Michener, Ben Miyamoto, Caroline Montojo, Megan Mullin, Michael Neblo, Chris O'Connell, Tom Pepinsky, Hannah Safford, Jen Selin, John Sides, Kathy Stack, Dara Strolovitch, Lauren Supplee, and Josh Trapani.

I've been incredibly grateful to present the ideas in this book in a wide variety of venues, which has always opened my eyes to new ways of thinking about the science of collaboration. I want to acknowledge excellent feedback, questions, and engagement from audiences at several academic spaces including UCSD Political Science, USC Price School, The University of Hong Kong, Yale Political Science, University of Wisconsin-Madison Life Sciences Communication, University of Birmingham, London School of Economics, Yale Program on Climate Change Communication, University of Auckland Business School, Northwestern Political Science, NYU School of Global Public Health, Temple University Center for Public Health Law Research, and Boston University. I am also extremely grateful for excellent feedback, questions, and engagement from audiences in several cross-sector spaces, including the Civic Science Fellows, several convenings at the National Academies, Columbia World Projects, Simons Foundation, Rare's Climate Roundtable, Research Impact Summit, Spencer Foundation, Scholars Strategy Network, Maryland Governor's Office on Service and Voluntarism, White House Evidence Forum, Pew Charitable Trusts' Evidence Project, Midwest Transitional Justice Network, and the federal Agency for Healthcare Research and Quality.

I also owe many thanks to Robert Dreesen at Cambridge University Press. The initial idea for this book – the very idea that it could and should be a book – came from a conversation we had in May 2019. I casually mentioned some of what I was observing with research4impact and subsequent research studies, and Robert immediately asked: "When can you write that book?" And I was off!

And beyond all others, I am thankful for a wonderful family that stretches over several states and time zones. There is absolutely no doubt that they have always been in my corner, cheering me on, and for that I am immensely thankful. This is especially the case for one very special family member: my partner-of-19-years-who-officially-became-my-husband-while-writing-this-book, Bryce! He has provided so much encouragement, so much love, and extended so much grace when my head was clearly buried in writing. He also cheerfully engaged in so many rich and thoughtful conversations about the book – what to call it (he came up with the title!), how to structure it, how to tackle methodological challenges, what the audience can and should be, and why it's important. To Bryce: Thank you, from the bottom of my heart.

Expertise and Collaborative Relationships in Civic Life

In 2017, Don Green, Jake Bowers, and I launched a LinkedIn-style online platform to foster new collaborative relationships between researchers, nonprofit practitioners, and policymakers. We called it research4impact. The platform enabled people to build a profile and then reach out to others directly.

We knew that there was demand for new cross-sector connections. They each bring unique expertise to understanding and solving many problems facing communities they care about, such as climate change, poverty, low education, poor health, racial inequity, and voter disengagement.

The mix of people who built profiles was wide, and included grassroots activists, nonprofit program leaders, deep canvassers, policymakers, and researchers. For instance:

- A nonprofit leader who was designing new after-school programs to improve educational outcomes for young children growing up in poverty.
- An organizer who was building a local chapter of a nationwide network to raise awareness of climate change.
- A frontline grassroots leader focused on improving access to clean energy technology, like solar panels, in local neighborhoods.
- A researcher studying voter turnout among marginalized populations.

Overall, what they shared in common was a desire to improve communities they care about. Yet they often remained apart. Our goal was to build a platform to enable new connections.

At one level, the site was a huge success – 388 people built profiles within the first ten months! This means they recognized that collaborating with diverse thinkers in the network would be valuable for tackling the problems that they care about. It also means that, at some level, they had time available for this kind of engagement.

In short, they demonstrated interest and capacity and had leveraged an existing opportunity that was designed to substantially reduce barriers to forming new collaborative relationships. Based on traditional models of civic engagement that stress motivation, resources, and opportunity (Verba et al. 1995), we had every reason to expect they people in the network would initiate a flurry of new connections.

Yet they didn't. During the first ten months in 2017, only seven (!) people contacted someone else in the network.

This was puzzling. In part, it was puzzling in light of the aforementioned research literature on civic engagement and the fact that network members had already overcome so many hurdles. Yet it was also puzzling because, while there is substantial research on the consequences of new collaborative relationships in civic life and why these relationships are normatively desirable, what we were observing was evidence of a different phenomenon. We were observing how new collaborative relationships that people would value (given that they had chosen to create profiles on the site) may not arise in the first place. Rather, there can be an *unmet desire to collaborate*.

And it turns out that our experience with the research4impact online platform was not unique. New collaborative relationships between people with diverse forms of expertise often do not happen on their own, even among those who are interested and would value them. My goals in this book are to understand why this desire can remain unmet, as well as how to surface and meet it. What emerges is a new window into what the role of expertise in civic life is and can be, as well as new understanding and new tools for fostering collaborative relationships.

FUNDAMENTALS OF CIVIC LIFE

Those who seek change – grassroots activists, policymakers, researchers, nonprofit managers, people on the research4impact online platform, and community members – share much in common. First and foremost, they need to work with others. Collective action is a fundamental feature of civic life.

They also need to strategize about what to do. Recognizing a shared interest is just the starting point. Civic actors still have to agree on the underlying nature of the problem they want to address – a shared reality – and then decide what course of action to pursue.

This is where expertise comes into play. When strategizing, individuals bring unique expertise to the table. Expertise is "a superior quantity or level of knowledge in some domain and an ability to generate new knowledge in answer to questions within that domain" (Goldman 2001:91). Expertise in civic life may stem from knowledge gained via credentials, skills, and/or the lived experience of deeply understanding a local context. This is what it means to have expertise, though it may differ from whether that expertise is socially recognized.

Domain-specific expertise is useful because it can reduce uncertainty about the consequences of different courses of action. At the same time, those who seek change typically face problems with multifaceted causes and consequences that affect different groups in different ways. In these cases, no single individual knows everything that's needed to understand and effectively tackle a problem.

That's why civic actors can strategize by initiating and engaging in new *collaborative relationships*, which entail back-and-forth interaction ("talk") between people who bring diverse, task-relevant expertise to understanding and solving problems in their community (Ostrom 2010, Gazley 2017, Peter Levine 2022).[1] They are an example of one of the most essential elements of civic life: engaging with others across lines of difference (Allen 2023).

The knowledge exchange that happens during collaborative relationships facilitates an expanded understanding of the problem beyond what individuals could generate on their own. That's how civic actors go from recognizing a problem (e.g., children from marginalized backgrounds are underperforming in school) to reaching a deeper understanding of

---

[1] My use of the term "collaborative relationship" (and my argument that it is an important precursor to collective action) is akin to what other authors who study collective action have variously called talk, communication, interaction, and relationships (see Ostrom 2010 for an overview from the collective action literature; see Gazley 2017 for an overview from the collaboration literature; see Peter Levine (2022) for an overview from the civic engagement literature). Collaborative relationships would also count as a form of what civic engagement scholars Cook et al. (2007:7) call discursive participation: "citizens coming together with others in formal or informal settings – face-to-face or via the telephone or the Internet – to discuss local, national, or international issues." I further situate this book in both the collective action and the political talk literatures later in this chapter.

why the problem exists and devising a strategy about what to do (e.g., we need an after-school program, we need policy change, here's how to achieve those goals, this is how to evaluate our efforts, etc.).

As I highlight throughout this book, there is a wide variety of civic actors who are working to improve their community and would value the opportunity to engage in new collaborative relationships. This non-exhaustive list of the kinds of new collaborative relationships that people are seeking includes:

- Advocacy leaders with each other
- Philanthropists with each other
- Federal government staff with colleagues from other agencies
- State policymakers and in-state researchers
- Local policymakers and local researchers
- Citizen advocates and their representatives
- Community organizers and researchers
- Nonprofit leaders and researchers

For instance, suppose a program leader at a local nonprofit is designing a new after-school program to improve educational performance among neighborhood children.[2] He has already gathered a significant amount of socially dispersed information: reasons why school performance is low, what's been tried in the past, and how much money is available for a new intervention (and thus what's affordable and what trade-offs may be required). Yet because research findings are often hidden behind paywalls and jargon, it is unlikely he has access to what the broader research literature says about the educational impact of different kinds of after-school programs. Further suppose an education researcher at a local university has this detailed knowledge and shares a desire to improve educational performance, but also recognizes that much of the existing research was conducted in an entirely different context and thus may not test direct links between after-school programs and the specific performance indicators that matter most for this neighborhood. The implications of that work for the local context must be determined based on a detailed understanding of that context, which the researcher lacks.

In this example, we may reasonably assume that both the practitioner and the researcher would be interested in a collaborative relationship – that is, they would value the opportunity to engage interactively to talk through what is happening on the ground in this neighborhood as well as

---

[2] This is based on a real-world example discussed in Levine (2020a).

what the research literature says and how it could inform an effective strategy for the local context. Interaction is essential because the relevance of the research findings will not speak for itself. If instead the researcher just emailed links to existing articles, it is unlikely that the take-home messages about what would work best in this particular context would be clear (and even that assumes an ability and willingness to cut through the research jargon). Moreover, the researcher would miss an opportunity to learn about the local neighborhood and potential applicability as well as limitations of the existing research literature. All of that could inform strategic decisions about what topics the researcher chooses to focus on going forward.

All of that said, most practitioners and researchers are embedded in very different professional networks and may not already know each other. Thus in addition to demonstrating many fundamentals of civic life mentioned earlier, this example also points to one not yet mentioned: the kinds of collaborative relationships that are needed are often between people who start off as strangers. Strangers tend to remain strangers if left to their own devices.

One final aspect of this example is worth noting. When I say that the researcher and practitioner may value a collaborative relationship, there are arguably two broad types of goals they may pursue. They may wish to collaborate solely for the purpose of knowledge exchange to inform strategic decision-making (i.e., "informal collaboration") and/or they may wish to interact with the goal of partnering to design, implement, and evaluate a new after-school program together (i.e., "formal collaboration"). And these goals are not mutually exclusive – they may initially just pursue knowledge exchange, and then over time start talking about what a formal partnership could look like. Or they may start out with the goal of partnering on a project yet decide over time that solely focusing on knowledge exchange is preferable.

Either way, the general point is that it is critical to explicitly distinguish between, and legitimize, both goals. Everyday uses of the term "collaboration" often connote formal projects over which collaborators share ownership, decision-making authority, and accountability. Yet *informal* collaboration oriented solely toward knowledge exchange is important its own right and is sometimes all that potential collaborators have the need and capacity for. Indeed, this example underscores one of the key implications of this book: that we need to broaden the scope of what we often think of and label "collaboration."

In sum, this book rests on several features of civic life. Change requires collective action, collective action requires strategy, and strategy requires talk. These collaborative relationships arise between people with unique, task-relevant expertise who often start off as strangers to one another. Engaging in collaborative relationships with diverse thinkers, with the goal of either informal or formal collaboration, is a key type of civic activity.

WHY THIS BOOK?

Because collaborative relationships are a fundamental feature of civic life, many researchers have written extensively about them (and even if they do not use this precise term, they use terms such as engagement/talk/communication to denote similar back-and-forth interaction between civic actors who bring diverse task-relevant knowledge to problems). One line of work puts forth powerful normative arguments about why they should happen – why they are valuable and how to design effective and equitable institutions to foster new ones (e.g., Allen 2003, 2016, Anderson 2006, Farrell and Shalizi 2015, Pamuk 2021, Levine 2022). Another line of work empirically studies the consequences of collaborative relationships that have already formed, focusing on how variation in their structure or process (i.e., who's involved, how interaction is structured, etc.) can produce more creative and effective strategies for solving problems and/or spur the kinds of plans and commitments necessary for successful collective action. Some of this work examines new connections between diverse thinkers in general (e.g., Ostrom 2010, Page 2017, Phillips 2017), whereas other work focuses on particular pairs of diverse thinkers such as researchers and policymakers, among others (e.g., Bogenschneider and Corbett 2010, Hall et al. 2018, Bogenschneider et al. 2019, Crowley et al. 2021, Levine 2021a).

We thus have a rich understanding of why collaborative relationships (a) are normatively important in civic life and (b) can be empirically consequential once they've arisen. Yet we know less about how they arise in the first place, and why some arise while others that could have arisen do not.

This is nontrivial. We saw with the research4impact online platform one example of how new collaborative relationships that people would value may not arise on their own. And it turns out that this phenomenon of unmet desire occurs in many other settings as well. Consider these examples:[3]

---

[3] Many of these examples come from personal conversations with organizational leaders, and any unattributed quotes in this section come from those conversations. I mention this point in part because citing sources is important, and also because it underscores how unmet desire as such is not a phenomenon that we typically see written about in print. In these examples, I only learned about it because I happened to ask these leaders

- *Activists advancing transitional justice:* The Midwest Transitional Justice Network is a growing network of activists and scholars who share a desire to use transitional justice tools in their region. Network leaders know that new members join because they want to exchange actionable ideas and work with others who share their goals. At the same time, new members typically take time to figure out their place in the network and how best to reach out to others anew especially if they live in other cities and towns. They are interested in new collaborative relationships yet not always certain how and with whom to initiate them.

- *Grantees who face similar challenges in their work:* The Simons Foundation funds research that advances the frontier of mathematics and the basic sciences, and also has a division focused on science engagement. As part of that mission, the foundation aims to "create strong collaborations and foster the cross-pollination of ideas between investigators, as these interactions often lead to unexpected breakthroughs."[4] Moreover, foundation leaders are keenly aware that these connections often don't happen on their own and thus seek to actively build new ones. One example comes from the Foundation's Science Sandbox – an initiative that funds programs to create opportunities for individuals who don't necessarily think of themselves as science enthusiasts, as well as communities that have traditionally been "left out" by science engagement. Science Sandbox leaders know that many of their grantees are facing similar kinds of challenges in their work and feel "really ready to connect" with each other to share knowledge and/or possibly work together to tackle these challenges.

- *Evidence champions in the federal government:* in April 2022, the White House announced the Year of Evidence for Action, a new initiative to "increase connection and collaboration among researchers, knowledge producers, and decision makers inside and outside of the Federal Government."[5] Encouraging new collaborative

---

if there were challenges that either they or others in their organization were facing that would benefit from new engagement with diverse thinkers (or, in some cases, organizational leaders learned that I was writing this book and then shared examples with me unprompted). Indeed, this invisibility underscores why I believe new research on this topic is so critical.

[4] www.simonsfoundation.org/about (Accessed December 16, 2022).

[5] www.whitehouse.gov/ostp/events-webinars/year-of-evidence-for-action/ (Accessed December 16, 2022).

relationships is important in this domain given that individual agencies are often facing similar challenges and also because the success of any government program often depends upon the work of others. Indeed, one part of the Year of Evidence entails identifying "evidence champions": federal employees who already have an idea of the kind of information that would help improve the performance of their programs, and a desire for new collaborative relationships with others who have that information.

- *State policymakers*: several years ago, the North Carolina Office of State Budget and Management (OSBM) recognized that there was desire among state agency staff for new cross-agency collaboration as well as new collaboration with outside researchers and nonprofits. Yet it wasn't happening on its own, and so to meet this need OSBM created the Office of Strategic Partnerships (OSP) and the North Carolina Project Portal, an online portal in which state agencies could advertise questions they are tackling in their work and the kinds of diverse thinkers they would like to engage with to address them.[6] OSP, in turn, would help with every step along the way. In some cases, agency staff are looking for informal knowledge exchange – for instance, staff at the Secretary of State's office were looking for conversations with researchers to decide what kind of data they should collect to better understand the factors that influence business survival and success in the state. These conversations, in turn, would inform state economic policy. In other cases, agency staff are focused on formal project partnerships with other state agencies, nonprofits, or outside researchers. For instance, one opportunity posted by the NC Department of Justice led to a study of needs for reentry services and support for formerly incarcerated individuals in communities across the state, via a partnership with several nonprofits.

- *Local policymakers:* in the United States, local policymakers are responsible for almost $2 trillion of spending annually and are directly responsible for many areas in which technical knowledge and policy analysis research is both relevant and helpful. And, as it turns out, majorities of local policymakers, including those from across the political spectrum, are disconnected from researchers

---

[6] For more information, see projectportal.nc.gov. The portal was supported by The Policy Lab at Brown University, which has a Project Portal Initiative helping state and local governments stand up capacity to identify new collaborative relationships between government and external researchers.

yet express a desire for more collaborative interaction with local researchers to discuss policy challenges they are facing (see Chapter 5 for more detail).

- *Funders*: many funders, in both the private and public sector, share a desire to support scientific evidence that can help improve outcomes – to improve public health, reduce educational inequities, mitigate the impacts of climate change, and so on. While there have long been networks and spaces for convening around individual policy topics, what was lacking for a long time was the opportunity to connect around how to most effectively support and use research evidence to achieve these goals. Indeed, through individual conversations with many of these funders over the last few years, The Pew Charitable Trusts' Evidence Project and The William T. Grant Foundation realized that there was great demand for new collaborative relationships along these lines that were not happening on their own. That's what led them to create the Transforming Evidence Funders Network, which convenes "public and private funders who are driving change in the generation, mobilization, and use of evidence across a wide range of issue areas and policy sectors worldwide."[7] The goals entail both informal knowledge exchange about what colleagues are doing to foster effective and equitable use of evidence (e.g., supporting research practice partnerships, coproduction, etc.), as well as formal collaborations to tackle larger challenges, such as changes in the research workforce, measures of success, and incentives (Bednarek and Tseng 2022).
- Climate Advocates: Citizens Climate Lobby is a nonprofit, nonpartisan advocacy organization that seeks to build political support for climate action. One of its big activities is an annual lobby day in Washington DC, in which advocates from across the country meet directly with their representatives on Capitol Hill to hear their ideas and request climate action. Prior to the lobby day, the organization runs a Climate Advocate Training Workshop for first-timers. The members who attend are highly motivated, and recognize that the goal of these meetings is collaborative relationship-building, not just disseminating information. Yet organizational leaders created this training workshop in part because they knew that many first-timers were quite hesitant about engaging in new collaborative

[7] www.pewtrusts.org/en/research-and-analysis/fact-sheets/2022/04/the-transforming-evidence-funders-network (Accessed March 5, 2023).

relationships with representatives. One common source of hesitation is about what to say – for instance, is it appropriate and effective to talk about personal values during these interactions or should they instead just focus on the science and locally-relevant data?

On top of these examples are others that I became familiar with when I began running workshops on the science of collaborative relationship-building in 2019. The people who reached out to me to host a workshop were typically organizational leaders who, much like the people in the previously discussed examples, knew that there were people in their organizations who were working to improve their community and would value the opportunity to collaborate with others who bring diverse forms of expertise to the problems they were addressing, yet for a variety of reasons these collaborative relationships were not arising on their own. For instance, there were teachers in Ontario, Canada, who wanted to collaborate with parents to voice concern about new education funding cuts. And there were sustainability professionals at a nonprofit in Cebu, Philippines who wanted to collaborate with local officials to reduce over-fishing. And there were climate advocates across the United States who wanted to collaborate with local community leaders to promote locally rooted adaptation strategies.

Across the examples mentioned in this section, the contexts vary tremendously (and in Chapter 5, I cite several other examples of cross-sector and cross-organization networks that have been created precisely for the purpose of creating valuable new collaborative relationships that were not already arising on their own). Yet at a fundamental level, they are all examples of the same underlying phenomenon: collaborative relationships between people seeking change in civic life and who bring diverse, task-relevant expertise to the problems they are addressing do not always arise on their own.

And, because of this, one of the key implications of this book is that those who want to use their expertise to seek change in civic life (including those who lead organizations that seek change) should pose and answer the following kinds of questions: do we have the collaborative relationships we need to tackle problems we care about? Is there information that would help us achieve our goals more effectively? Who has that information? What kinds of hesitations do we have about interacting with them, and might they have about interacting with us? Are there new projects or initiatives we might want to pursue together? Why don't these collaborative relationships exist already? Posing, answering, and acting upon the answers to these questions can be highly consequential, as I show in several ways throughout the book.[8]

MAIN ARGUMENTS

Expertise becomes useful in civic life[9] when people share it with others, which often means engaging in new collaborative relationships. Initially,

---

[8] Here is one example of what's possible when organizational leaders pose, answer, and act upon the answers to these kinds of questions. In 2021, Massachusetts had a clean energy plan that entailed, among other goals, converting 1 million homes from oil- and gas-burning heating systems to electric heat pumps by the year 2030. The plan called for 100,000 conversions a year and included several programs that would help subsidize the cost of conversion to individual homeowners. The only problem was that it quickly became apparent that the pace of conversions was too slow and that the goal was unlikely to be achieved using these programs alone ("Massachusetts Should Be Converting 100,000 Homes a Year to Electric Heat. The Actual Number: 461." By Sabrina Shankman. *Boston Globe*, August 21, 2021).

Also, during this time, the Gas Leaks Allies coalition along with the nonprofit organization HEET (Home Energy Efficiency Team) had developed expertise associated with alternative strategies, such as networked geothermal energy (which uses a network of ground source heat pumps to heat and cool buildings), that could help Massachusetts meet its clean energy goals. This coalition forged new collaborative relationships with state legislators and other officials to introduce and explain these alternatives. The expertise that this coalition brought to the issue reflected a deep understanding of the core barriers and risks of clean energy transitions – hidden upfront costs and barriers that individual families face, the need to ensure that the broader electrical system can handle all of these new heat pumps at every scale, and the risk of rising costs for low-income families remaining on fossil fuels. This expertise is valuable for achieving clean energy goals, but had not been central to the conversation in Massachusetts up until that point. It didn't become part of the conversation, let alone influence decision-making, until this coalition created these valuable new collaborative relationships.

[9] In the book's title, and also throughout the main text, I mean "civic life" to refer to any situation in which people are engaged around problems of the common good in communities they care about. One question that sometimes arises is about the distinction between activity that is civic as opposed to political. Here I think it's important to acknowledge that the content of collaborative relationships (i.e., the strategy being discussed for tackling problems and improving the community) often varies in terms of the degree to which it is overtly political – that is, the degree to which the strategy seeks to influence elections, government, and/or policy-making. In some cases, collaborators may focus on most immediately influencing the activities of people involved with a civic organization. For instance, a collaborative relationship may entail strategizing about how to better provide services at a local free health clinic. In other cases, however, like when one of the parties to a collaborative relationship is a policymaker, the content may aim to more directly influence policy-making. Either way, I agree with the AAAS Commission on the Practice of Democratic Citizenship (2020), who write that it is often difficult in practice to assess whether a given activity is purely civic or political; in practice, many actions have shades of both. For

we might expect that having a back-and-forth interaction about a topic one cares about should be relatively easy and straightforward. After all, it's "just" an interaction, and we interact with people all the time.

Yet new collaborative relationships do not always arise on their own. That's my first argument: even when people who seek change in civic life would value connecting with others who bring task-relevant expertise to the problems they care about, these new collaborative relationships may not arise for a variety of reasons. This first argument simply names the *unmet desire to collaborate* as a phenomenon that arises in civic life.[10]

Next, why might desire remain unmet? As with other forms of civic engagement, resources and motivation are important (Verba et al. 1995). Indeed, I often find that when people encounter the argument about unmet desire for the first time, the explanatory factors that immediately come to mind are lack of time and/or, if the person is part of an organization, lack of incentives within that organization. While I completely agree that these factors are important, the research4impact online platform experience as well as many of the examples from the previous section[11] underscore how they do not capture the whole story.

Another possible explanation that people sometimes raise to me, and that I've had potential collaborators directly express on several occasions, is that they do not know how to find the right person to engage with. At first blush, this may sound like an alternative way of expressing a lack of time, yet in this case I would argue that we need to probe

instance, in the case of the free health clinic and given that better health often leads to more voter participation, there could certainly be downstream political consequences, yet that is not the most immediate goal of the collaborative relationship. I choose to use the phrase "civic life" instead of possible alternatives (e.g., "civic and political life") with the understanding that the collaborative relationships I investigate vary in terms of how much overt political strategy they entail.

[10] This point speaks to a separate question, which is: where does the *desire* in unmet desire come from? In this book, I take it as given that this desire exists – that is, that people who seek change see interacting with others who bring diverse forms of expertise as valuable to their work. This desire may arise organically (e.g., based on individual introspection, life experiences, etc.) or it may arise because people are presented with an opportunity that leads them to think anew on the kinds of new collaborative relationships that would be valuable for their work. In this book, I do not interrogate the sources of desire in each situation, but instead my starting point is that it may be unmet regardless of its origin. I also return to this point about the origin of the desire for new collaborative relationships in Chapter 6, when I present a tool that can be used to foster them anew.

[11] For instance, the organizational leaders who reached out to host workshops on collaborative relationship-building typically did so when their members and colleagues already had at least some spare time as well as when the leaders knew that they could identify reasons why a new collaborative relationship would be valuable (i.e., they clearly demonstrated both capacity and interest).

deeper to understand what people mean when they express this senti-ment. We need to ask: what makes it difficult to find the right person? And: when faced with the prospect of engaging with someone new who brings diverse expertise to a civic challenge they are working on, what might people be uncertain about?

These considerations help to motivate my second argument. I argue that unmet desire can arise because the new collaborative relationships that people would value often entail interacting with others they do not know. Moreover, strangers can be uncertain about how to relate to one another, and in particular, whether a potential collaborator will relate to them in ways they would like, and whether they will be able to success-fully relate to the other person. This uncertainty is a cause for concern that reduces the likelihood of engagement.

To unpack this second argument, I build from two key theoretical con-siderations. One is that when interacting with others, people care about what I call *relationality* – whether the other person will relate to them in ways that they would like, and whether they believe they will be able to successfully relate to the other person. Relationality can be challenging in practice, however, because "relating to others" is layered and may encompass many different elements, and not everyone will be concerned about the same elements in each context.

For instance, when I study new collaborative relationships that entail researchers with either nonprofit practitioners or policymakers, I find that people in these sectors raise some of the following questions, each of which speaks to a potential source of concern about "relating to others":

Will the other person be interested in interacting with me?

Will the other person value my knowledge and experience on the issue?

Will they believe that I value theirs?

Will I be able to competently share what I know?

How should I start the conversation?

What is appropriate and inappropriate to say?

Will the other person respect my time and organizational constraints?

Is the other person a trustworthy source of information?

Does the other person have practical information to share with me?

But typically no single person raises all of these questions. Rather, which elements matter depends upon the potential collaborator and the context.

Moreover, in other contexts, potential collaborators may raise entirely different sources of concern. Coming back to the White House Year in Evidence example mentioned earlier, and the possibility of new collaborative relationships involving "evidence champions," one aspect of successfully relating to those in other agencies or outside the federal government is the need for explicit permission. This is the idea that people within the federal bureaucracy may not feel like they can initiate new collaborative relationships with diverse thinkers outside their agency if they do not have explicit permission to do so.[12]

Stated at a general level, my focus on relationality may sound tautological – of course, relating to people is important for relationships! Indeed, that was often the response I received from people when I told them I was writing a book that centered this concept. I would receive responses like: "Don't we already know that being nice matters?" or "Of course you need mutual respect!" My response is that naming relationality and explicitly measuring the elements that matter to people in particular contexts is what's needed in order to influence behavior. If the argument is that potential collaborators need to be mutually respectful, then the action item is often unclear. Is it enough for a potential collaborator to just state "I am respectful" or "I am nice"? Or will those statements come off as awkward and/or disingenuous? The general point is that we need more information about how people define respectful behavior in a given context, or what they want the experience of interacting with a diverse thinker to be like, and only once we do that can we operationalize relationality and then form new collaborative relationships. This information is needed to "convert a social relationship that is initially costly – in that it starts without a preexisting supply of shared tacit social understandings – into one that brings mutual benefit" (Allen 2023:121).

Moreover, by paying close attention to relationality, we are taking seriously that interaction is more than simply two people engaged in one-way dissemination of information. As Page (2017:93) writes, "People do not walk into a room, dump their ideas on the table, and leave. Ideas are shared, challenged, refined, and recombined." Building on this point, I find that the elements of the experience that people care about can include a combination of the information being shared and also what it feels like to interact with the person who is sharing that information.

---

[12] For more on this point, see this policy memo: https://fas.org/publication/how-unmet-desire-surveys-can-advance-learning-agendas-and-strengthen-evidence-based/ (Accessed September 20, 2023).

The fact that people care about relationality is one key theoretical building block of my argument about why unmet desire arises. Yet by itself it doesn't tell us why people may be hesitant to engage in new collaborative relationships. For that, it also matters that new collaborative relationships are often between people who start off as strangers to one another. It's not only that people care about relationality, but rather that because potential collaborators are strangers, they may be *uncertain* about relationality. In particular, they may be uncertain that a potential collaborator will relate to them in the way they would like, and also be uncertain that they will successfully relate to other person, and both can be cause for concern.[13] The specific concerns people express will vary. One person may be mostly concerned that a potential collaborator won't value their task-related expertise. Another person may express script concerns, in which they are uncertain about what is appropriate and inappropriate to say to a potential collaborator. A third person may express both, or entirely different concerns altogether.

Overall, I find that this uncertainty about relationality can help explain why desire remains unmet. It leads people to refrain from engaging in new collaborative relationships, even if they believe that these relationships would be beneficial. It also helps explain what people mean when they say things like "I don't know how to find the right potential collaborator." This often reflects uncertainty about what precise expertise a given individual may have and/or what the experience of interacting with that person will be like.

This brings me to the next major part of my argument: how to meet unmet desire. One way is to create new opportunities that reduce uncertainty about relationality. As a general matter, being presented with opportunities can increase the likelihood that people engage in voluntary civic activity for a variety of reasons (Brady et al. 1999).[14] Here I

[13] Some people may use different words than uncertainty to describe this concern, such as ambivalence or even skepticism. Yet I would argue both of these imply being uncertain about whether the collaborator will be relational or not, and whether the collaborative relationship will be fruitful or not. This is why I choose to use the term uncertainty throughout the book. In Chapter 2, I discuss common sources of uncertainty about relationality when interacting with strangers.

[14] For instance, by providing information that reduces the cost associated with taking action, highlighting the benefits of taking action, applying social pressure, and expanding one's sense of possibility (as people may not have previously thought about it).

examine two ways to create opportunities for new collaborative relationships that specifically reduce uncertainty about relationality. One way is for potential collaborators to explicitly communicate in a relational way. This may sound obvious, but it turns out that it's easier said than done. In part that's because the need to be relational is not always salient to people in interpersonal settings. Instead we tend to focus on making sure that we competently convey what we know that is task-relevant rather than explicitly communicating how we will relate to others in ways that they would like (Wojciszke 1994, Kumar and Epley 2018). For instance, we are more likely to be focused on whether we are effectively sharing what we know, rather than making sure that the other person knows that we value their expertise on the issue. It's also easier said than done for the reason mentioned earlier: people may be uncertain about what elements of relationality matter most to their potential collaborator.

The upshot is that when we know what elements of relationality matter the most to potential collaborators, and we explicitly communicate in ways that overcome uncertainty about them, then others' desire to engage with us increases. For instance, if we know that a potential collaborator is uncertain about whether we will value their knowledge and experience, then in advance we can tell them explicitly about how we're interested in their work and looking forward to learning more. As I show in Chapter 5, this kind of explicit relational language can make a real difference.

A second way to create opportunities that reduce uncertainty about relationality is to enlist third parties. Third parties can include either individuals or organizations who are able to offer opportunities that entail providing information that overcomes initial concerns that potential collaborators may have. The argument here about third parties providing the right kind of opportunity is similar to that espoused by Neblo et al. (2010), who study the demand for public deliberation. In their study, they are a third party that offers a new opportunity to citizens to participate in an online deliberative forum with their Member of Congress. They reframe one of the key questions in the study of deliberation from "Who deliberates?" to "Who is willing to deliberate?," and in the process of doing so, their research question focuses on how we can create attractive new opportunities to discuss public issues. They find, for instance, that if offered new opportunities that depart from "politics as usual," then a more diverse set of people chooses to attend than the typical set of participants.

Their findings also speak to a broader point beyond deliberation per se: the power and possibility of third parties to create new opportunities for engagement across lines of difference. I find something similar with collaborative relationships between diverse thinkers who are working to tackle problems in their community. I study the impact of third parties who act as matchmakers (or what are sometimes called "boundary spanners"; Bednarek et al. 2018) as an example of an institution that helps build what Allen (2016) calls "a connected society." Matchmakers create new ties between members of diverse communities and, in the process of doing so, expand the set of personally valuable relationships that individuals can enjoy. They are third parties that can overcome uncertainty about relationality in a new context and also help grease the wheels of conversation in ways that the participants themselves may be unable to do.

Along these lines, and as I'll discuss more in Chapters 4 and 5, while the research4impact online platform presented researchers and practitioners with a new opportunity to connect with each other, it turns out it did not go far enough in reducing uncertainty about relationality. Concerns about how to engage across lines of difference stopped people from initiating new collaborative relationships. From the perspective of potential users, it wasn't the right kind of opportunity.

A final example is perhaps beneficial here. Consider how in some new collaborative contexts we entirely take strangers' relationality for granted. For instance, think about the experience of going to a new restaurant. While we do not typically describe this experience using mouthfuls like "a collaborative relationship between strangers to enable successful collective action," that is precisely what a dining experience depends upon: requesting a seat from a host and then interacting with the server to learn about the specials, order food and beverages, ask for refills, respond to questions about food preparation, and payment. When we do not know the servers, all of this occurs with a stranger.

Yet in these cases, many people don't give relationality a second thought. It's not that they don't care about it, but instead they just aren't uncertain about it. Why not? I would argue it is because we generally feel like we understand the script (what's appropriate to say and what's not appropriate to say) and we share expectations about this script with the people we're interacting with. We also believe that the people we're interacting with are knowledgeable and not trying to mislead us. In short, we are typically not uncertain about the elements of relationality that matter most in this interaction, and thus how to establish successful collaborative relationships anew.[15] This example underscores how caring about relationality and being uncertain about it are not equivalent. The contexts I study in this book largely give people pause because of this uncertainty.

Collaborative Relationships Can Have Two Main Goals

The core element of collaborative relationships is that they entail interaction between people who bring diverse forms of expertise to issues that affect a community. They are important in civic life because they help make collective action possible. Yet one question that arises relates to the goals of these interactions – when I say that they help make collective action possible, what does that look like from the perspective of the decision-makers engaging in them? What are their goals?

Recall the example of the after-school program discussed earlier in the chapter. There I identified two goals that the practitioner and the researcher may have when engaging with each other to promote higher educational attainment in the local neighborhood. They may solely want knowledge exchange to talk about what an effective after-school program should look like (also known as "informal collaboration"). And/or they may want to interact with the goal of directly partnering with one another to design, implement, and evaluate a new after-school program (also known as "formal collaboration"). One key distinction between these two goals is the degree of interdependence that they entail. When the goal is knowledge exchange, the practitioner and researcher remain independent decision-makers. When the goal is to partner on the new after-school program, then they are seeking a degree of formalized interdependence between them.

Stepping back from this example, we can distinguish between two types of goals that collaborative relationships may have: influencing collective action indirectly (via knowledge exchange, or "informal collaboration") and directly (via new shared projects/initiatives, or "formal collaboration"). Both can be impactful, and I discuss each in turn. One of the main arguments of this book is that it is important to distinguish between and legitimize both goals, and that's especially the case when trying to surface and meet people's unmet desire to collaborate.

---

[15] To be sure, this does not preclude the possibility that people still end up being wrong about the elements of relationality that matter most in a given restaurant interaction. Many of us have experienced interactions in restaurants that lead to misunderstanding. My point is simply that this is a situation in which, relative to those I focus on in this book, people may not feel uncertain about how to relate to others.

Collaborative Relationships That Influence Collective Action Indirectly ("Informal Collaboration")

The first way that collaborative relationships help make collective action possible is the indirect route. In this case, one of the people involved is a collective action leader – such as a community organizer, a policymaker sponsoring a bill, a nonprofit administrator who runs a team tackling a local problem, a researcher leading a research team, and so on. Leaders are important because collective action often arises in the first place, and is maintained over time, due to their extraordinary efforts to convene others and create new opportunities (Wagner 1966, Salisbury 1969, Frohlich et al. 1971, Baggetta et al. 2013).

These leaders need to strategize, and it can be helpful to seek out collaborative relationships with people outside their organization who bring unique, task-relevant forms of expertise to the problems they are tackling. I say that these collaborative relationships *indirectly* influence collective action because the people interacting are not themselves engaged in a shared project. The leader and the diverse thinkers she chooses to engage with remain independent decision-makers rather than seeking to initiate a new formal project together. Instead, the immediate goal of the relationship is for the leader to gain an expanded understanding of her strategic options – for instance, paths forward that might be most effective and/or perhaps stronger justifications for a particular course of action.[16] Or, put differently, the goal of the collaborative relationship is to help the leader answer the question "What should I do?" when making strategic decisions.

The existing research literature provides many examples of organizers, policymakers, program leaders, and others engaged in important

---

[16] A word on terminology, and how the terminology I use in this book relates to what I and others have used in other work on collaboration in particular (the content of this footnote appears in various parts of the main text, but I include it here as well so that everything is in one place). First, as noted in the main text, I define "collaborative relationship" as back-and-forth interaction between diverse thinkers who share unique forms of expertise relevant to solving problems that their communities face. When they are meant to indirectly influence collective action, collaborative relationships help leaders expand their understanding of a problem and possible strategic responses, while remaining independent decision-makers. In other work, I (and other authors) have used the term "informal collaboration" to refer to interaction with this goal in mind (Murray 1998, Levine 2020b). When they are meant to directly influence collective action, collaborative relationships have the goal of a new formal project/partnership/commitment among those who are interacting. In other work, I (and other authors) have used the term "formal collaboration" to encompass interaction with this goal in mind (Murray 1998, Levine 2020b).

new collaborative relationships with diverse thinkers to inform strategic decision-making in this way. For instance, studies of policymakers have found that they seek out collaborative relationships with researchers for a wide variety of reasons, including specific issues but also for exploratory conversations "to provide 'outside the square thinking' to expand their horizons and to enliven and inspire them" (Haynes et al. 2011:572). These back-and-forth interactions build awareness of a new problem not previously considered (Allen 2016) and facilitate the formation of more effective policy that leverages locally rooted knowledge (Ober 2008). State and local policymakers also want to interact with others from similar and neighboring locations to learn about public policies that have been successful elsewhere (Butler et al. 2017, Einstein et al. 2019). Community leaders – organizers, social movement leaders, program leaders, and school administrators – want to interact with researchers and others for evidence-informed strategic decision-making so that the people they are leading are being most effective (Farrell et al. 2019, Levine 2020a). Executive directors and high-level staff of nonprofit social service organizations want to learn about new modes of service delivery and advocacy, as well as gain valuable technical assistance (Alexander 2000, Gazley 2017). Finally, the success of deep canvassing[17] depends upon volunteers who are willing to initiate new collaborative relationships with voters on their doorsteps (Kalla et al. 2022). The same is true of deep canvassing initiated by candidates running for office.

Overall, when I say that collaborative relationships make collective action possible indirectly via knowledge exchange, it is an example of what scholars of collaboration have referred to as "informal collaboration" because it entails a minimal degree of interdependence between the parties involved (Murray 1998). Collaborative relationships that only entail knowledge exchange, even in the form of single conversations, can substantially impact strategic decision-making (Levine 2021b), a point that I provide further evidence for in Chapter 5.

Collaborative Relationships That Influence Collective Action Directly ("Formal Collaboration")

The second way that collaborative relationships make collective action possible is the *direct* route. In this case, there is also knowledge exchange

---

[17] Deep canvassing is a model for engaging directly with voters that involves two-way interaction between canvassers and voters about lived experiences relevant to an important issue, rather than canvassers only disseminating talking points.

that happens, but this interaction occurs among the set of people who aim to voluntarily pool their resources (and/or those of an organization they run) toward a project that entails shared ownership, decision-making authority, and accountability. In this case, the key question civic actors aim to answer is: "What should we do?" (Peter Levine 2022) and decision-makers seek a higher degree of interdependence. Directly working together typically requires individual sacrifice and some may be tempted to free-ride (Olson 1965, Wilson 1973, Rosenstone and Hansen 1993, Verba et al. 1995, Ostrom 2010). Interaction helps them strategize and also generate shared commitment to follow through on whatever strategy is decided.

Several lines of research, across the social sciences, provide examples of collaborative relationships directly influencing collective action. For instance, people who share a mutual interest in producing a public good or common-pool resource are far more likely to successfully produce it when they interact ahead of time to establish trust and shared identity (Ostrom 1990, 2010). Social movement leaders need to interact with each other and with new coalition partners to decide what strategies to pursue and especially to learn about tactics that have worked well for others (Ganz 2000, Teles and Schmitt 2011, Wang and Soule 2012, 2016, Van Dyke and Amos 2017, Han et al. 2021). Organizers directly interact with, strategize with, and hold accountable new budding leaders in order to build powerful new constituencies that are better equipped to respond to uncertain and changing political environments (Warren 2001, Han 2014, Han et al. 2021). Interaction is also essential when new cross-sector partnerships are taking root, such as when researchers are partnering with schools, development agencies, governments, or nonprofit organizations (Karlan and Appel 2016, Penuel and Gallagher 2017, Tropp 2018, Levine 2021a).

In all of these examples, the details are different, but what they share in common is that the people who are interacting are also the ones who aim to coordinate their behavior toward addressing a community problem they care about. Here, collaboration researchers would say that the goal is "formal collaboration" because it entails a much higher degree of interdependence than solely knowledge exchange (Murray 1998). This is encapsulated in the fact that the core question here is "what should *we* do?" rather than "what should *I* do?"

In practice, there are often degrees of formality. For instance, collaborators may decide to hold themselves mutually accountable to each other, yet not necessarily share much decision-making authority and/

or ownership. During the Covid pandemic there were several examples of autonomously-operating local public health officials who agreed to coordinate messaging, even though they did not officially share decision-making authority or ownership over a particular output. This point underscores how, once we are talking about collaboration goals beyond knowledge exchange, there are many different types of shared projects/initiatives that can arise. All of that said, for ease of exposition throughout this book I refer to formal collaboration as projects/initiatives entailing shared ownership, decision-making authority, and accountability given that most of the examples I highlight have all three attributes.

Summarizing the Book's Main Arguments

Figure 1.1 displays a summary of the book's main arguments. Several points are worth underscoring.

First, as shown in the second box, it is important to explicitly distinguish between the two possible goals of collaborative relationships in civic life: informal collaboration (knowledge exchange that indirectly influences collective action) and formal collaboration (new collective projects that entail shared ownership, decision-making authority, and accountability). Making this distinction explicit is important because, as mentioned earlier, when people think about "collaborating" or "collaboration," what often comes to mind is the formal goal – things like new shared projects, or serving on a task force together, or taking on an official role in an organization. Examples like these are certainly important. And they are often visible to outsiders,[18] which makes them both salient and also relatively easy to measure by organizational leaders, funders, educational administrators, policymakers, tenure review committees, and others. At the same time, they entail an ongoing and intensive exchange that people may not always have the need or resources to pursue, and thus can feel like a "big lift."

A collaborative relationship focused solely on knowledge exchange, which may take the form of a single conversation or a short series of

---

[18] To be sure, not all formal collaborations are visible to outsiders, but it is reasonable to say that examples are all around us. For instance, the product of a formal collaboration – the creation of a new after-school program or a new research project – is often immediately visible to outsiders. In other cases, the very existence of a formal collaboration may be newsworthy on its own, such as the launch of a new task force. In contrast, informal collaboration often happens in private between the people engaged in that knowledge exchange, not because it is necessarily secret but rather because of the nature of the activity.

conversations, is a much "lighter lift" and thus is more accessible to more people at a given time, especially those with severe time constraints. And it can be impactful precisely because it indirectly influences collective action (as I show in Chapter 5).

In addition, one goal does not preclude the other. Informal collaboration may segue into a formal partnership over time, or a collaborative relationship oriented toward a shared project may ultimately end up only entailing informal knowledge exchange.

For all of these reasons, one of the core arguments of this book is that, at a very fundamental level, we need to explicitly distinguish between and legitimize *both* goals of collaborative relationships. As I mention in the bottom box of Figure 1.1 (and describe in more detail in Chapter 6), individual civic actors can do that in their own work. So, too, can organizational leaders, who can foster new collaborative relationships by creating infrastructure that supports surfacing and meeting the unmet desire to collaborate among those within their organization, and also by demonstrating that they value forms of collaboration that are less resource intensive, such as informal collaboration, in addition to new formal projects and partnerships.

Second, the arguments in the third and fourth boxes in Figure 1.1 do not boil down to simply "relationality matters." The reason is because even when people know why they would value engaging with diverse thinkers, and even if they know that relationships matter in some general sense, the core challenge is that they are uncertain about how to engage. They are uncertain how to get from here to there. This is why my argument is not that we just need to remind people that relationality matters and leave it at that. A statement like that is not actionable for many people in many contexts.

Third, some of the examples cited earlier, like with the research4impact online platform, involve researchers as one of the potential collaborators. Yet many do not, and in general, the research literature (along with the examples of unmet desire discussed earlier in this chapter) identifies many instances of potentially beneficial collaborative relationships between non-researchers that also may not materialize on their own. Uncertainty about relationality is a barrier that is not unique to interactions with researchers.

Fourth, while unmet desire to collaborate may arise due to limited resources and lack of organizational incentives in addition to uncertainty about relationality (as shown in the fourth box in Figure 1.1), the large majority of this book focuses on relationality. In part this is

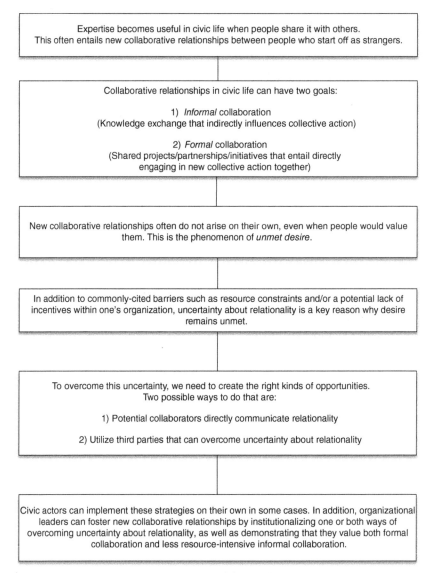

FIGURE I.I Summary of the book's arguments

because it is theoretically the most novel and understudied. It's also, in my experiences interacting with organizational leaders who are interested in fostering new collaborative relationships, the part most likely to be overlooked. Thus, the new theory and empirical work in Chapters 2 to 5 largely focus on unpacking what relationality is, why people may be uncertain about it when interacting with strangers, and how to create new opportunities that foster new collaborative relationships that overcome this uncertainty.[19] All of that said, in Chapter 6, I discuss a set of tools that organizational leaders can use that involve gathering information that overcomes uncertainty about relationality while also mitigating resource and incentive barriers that may exist.

EXAMINING THE BOOK'S SIGNIFICANCE FROM THREE OTHER ANGLES

Having presented the motivation for this book and its main arguments, in the remainder of the chapter, I examine its significance from a few other angles. First, I examine the way in which participating in collaborative relationships can cultivate our sense of democratic agency in important ways. Next, I discuss how many of the results speak to what some have called the "sorry state of science-society relations." Then I link the book's argument with three further strands of research in addition to the work on collaboration discussed so far.

Cultivating Democratic Agency

Thus far, when talking about the benefits of collaborative relationships, I have largely focused on strategic decision-making – how these interactions help people to better understand the nature of the problem they want to address, the range of possible solutions, the likely effectiveness of those solutions, and the possibility of partnering. Collaborative relationships with strangers make collective action possible because it helps people strategize in these ways.

However, that's not the only reason why they are valuable. They can also impact people's perceptions of their own agency as democratic citizens.[20] To see why, first note that in the original Greek, the word

[19] A core set of assumptions underlying Chapters 2 to 5 is that there is a set of decision-makers who would value interacting with diverse thinkers and also see themselves as having at least some discretionary time for new collaborative relationships (and at the very least are not disincentivized from engaging). The research4impact experience, along with the unmet desire examples mentioned earlier in Chapter 1 as well as examples of thriving third parties in Chapter 5, suggests that these assumptions are reasonable in many circumstances.

[20] One could easily think of other possible benefits from bringing strangers into interaction with each other, such as prejudice reduction and more positive inter-group attitudes

democracy literally translates into "people power," a form of government in which the people are empowered to "protect themselves against domination" (Allen 2013:1). One way people do this is through collective action – working with others to improve communities that they are part of. That work sometimes entails voting, but it often entails a much more diverse set of activities in which many paths are possible and choosing among them (i.e., strategizing) is essential. Indeed, that's why Peter Levine (2022) has written that working with others to improve communities we are part of and also engaging in collaborative relationships to strategize about how to do that are essential elements of citizenship. It's also why a common definition of democratic citizenship entails "an ethical notion of being a prosocial contributor to a self-governing community" (AAAS 2020:65).[21] As Alexis De Tocqueville observed in the early nineteenth century, Americans' self-understanding of active citizenship has long entailed people choosing to join with others in their community to identify collective problems, think about potential solutions, devise a theory of change, figure out what decision-makers need to be involved, communicate with those decision-makers, and ensure that solutions are implemented.

With this broad notion of citizenship in mind, collaborative relationships can enhance individuals' democratic agency in several ways. One is that, particularly when they involve strangers and/or people from other groups, they are an opportunity to learn that there are people we do not normally interact with who we can trust and who want to engage with us.[22] This kind of realization provides a "sense of freedom and empowerment" (Allen 2003:161) that is essential for being a prosocial contributor to a community. It enhances our own sense that we can play a role in improving our community in ways that we may not previously have imagined.

For instance, when I interact with researchers and practitioners who are connecting for the first time, this meta-cognition is something that they frequently share with me. Because such interactions are not common, and also because of stereotypes and other cultural barriers that

---

(e.g., Broockman and Kalla 2016). For a recent overview of the literature on the "contact hypothesis," see Busby (2021). For a test of the impact of fostering new cross-party dialogue, see Levendusky and Stecula (2021).

[21] Note that this definition is a broader notion of citizenship than another common definition: formal status within a state. This broader definition deliberately incorporates participation in common life and contributions to the collective good, all toward the goal of improving communities we are part of.

[22] To be sure, the opposite can happen too.

make relationality uncertain, it is not unusual for people to be uncertain about whether the other has anything useful to offer in advance of interaction. Direct engagement is one powerful way to demonstrate that fruitful interaction is possible, even in situations where people may not have previously considered it.

Another way that collaborative relationships with strangers can enhance democratic agency is by providing an opportunity to practice and develop skills associated with engaging across lines of difference. The collaborative relationships I study entail engaging across lines of difference that are defined, at least initially, based on having diverse forms of task-relevant expertise (though of course that often goes hand-in-hand with other lines of difference as well). They offer practice with the kind of talk that is important for democracy writ large (Anderson 2006, Farrell and Shalizi 2015).[23] The challenge, which echoes a key part of my argument in this book, is that realizing this benefit is not automatic. People who are diverse and otherwise strangers may not feel comfortable, nor have opportunities, to interact with each other. These skills must be practiced.

At the individual level, then, collaborative relationships are important because they enable new collective action and also because they further individuals' sense of democratic agency by providing an opportunity to practice core skills. For this reason, collaborative relationships – the act of interacting with others you may not already know and who bring diverse forms of expertise to community problems you care about – are a vital form of civic engagement. To be sure, any individual interaction may not be considered "successful" and in fact may be downright disappointing, or worse. Yet as with any new endeavor, each one presents another opportunity to further instill within people a sense that they have the ability and tools to interact with others in ways that are important for solving problems in their communities.

The above benefits all pertain to individuals. Yet they can aggregate in important ways. Here I highlight one societal-level benefit that can arise from fostering new interactions between diverse thinkers, which is that each new connection can also contribute to reducing inequalities in access to vital information in society. To see why, note that while everyone can potentially benefit from interacting with new people who bring diverse forms of expertise to challenges they are facing, it is also the case that some are likely to need these epistemic benefits more than others

---

[23] I discuss talk across another major line of difference – that between people who hold oppositional views on policy and electoral issues – later in this chapter.

at any given time. For instance, large well-resourced nonprofit organizations like the National Rifle Association have a substantial amount of researchers on staff and the capacity to keep up on the latest research relevant to their goals. Even if one might argue that they would normatively benefit from interacting with certain kinds of strangers, the people who work there may not feel that way. In contrast, a leader of a small, grassroots, purely volunteer-led gun violence organization likely does not have access to such an extensive research staff. If this grassroots leader is going to use research evidence to inform strategy, then he likely needs to engage with others that he doesn't already know. This example underscores how each new connection has a small part to play in democratizing access to valuable knowledge (it also underscores the importance of institution-building as well, a key theme throughout this book).

In sum, new collaborative relationships with strangers can yield three major benefits, two for the individuals involved and one for society. They can provide vital strategic information that makes collective action possible, help build individuals' sense of democratic agency, and reduce inequalities in access to knowledge.

"The Sorry State of Science-Society Relations"

My argument about unmet desire and uncertainty about relationality applies broadly to any situation in which diverse thinkers may wish to form new collaborative relationships (and especially when they start off as strangers to one another). The wide array of examples presented earlier, including advocates, federal government employees, grantees, and so on, echoes this point.

That said, my initial inspiration for this book was the lack of engagement on the research4impact online platform and my desire to better understand why that happened and what might be more successful. With that use-inspiration in mind, many of the settings in which I study the formation of new collaborative relationships in this book involve particular types of strangers: researchers based at colleges and universities (especially social scientists, and mostly in the United States) with either practitioners (especially nonprofit leaders, organizers, and grassroots activists) or policymakers (especially local policymakers in the United States).[24]

---

[24] I acknowledge that the distinction between researcher and practitioner is not always airtight given that (a) many nonprofit organizations employ researchers and (b) universities employ many people who are not researchers.

Given that, here I take a step back to pose the following question: why is it that researchers are so often strangers to practitioners and policymakers in the first place? And how does the argument in this book jive with growing calls to increase the societal value of science, or, as Hilgartner et al. (2021:893) put it, to repair "the sorry state of science-society relations in the United States"?

To answer the first question, the immediate post-World War II period is a reasonable starting point. During the war, the American research enterprise helped produce several advances that were crucial to the Allied victory, including the atomic bomb, radar, and the mass production of penicillin. As the nation looked toward peacetime, President Roosevelt asked Vannevar Bush, then the head of the wartime Office of Scientific Research and Development, to envision the role of American science going forward. Bush, in turn, argued in favor of major federal government investments in research to ensure the nation's health, prosperity, and security (Bush 1945).

Bush's proposal, *Science – The Endless Frontier*, ushered in a dramatic new era for researchers at colleges and universities across the country. This included a new argument about the role of science in peacetime along with an argument in favor of researcher autonomy to decide how the new government funding should be spent. In his report, Bush wrote: "Scientific progress on a broad front results from the free play of free intellects, working on subjects of their own choice, in the manner dictated by their curiosity for exploration of the unknown."

His document paved the way for a massive increase in government investment into scientific research over the ensuing decades (including a fortyfold increase for research at colleges and universities from 1953 to 2012; Sarewitz 2016) as well as the institutionalization of an ethos in which researchers are primarily accountable to their disciplines. Other scientists, via the grant-making and peer review processes, are their main constituency.

Over the ensuing decades, this ethos infused the large research universities as well as increasingly the entire landscape of higher education (Boyer 2016 [1990]), including those who do not depend upon large grants to conduct their work. While public engagement and teaching are valued more explicitly in some parts of academia, by and large the situation for researchers at colleges and universities in the United States is consistent with this summary offered by Christopherson et al. (2018:48):

Scientific culture does not typically nurture public engagement by scientists, and often discourages it. The guiding mantra for most scientists' careers is "publish or perish." Scientists must focus on writing grants, doing research, publishing, and teaching. Even if scientists want to take part in [new collaborative relationships], many universities do not adequately incentivize engagement, and professionals who enable effective communication about science often lack adequate support.

The result can be a gap between the boundaries of scientific knowledge and whether problems are being solved in the world (Sarewitz 2016). Thomas Insel, the former director of the National Institute of Mental Health, recently illustrated this point (2022). He wrote about a "disconnect between the work ... supporting brilliant scientists and dedicated clinicians and the challenges that faced more than 14 million Americans living, and dying, with serious mental illness." He notes that while there have been great advancements in understanding the causes of addiction, the neuroscience of depression, the genes associated with schizophrenia, and so on, there was far less systematic knowledge on the care that's needed to directly help people facing mental health issues and the poverty, homelessness, and incarceration that often accompany them.

Thus, the answer to the question of why researchers at colleges and universities are so often strangers to practitioners and policymakers stems in large part from the institutions and culture they are part of. First and foremost, they are generally accountable to the scientific community. This in turn has produced an equilibrium, in which they often don't reach out and at the same time, practitioners and policymakers also recognize the challenges associated with productive engagement. Strangers remain strangers, as each refrains from initiating contact and thus does not gain experience building new connections.

Some observers take this equilibrium as an opportunity to criticize science policy, the tenure system, and the value of using public dollars to fund certain kinds of scientific research. In recent years, such critiques are often well-publicized, as they feed into a broader narrative about anti-intellectualism and the death of expertise in American society (Hofstadter 1966, Nichols 2017).

Yet it is also worth noting that this equilibrium is not necessarily the way that people would like it to be. Many policymakers and practitioners welcome more interaction (a point I return to in Chapters 3 and 5 when I present further empirical work underpinning an unmet desire to collaborate). And researchers are not always satisfied either. A growing body of writing identifies effective new ways that they are working to bridge the divide, such as improving communication strategies (Lupia 2013, Scheufele 2014, Druckman 2015) and publishing blogs and policy briefs (Sides 2011, Skocpol 2014, Nyhan et al. 2015). In addition, there are some who intentionally seek out opportunities to co-design research projects with marginalized communities (Cooper et al. 2021),[25] non-profit organizations (Coburn and Penuel 2016, Karlan and Appel 2016, Butler 2019, Levine 2021a), and governments (Bowers and Testa 2019). That said, as of this writing, it is reasonable to conclude that, in general, researchers, practitioners, and policymakers remain "travelers in parallel universes" (Brownson et al. 2006).

This brings me to the second point about the "sorry state of science-society relations": a growing body of research that studies how to increase the societal value of science (e.g., Brownson et al. 2006, Palinkas and Soydan 2011, Oliver et al. 2014, Christopherson et al. 2018, Bogenschneider et al. 2019, Oreskes 2019, Hilgartner et al. 2021).[26] This work finds that one of the most impactful ways of making scientific expertise more useful is to build new collaborative relationships between researchers and non-researchers, thus bringing people with diverse forms of expertise into direct back-and-forth conversation with each other (Hird 2005, Nutley et al. 2007, Haynes et al. 2011, Dietz 2013, Oliver et al. 2014, Scheufele 2014, Druckman 2015, Bowers and Testa 2019, Peterson 2018, Bogenschneider et al. 2019, Levine 2021b).[27] For instance, Hilgartner et al. (2021:894) write that "building a … more inclusive dialogue between science and citizens is crucial for informed, democratic governance." And Crowley et al. (2021:1) note, "Growing scientific study of how to improve the use of scientific evidence has shed light on the 'social side' of successful research translation and evidence-based policymaking." During the Covid pandemic, for example, there were calls for new collaborative relationships between scientists and

---

[25] These co-designed projects are often called participatory research. There are several models of participatory research, as discussed in Cooper et al. (2021).

[26] Here I am largely focused on research with decision-makers as the intended audience, yet there are certainly other ways to increase the societal value of science for other audiences – for instance, improving science education and informal science opportunities for children, and creating science fairs and science cafes that seek to raise awareness among the broader public.

[27] The findings in this book are also relevant to our understanding of the Science of Team Science, which focuses on the impact of science teams (i.e., formal cross-disciplinary collaborations between people with a shared scientific goal). In their review of the literature, Hall et al. (2018) argue that more work is needed on researchers' decisions to participate in new cross-disciplinary collaboration (see pages 542–3). Along those lines, the findings in this book are especially relevant for thinking about when researchers wish to connect anew with those who have relevant expertise yet they don't already know. Indeed, on their own, researchers tend to work on science collaborations with those they've worked with in the past and/or those who work in close physical proximity that enables face-to-face contact (e.g., Lungeanu et al. 2014, Long et al. 2014, Vacca et al. 2015).

community leaders such as elected representatives, trusted faith leaders, and community advocates in order to broaden the participation of marginalized communities in both clinical Covid-19 vaccine trials and then later on again to reduce vaccine hesitancy and increase uptake (Warren et al. 2020, Public Health on Call Podcast 2021).

In all of these cases, the reason why collaborative relationships are so important is because they involve a back-and-forth exchange to clarify what the science says and also think deeply about how it would apply (or would not apply) in a particular organization, location, or context. Indeed, this was the situation of the researcher and practitioner in the after-school program example discussed earlier in the chapter. These relationships can improve the effectiveness of decisions – that is, strengthen confidence about the likely effects of a course of action. They can also make scientific research more useful in civic life by enabling non-researchers to question the assumptions, biases, and limitations that underlie scientific results (Pamuk 2021) and, in some cases, directly work with researchers to design new studies.[28]

A final consideration related to collaborative relationships as a core mechanism for increasing the societal value of science stems from the other side: why researchers should want to engage in new collaborative relationships with non-researchers. One reason is that people typically choose research-based careers with the twin goals of advancing scientific understanding and helping to solve real-world problems in communities that they care about (Levine and Matias 2021). Yet over time the incentives can make it easier to solely choose research questions that fill an identifiable gap in the scientific literature (given the fact that researchers are held accountable to the scientific community). Collaborative relationships oriented toward knowledge exchange with practitioners

---

[28] There is also a robust literature on how policymakers and practitioners use the research discussed in collaborative relationships. This work finds that a direct translation of research into policy and practice is possible but unlikely (Weiss 1989, Nutley et al. 2007, Brossard and Lewenstein 2009, Bogenschneider and Corbett 2010, Cartwright and Hardie 2012, Cairney 2016). Instead, policymakers and practitioners are more likely to use it to gain an overview of a research literature that advances strategic decision-making, help inform an immediate evidence-based decision, re-think how to conceptualize and measure the impact of their work, build a broader coalition of support, and/or justify existing decisions. Some, too, use it as a basis for forming new formal partnerships or task forces (Haynes et al. 2011, Levine 2020a). Overall, when we think about the possible uses of research in policy and practice, Gamoran (2018:185) notes: "A realistic goal is to have [information] present for consideration rather than assuming it will dominate the decision process."

and policymakers can be a relatively easy and low-cost way to gather feedback on community priorities and also take stock of how well (or not well) the scientific literature speaks to them. This feedback may not always dominate researchers' decision processes, yet it can help ensure that community needs are present for consideration when scientists are deciding what to study. That exchange is valuable as an end to itself or with the goal of a formal research partnership.[29]

Further Links to Existing Research

By unpacking the phenomenon of unmet desire to collaborate in civic life, and investigating ways to meet that desire, the theory and findings in this book are relevant to several strands of research. Three have already been mentioned: previous research on collaborative relationships (i.e., research on their consequences and normative desirability), the use of research evidence in policy and practice, and the role of expertise in democracy writ large. In this section, I identify three other strands: the literature on voluntary collective action, political talk, and civic competence.

Voluntary Collective Action
A large number of scholars have studied the conditions that make collective action possible (e.g., Olson 1965, Salisbury 1969, Wilson 1973, Ostrom 1990, Walker 1991, Rothenberg 1992, Rosenstone and Hansen 1993, Verba et al. 1995, Baumgartner and Leech 1998, Berry 1999, Ganz 2000, Putnam and Feldstein 2003, Skocpol 2003, Goss 2006, Strolovitch 2007, Han 2009, Jacobs et al. 2009, Munson 2009, Balliet 2010, Green and Gerber 2010, Teles and Schmitt 2011, Garcia Bedolla and Michelson 2012, Sinclair 2012, Wang and Soule 2012, 2016, Baggetta et al. 2013, Ahlquist and Levi 2014, McKenna and Han 2014, Albertson and Gadarian 2015, Levine 2015, Klar and Krupnikov 2016, Van Dyke and Amos 2017, Green and Gerber 2019, Neblo et al. 2019, Hersh 2020,

---

[29] Here I am largely focused on why researchers should want to engage in new collaborative relationships in general with practitioners, policymakers, and other community members (i.e., why they should value back-and-forth interaction with these types of diverse thinkers oriented toward an expanded understanding of a problem they are studying and interested in). As noted in the main text, the goal of these collaborative relationships can be either knowledge exchange itself, or more formal collaboration. For those who have formal collaboration entailing research as their goal (i.e., collaborative relationships with the goal of conducting a research project together), I include a step-by-step guide for doing so in Appendix C.

Han et al. 2021, Hayes and Lawless 2021, Lacombe 2021, Levine 2022, Kalla et al. 2022). Many of these studies, like mine, emphasize the importance of back-and-forth interaction as vital precursors to successful collective action. Yet once we know that interaction is important, it remains an open question how that interaction arises in the first place and why it arises in some cases and not others. Sometimes new collective action may arise among people who already know each other and need to talk only for the purpose of making commitments. In those cases, people are not strangers, and so uncertainty about relationality may not apply. In other cases, factors such as geographic proximity or organizational affiliation may mean that talk is not voluntary in any meaningful way. Yet in situations where the people who want to share expertise begin as strangers, and they face the decision of whether to interact in the first place, then overcoming uncertainty about relationality is a vital and non-trivial precursor.

My focus on relationality – what it is, why people may be uncertain about it, how uncertainty impacts the demand to engage with strangers around shared community problems, and how to create opportunities to overcome this uncertainty – aims to fill this important gap, and thus contributes new understanding to our knowledge of the conditions that make collective action possible.

Last, I should acknowledge that many of the studies cited above focus on important precursors to collective action other than interaction (e.g., attributes of individuals being targeted, type of communication being used, etc.). The findings in this book are relevant for those studies as well because, in any situation in which an organization is communicating in a way intended to activate others, there was likely some set of collaborative relationships that had to develop beforehand in order to strategize – to decide to pursue one communication strategy versus other possibilities. Thus, even if this strategy-setting was not the focal variable being studied in previous research, it was nonetheless an important background condition. Focusing on relationality provides a basis for interrogating participation in those strategic decisions, and leads us to ask questions about who might have chosen to take part and who may have refrained.

Talk

The second strand of related work examines the prevalence of talk in civic life, or what is alternatively called discursive participation, political conversation, or deliberation. As mentioned earlier, interacting directly with others, and in particular communicating across lines of difference, has long been seen as an essential element of a healthy public square (e.g., Mill 1956, Habermas 1989). Many studies of talk in civic life focus on interactions with others who espouse conflicting views (Huckfeldt et al. 2004, Mutz 2006).

The present study of collaborative relationships builds on and contributes to this literature in two ways. First, while collaborative relationships are also examples of communication across lines of difference, they differ in the sense that the "line of difference" is based on having diverse forms of task-related expertise instead of conflicting views on political matters. Previous work that emphasizes the latter focuses on discussion between people who differ based on party identification, vote choice, demographic attributes, and perceptions of whether others share or oppose one's own political views (Mutz 2006, Eveland et al. 2011). To be sure, those with diverse task-related expertise may also differ along these lines, but they also may not, and in any event, it is the diverse forms of expertise that are the initial impetus for engagement in the collaborative relationships I am studying.

The present book also contributes to our understanding of talk across lines of difference by examining a different form that it may take. Past work focuses on two broad forms: informal conversation and formal deliberation (or what is sometimes called "public deliberation"). Informal conversation entails "interpersonal and small-group interactions about the broad topics of politics that take place outside of formal deliberative settings" (Eveland et al. 2011:61). Formal deliberation entails rule-bound settings that convene a group of people to discuss a public issue that affects people. Some of the most common forms are deliberative town halls, deliberative polls, Citizens Initiative Reviews, and participatory budgeting (Fung 2003, Gastil and Levine 2005, Fishkin 2011, Neblo et al. 2010, 2019). It may also include small, rule-bound discussion groups (e.g., Frohlich and Oppenheimer 1992, Karpowitz et al. 2012).

At some level, the collaborative relationships that I focus on in this book would be considered an example of informal political conversation (Eveland et al. 2011). Just like those, they entail the exchange of information between people who bring diverse forms of expertise to an issue that pertains to the community writ large. Yet there are two key ways in which they are distinct from the types of informal conversation that have typically been the focus of past work. One is that they often occur between strangers, whereas the types of informal conversations that have been the focus of past work entail people who already know each other (e.g., Wyatt et al. 2000, Cramer Walsh

2004, Jacobs et al. 2009, Cramer 2016). Cramer studies pre-existing coffee klatches, and Jacobs et al., in their nationally representative survey, ask respondents about how often they engage in "informal face-to-face or phone conversations or exchanges with people you know about public issues that are local, national, or international concerns." The second difference concerns content. As defined, the content of most existing studies of talk is public issues (e.g., the wording that Jacobs et al. use, as noted in the previous sentence). The collaborative relationships I am studying are also about issues that face a broader community, but in addition to that they are distinctly action-oriented. They are about strategies that individual actors should adopt, alone or with others, in order to address a problem that the community faces.

The collaborative relationships I am studying are also, at least in some cases, different from previous studies of informal political conversation in a third way too. Many of those previous studies (implicitly if not explicitly) are about ordinary citizens who do not have official policy-making roles. While that is true of many participants in the collaborative relationships that I am studying, in some cases my data and examples do pertain to policymakers.[30]

In sum, one way this book contributes to the literature on talk is by identifying and then studying a distinct form of interaction called collaborative relationships. In addition, it also contributes by centering the inception of talk. Talk requires that people choose to do it in the first place. My focus on the possibility of unmet desire, and how uncertainty about relationality can help explain it, uncovers invisible yet important barriers to this decision. It also echoes similar arguments about authority and voice within already-formed groups, especially those engaged in formal deliberation (Mansbridge 1983, Sanders 1997, Karpowitz et al. 2012, Lupia et al. 2013). Here I study how these elements influence decisions to enter the room, so to speak. Last, this book also responds to calls by several other scholars (e.g., Neblo et al. 2010, 2019, Eveland et al. 2011, Allen 2016) for new research on the conditions under which talk arises and how we can create attractive new opportunities for it.

---

[30] Though having said that, arguably even the collaborative relationships that involve policymakers in my empirical analyses would still count as informal political conversation given that they occur outside of official meetings and between people whose roles are not formally connected to each other (c.f., Haynes et al. 2011).

Civic Competence

Research on civic competence studies whether citizens are making "reasoned, well-considered policy and vote choices" that are in line with their interests (Cramer and Toff 2017:755). While much of this work focuses on citizens in their capacity as voters, the core ideas are meant to apply to community matters writ large (thus, we often speak of *civic* competence, not just *voter* competence). One model of civic competence entails identifying tasks that citizens engage in, criteria for evaluating them, and standards for mapping performance onto evaluative criteria (Kuklinski and Quirk 2001). Traditionally, the standard applied was awareness of batteries of factual information about politics and public affairs. Using these criteria, most citizens were (and are) woefully uninformed about politics (Delli Carpini and Keeter 1996) and thus considered incapable of making high-quality decisions.

More recently, however, scholars have raised questions about evaluative criteria based on factual information batteries. One critique argues that we need to delineate precisely what information is necessary and sufficient for citizens to successfully complete civic tasks (Lupia 2006). A second critique centers the importance of not just what people know, but how they use what they know (Lupia 2016). Here, for instance, Cramer and Toff (2017) argue that personal experience is a key lens through which people interpret and make sense of factual information, and they present evidence of this point among ordinary citizens as well as elected officials.

Taken together, these two critiques point toward new criteria for civic competence. While citizens can (in theory at least) learn objective facts in the privacy of their homes by reading or surfing the web, learning about others' experiences and how those experiences shape people's view of community problems requires talking to them. Thus, Cramer and Toff argue in favor of normative criteria of civic competence that centers talk:

Rather than placing knowledge of objective facts alone at the center, this view of democracy also values the ability of citizens to interact with one another and share experiences ... Civic competence requires an openness to understanding the lived experiences of others, not just knowledge of facts. (758)

I concur, and I would argue that collaborative relationships are one example of the type of talk that's needed. By studying when people choose to engage with others in this way (and when they do not), my findings help enrich our understanding of how to realize this new approach to civic competence.

In sum, the theory and findings of this book contribute to research literatures across the social sciences that focus on collaborative relationships, the use of research evidence, the role of expertise in democracy, voluntary collective action, talk, and civic competence. In addition, as I describe more in Chapter 2, my theory of relationality builds on empirical work from the research on diversity in groups (e.g., Ridgeway 2001, Page 2017, Phillips 2017, Van Dijk et al. 2017) as well as the empirical literature on interactions between strangers (e.g., Epley and Schroeder 2014, Sandstrom and Boothby 2020). My hope is that researchers in those areas will find inspiration in seeing their ideas applied in new settings as well.

PLAN OF THIS BOOK

The book proceeds as follows. In Chapter 2, I present a theory of relationality and why it matters for explaining the phenomenon of unmet desire. This relatively brief chapter develops the main hypotheses, building on foundational work in sociology and psychology.

Chapter 3 provides the first set of evidence in support of this theory, using a combination of interviews and surveys to see if people use elements of relationality to describe why they would choose to engage in (or refrain from engaging in) new collaborative relationships. The chapter includes interviews with a wide range of practitioners, local policymakers, and researchers, as well as two national surveys of local policymakers and AmeriCorps program leaders. The survey results underscore how relationality in general matters, but the specific elements of relationality that matter most (and that potential collaborators may be uncertain about) vary across people and contexts.

Chapters 4 and 5 marshal a wide range of evidence – comparative case studies, field experiments, and observational data – to show several examples of unmet desire to collaborate in civic life, how uncertainty about relationality impacts it, and how the introduction of two types of interventions (third parties and direct communication) can overcome this uncertainty to create the kinds of collaborative relationships that people value. Chapter 5 also presents evidence on the impact of these collaborative relationships – that is, how expertise becomes useful in new ways in civic life.

Last, Chapter 6 pivots to talk about how to put the main results from this book into practice. I discuss three strategies that may be helpful, identifying the benefits and limitations of each. I also present a new tool, called an unmet desire survey, that along with follow-up matchmaking can aid implementation of the strategies. Last, I identify two key policy implications that (a) help institutionalize ways to surface and meet unmet desire, and (b) provide the foundation for needed future research on this topic.

The pivot in Chapter 6 to focus on being actionable underscores how my goal in writing this book is to reach two types of constituencies (which likely overlap): first, those who aim to deepen their theoretical understanding of civic life and, second, those who seek change in their community and are looking for practical guidance forming new collaborative relationships that would be helpful for doing that. The latter group includes the kinds of people who are featured in many of the examples in this chapter and throughout the book, such as those who are directly working to bring change to communities they care about as well as organizational leaders who see new collaboration as essential to achieving their goals.[31] They recognize that new collaboration often doesn't happen on its own.

My goal in writing a book that posits and tests a new theory while also providing actionable guidance for real-world civic engagement stems from its original genesis. The main idea for this line of research came

---

[31] For many organizational leaders who reach out to me about this topic, their entry point is a desire to foster "more collaboration" in an aspect of civic life that pertains to their work. Often I find that, at least initially, it can feel like there's a disconnect between wanting "more collaboration" and a book that focuses on fostering "collaborative relationships." The question naturally arises: are they equivalent or, if not, then what's the difference?

Given this frequent entry point to the topic, when I speak with organizational leaders who reach out to say that they are interested in fostering more collaboration, I often start by stating that this book is primarily about collaborative relationships for two reasons: (1) the term "collaboration" means different things to different people – as mentioned in this chapter, it can refer to either informal collaboration or formal collaboration, and (2) either way, the types of collaboration we're talking about often entail voluntary interaction between people who do not know each other or at the very least do not know each other in this capacity.

For both of these reasons, my argument is that we need to start with fundamentals: new collaboration in civic life often entails people with diverse forms of task-relevant expertise, who do not already know each other, choosing to engage in back-and-forth interaction with the goal of expanding their understanding of problems they care about. This is what I mean by "collaborative relationships." Thus, first and foremost, we need to understand the conditions under which people choose to do this (which is what the new empirical work in this book expands our understanding of). In addition, organizational leaders need to be clear about the differences between informal collaboration oriented toward knowledge exchange and formal collaboration oriented toward shared projects. They need to decide if they are open to one or both goals. Finally, given all this, then I offer tools leaders can use (such as the unmet desire survey described in Chapter 6) to help implement these ideas.

from the initial failure of the research4impact online platform. I was inspired to better understand why it did not work and if something else could be done.

In this way, my research is an example of *use-inspired basic research* (Stokes 1997). My rationale for doing the research began with a particular use in mind – meeting the unmet desire of researchers, practitioners, and policymakers for new collaborative relationships. But I also realized that achieving that goal requires advancing our fundamental understanding of why that desire may remain unmet in the first place. This meant that I needed to view the research4impact experience as one example of this broader phenomenon I've come to refer to as unmet desire, and then begin to unpack its origins. Doing so contributes to our fundamental understanding of when diverse thinkers choose to engage with each other (which is essential for civic engagement more broadly) and also informs the design of a reinvented (and as it turns out more successful) research4impact, which I discuss in more detail in Chapters 3 and 5.

Thus, on a personal level, I approached the topic of this book both as a scholar interested in the scientific study of collective action, civic life, and collaborative relationships, and also as a leader of research4impact hoping to apply the insights myself in that work. My hope is that the combination of scholarly insights and actionable guidance will prove useful for all readers regardless of their entry point into this topic.

2

A Theory of Relationality

Relationality captures whether we believe that others will relate to us in ways that we would like, and whether we believe that we can successfully relate to others as well. What do these judgments look like, and why should we expect them to influence people's willingness to engage in new collaborative relationships? Stepping back, how can they help explain the phenomenon of unmet desire in civic life?

Those are the key questions that I tackle in this chapter, drawing on insights from a range of social sciences. I have endeavored to make this chapter theoretically rich and well-grounded, but also make sure that I do not wade into theoretical details more than is necessary to motivate my key hypotheses. Readers who are first and foremost interested in seeing what relationality looks like in the world may wish to skip ahead to Chapter 3.

THEORETICAL BUILDING BLOCKS

My theory of relationality stems from several fundamentals of social cognition. By focusing on the conditions under which people choose to engage in collaborative relationships that are the direct or indirect precursor to collective action, I am assuming a mindset that is task-oriented. In addition, I am assuming that potential collaborators are strangers to each other[1] and engaged in either paid or volunteer work that entails

[1] To be sure, relationality also matters when potential collaborators are not strangers to each other. Yet in that case, it is unlikely that people are uncertain about the elements that matter most to them, and so the core focus of my theory and findings would not apply.

better understanding and solving problems in communities that they care about.

When potential collaborators are strangers, how do they form judgments about whether they want to engage? Social cognition research finds that people quickly and unconsciously apply stereotypes to others (van Dijk et al. 2017). These stereotypes are beliefs and expectations based solely on others' group memberships that are salient with regard to a particular task. Group memberships may include attributes such as occupation, education, race, gender, income, age, nationality, and so on. They can also be tied to organizations that people are part of – for instance, professors are often identified not only as professors, but as professors at a particular institution. The same may arise in professional settings (people may speak of "Harvard-trained lawyers," for instance). Moreover, the attributes most likely to be salient (and that are the basis of the stereotypes that potential collaborators are likely to form about each other) are those in which "the actors differ on the characteristic ... or when the actors perceive the characteristic to be relevant to the [task]" (Ridgeway 2001:358).

In the absence of more textured, individuating information that we have about people we already know, stereotypes can be cognitively beneficial because they provide an efficient way to assess others. However, they also have a downside, which is that these assessments can be biased precisely because they do not take into account the unique task-relevant expertise that a potential collaborator brings to the table. In short, they open up the possibility that potential collaborators have highly valuable task-relevant information to share, but that people opt out of engaging with them because they are not expected to have highly valuable task-relevant information to share.

Decades of research identifies two broad dimensions of stereotypes about others. As Fiske et al. (2007:77) write, "When people spontaneously interpret behavior or form impressions of others, warmth and competence form basic dimensions that, together, account almost entirely for how people characterize others." Warmth captures traits related to liking and also trustworthiness (i.e., perceived intent, or whether the other person intends to help and harm). Competence captures traits related to ability/knowledgeableness/skill – whether the other person is able to successfully act on those intentions. Taken together, these judgments reflect both the intentions of the other person and the other person's ability to act on those intentions.

They also, in turn, influence behavior, such as whether people choose to interact with diverse thinkers in the first place. To see why, note that capacity and attention are scarce, and so a key decision that any potential collaborator has to make is whether it is worth the time and attention to engage with someone else (Lupia 2013). For the kinds of collaborative relationships that are the focus of this book – back-and-forth interaction between people who bring diverse forms of expertise relevant to problems facing a community – and where the goal is to influence the shape of collective action directly (by strategizing about how to formally work together) or indirectly (by helping a collective action leader gain an expanded understanding of his/her strategic options), I argue that these judgments are based on whether would-be collaborators perceive that the expertise others bring is likely to be (a) useful and relevant to solving the community problem that they care about and (b) trustworthy.

So far, everything I have written overlaps with what we would expect if speakers were only engaged in information dissemination. And indeed if that is all collaborative relationships entailed, then they would be successful so long as one person recited everything she knows and then the other person recited everything that he knows, and then they each went their separate ways. The value of the interaction would be simply the sum total of the private information that each person knew when they walked in the door.

Yet here the goal is more complex. In collaborative relationships, each party enters with a mindset in which they are open to learning from others and recognizing the limitations of what they know. They want to be collaborative in the sense of coming to an understanding of the problem that is deeper than anything they could come up with on their own.[2] And the ultimate success depends on a combination of what each person knows in advance along with their ability and willingness to engage in a back-and-forth dialogue about the problem.[3]

The importance of dialogue underscores how there is another major aspect of warmth judgments in addition to trustworthiness, which is what Fiske

---

[2] To be sure, there are certainly situations in which decision-makers may seek out interaction with diverse thinkers but only as a pretense for justifying existing positions and strategies or to persuade others that their pre-existing view is best. In those cases, I would say that their goal is not to be collaborative, and they are not seeking a collaborative relationship as I have defined it. This example underscores why my definition of collaborative relationship goes beyond mere information dissemination.

[3] This may mean that their beliefs about the best strategy to pursue do not change, yet they were open to their beliefs changing over the course of the interaction and at the very least have gained a broader understanding of why this strategy is valuable/legitimate.

et al. (2007:77) call "relationship development" or "friendliness" (or what some call "likeability"). In an interactive setting, people care about whether the experience of interacting with the other person is likely to be enjoyable in addition to the information that they have to share (Leary 2010).

There is robust research literature on "talking to strangers" that conceptualizes and measures people's views on this interactive component. This literature is based on the long-standing observation that social relationships are strongly related to people's well-being. While traditionally the focus was on so-called "bonding ties" with close family and friends, more recently research has found that interactions with strangers can also boost happiness (Epley and Schroeder 2014). This research focuses on everyday "small talk" situations – those that entail interactions with strangers on the bus or train during the morning commute, in a waiting room, in line at a store, or talking to a stranger on the street. As with most small talk, in these studies, the actual content of the conversation is typically beside the point. Instead they focus on people's decisions to have (and the impact of having) a back-and-forth interaction with someone they do not know.

One key finding is that people often underestimate how much they, and their conversational partner, will enjoy the interaction (Sandstrom and Boothby 2020). Given a frequent admonition not to talk to strangers, this is perhaps not surprising. Yet it turns out that people leave money on the table, so to speak, by forgoing what could be very enjoyable and uplifting experiences.

Moreover, researchers have identified several sources of concern that help explain why people may be reluctant to strike up new conversations with strangers in these everyday settings (Sandstrom and Boothby 2020). These include concern that they and their potential conversation partner may not be interested in talking with one another, concern that even if they do manage to strike up a conversation, then one or both of them may not enjoy it, and concern that one or both of them lack the ability to carry out the conversation. This last point echoes the fact that although the research on competence judgments in task-oriented settings has largely focused on the quality of information being shared, it is also the case that the ability to start and carry out the conversation without awkward silences or saying inappropriate things can be a source of concern. Last, all of these are aspects of likeability judgments (which themselves are, again, a type of warmth judgment) and thus to echo the earlier point, we would expect that people make them on the basis of social group membership as well.

In sum, people quickly and often implicitly form initial judgments of warmth (trustworthiness and likeability) and competence. These stereotypes are tied to potential collaborators' group memberships.

On top of that, there is a related line of work unpacking the ways in which competence stereotypes in particular are task-specific. These task-specific judgments are sometimes called status-based stereotypes, as they reflect not just group membership but in particular the status of social groups and the fact that some groups are widely viewed as having more useful information for specific tasks than others.

Ridgeway (2001) summarizes extensive research showing that at least in the United States, gender, race, age, occupation, educational attainment, and physical attractiveness are common bases of these status-based stereotypes. For instance, in professional settings there are stereotypes that "men are better at some particular tasks (e.g., mechanical tasks) while women are better at others (e.g., nurturing tasks)" (358). As another example, consider new collaborative relationships between members of marginalized communities and researchers at universities in the United States. Here, one attribute that is especially likely to be the source of salient status-based stereotypes is race. Higher education in the United States is highly racialized (Miller et al. 2021), and faculty at colleges and universities are disproportionately white relative to the broader population (as well as their own student bodies).[4] These institutions have also been responsible for long-standing racist research practices (Warren et al. 2020).[5] For all of these reasons, we have good reason to expect that race will be salient, and disadvantage the expertise that racial minorities bring to collaborative relationships about community needs and priorities.

Last, note that these status-based stereotypes can influence not only how people view others' task-relevant competence, but also how they see themselves. Research finds that, because they are based on widely shared cultural beliefs, even those who are disadvantaged by them often still accept them (Ridgeway et al. 1998). The upshot is that potential collaborators may have overly positive or negative views of others' task-relevant competence as well as their own depending upon whether salient social group characteristics are high-status or low-status.

---

[4] https://imdiversity.com/diversity-news/college-faculty-have-become-more-racially-and-ethnically-diverse-but-remain-far-less-so-than-students/ (Accessed December 16, 2022).
[5] One example is the infamous Tuskegee syphilis experiment. In addition to that, as Warren et al. (2020:1) note, there have been "centuries of well-documented examples of racist exploitation by American physicians and researchers."

Two Examples

Here are two more detailed examples that illustrate what these judgments can look like in practice when people are considering new collaborative relationships.

The first example entails status-based stereotypes tied to occupation. Here I return to the example from the beginning of Chapter 1: a nonprofit program leader is revamping an after-school program for underprivileged youth, and would like to use research on child development to inform its design. In this case, a collaborative relationship with a researcher could be quite helpful, and the researcher in turn could learn about how well (or not well) existing research applies in this context. The program leader and the researcher may remain independent decision-makers, but the interaction could yield an expanded understanding of how to address a problem they both care about: educational inequities. Together, they could think about evidence-based ways to improve the program and boost student achievement, and that make sense given local needs and constraints.

Yet while there is a good reason for them to connect, a connection may not automatically arise. In this example, I focus on the situation from the perspective of the program leader. In the United States, there are widely held stereotypes that researchers are highly competent on research-related topics but also not particularly likeable (Fiske and Dupree 2014). Thus, if all the program leader knows in advance is that the person is a university-based researcher, then he may unconsciously infer that the researcher is well-versed on the research literature but also may not be enjoyable to interact with. One possibility, for instance, is that the program leader may expect the researcher to see her role as simply disseminating research-based information as opposed to being collaborative – that is, as opposed to engaged in a back-and-forth interaction aimed at coming to a new understanding of the relevance of that research-based information to his specific context. I would expect this concern to give him pause, and thus may lead him to avoid reaching out in the first place and/or not respond affirmatively if a third party were to offer a connection.[6]

The second example illustrates why we need to distinguish between the two major aspects of warmth. This example comes from a chapter

---

[6] The researcher may, too, have concerns that give her pause and which may or may not match those of the program leader.

in Linda Tropp's edited volume *Making Research Matter*, which examines the formation of new collaborative relationships between educators and psychologists (Tropp 2018, Maruyama and Westerhof 2018). Two aspects are noteworthy. First, there is a clear distinction between likeability and trust. One section of the chapter, entitled "Schools Don't Need Saviors, but Partners," refers to the mindset that researchers need to adopt when interacting in these settings: "Researchers who go into schools thinking that they have all the answers are likely to be met with skepticism and distrust, for the professionals in school settings have been thinking about the issues for much longer and in more complex and nuanced ways than have most researchers" (125). An entirely different section entitled "Trust is Essential" focuses on trust, defined as "the belief that each member will commit to the partnership, bring expertise, and help other members meet their goals" (126). Here the focus is more on the information itself, and how it needs to be helpful.

Taken together, the juxtaposition of these two sections of the chapter underscores how likeability and trust are both important and also not equivalent. Further echoing this point, the authors note that distrust can be present at the beginning of new collaborative relationships, and likeability can help to build that needed trust over time (126): "Although distrust is common in the beginning of a partnership, trust can be fostered over time and with effort through the development of mutual respect and valuing one another's expertise and contributions … and by shared goals identified or developed across partners."

AN IMPORTANT INCONSISTENCY

People implicitly and frequently make judgments of competence and warmth (trustworthiness and likeability), and they influence behavior. It also turns out that warmth judgments tend to come first. As Fiske et al. (2007:77) note: "considerable evidence suggests that warmth judgments are primary: warmth is judged before competence, and warm judgments carry more weight in affective and behavioral reactions." For instance, research on the workplace finds that they are a more important predictor of decisions to engage with potential collaborators for creative problem-solving tasks or even just informally for advice (Casciaro and Lobo 2008:678).

That said, an important inconsistency often arises, in which people downplay the importance of warmth when talking about collaborative relationships. This occurs in several ways. One is that it influences how people talk about the relationships that they want to engage in. For instance, as president of research4impact, I am often asked about the best way to form new collaborative relationships. These questions are invariably phrased in competence terms – that is, the information that people hope to gain from interacting. A community leader might reach out to me to express a problem they are seeing in their neighborhood and phrase it as follows: "We don't have easy access to fresh fruits and vegetables." Then because they know that one purpose of research4impact is to connect practitioners with researchers, the follow-up request might be something like: "I would like to talk to a researcher about whether a community garden could work for us and what the research says about the best ways to design it."

This kind of language is totally reasonable, yet when I respond, I always try to point out the important warmth elements as well, perhaps by saying: "We also need to make sure to find someone who will value the expertise that you bring to the table. That's in addition to whatever subject-matter expertise they may have." I'll admit that when I say that, people often consider it to be obvious after the fact, yet it also sounds unusual to them because it's not typically how we talk about the collaborative relationships we want.

A similar idea applies to how we explain collaborative relationships we observe in the world. Consider an example of a new community garden that resulted from a formal partnership between a local leader and a researcher. A common way that outside observers would describe what happened would be in terms of the substantive goals: "A community leader and a local researcher led an effort to build a community garden because there was no access to fresh food in the neighborhood." Yet such a shared activity requires substantial collaborative relationship-building to decide where to locate it, what to grow, who needs to do which tasks, and so on. That part typically occurs in the background, and often in private (not because collaborative relationships are necessarily secret, but instead because their value typically resides in the back-and-forth exchange between a small number of diverse thinkers). Here I would argue we should also explicitly recognize the importance of likeability: "A community leader and a local researcher led an effort to build a community garden because access to fresh food was challenging and also because they felt comfortable engaging with one another and valuing each others' expertise every step of the way." Again this revised language probably sounds quite unusual and wordy, but that's simply because it departs from the language we typically use to describe what's happened.

A final source of inconsistency is that, despite the primacy of others' warmth judgments, when engaging with others in interpersonal, task-oriented settings, we tend to focus far more on and evaluate ourselves based on competence (Wojciszke 1994, Kumar and Epley 2018). Potential collaborators are more likely to worry about whether they are able to communicate what they know "just right" (e.g., "Will I be able to effectively share what I know?") and less on whether they are clearly and explicitly communicating how much they aim to be likeable (e.g., "Am I making sure the other person knows that I value their expertise?"). The result is that relational information is left unsaid and remains invisible. Yet if potential collaborators were to explicitly share this kind of relational information, and thus aim to resolve others' uncertainty along these lines, it could have a substantial impact on their willingness to engage in new collaborative relationships with each other.

EXPECTATIONS

The foregoing theoretical building blocks underscore how relationality (i.e., whether potential collaborators believe that others will relate to them in ways that they would like, and also whether they believe they will be able to successfully relate to others) depends upon both the information that is shared and experience of interacting. For collaborative relationships oriented toward better understanding and addressing a problem facing a community, potential collaborators want to be sure that the other person will share information that is useful and trustworthy, and that the experience of interacting will be enjoyable. Uncertainty along these lines may be cause for concern, which increases the likelihood that people refrain. All of this leads to my first two hypotheses:

Information hypotheses: people are hesitant to engage in a collaborative relationship with someone when they are uncertain if that person has useful, task-relevant information that is trustworthy.

Interaction hypotheses: people are hesitant to engage in a collaborative relationship with someone when they are uncertain that the experience of interacting will be enjoyable. These judgments reflect a combination of perceptions about one's own and the other persons' ability to interact and also about whether they and the other person will enjoy the conversation.

The core challenge is that new collaborative relationships often entail people who do not know each other. Potential collaborators can be highly uncertain about all or perhaps just some of these aspects about how to relate to others. This motivates a second set of hypotheses:

Intervention hypotheses: people will be more likely to engage in a new collaborative relationship with someone they do not know when:

    (a)   the potential collaborator directly communicates information that resolves uncertainty about relationality.

    (b)   a third party (such as an organization or an individual) creates an opportunity for a new collaborative relationship that resolves uncertainty about relationality.

As we'll see in the rest of the book, actually testing these intervention hypotheses, as well as putting these ideas into practice, requires digging a little bit deeper. With any potential new collaborative relationship, resolving uncertainty about relationality means knowing what, precisely, the people involved are most concerned about. Sometimes the main source of concern may relate to the information being shared (e.g., Will it be practical? Will it be trustworthy?). Other times it may relate to the experience of interacting (e.g., Do I know what's appropriate and inappropriate to say, or am I uncertain about that? What expectations will the other person have? Will the other person value my expertise?). Sometimes it may be all of the above. I unpack all of this in the chapters to come. And, along the way (particularly when testing the intervention hypotheses), I gather a wide variety of evidence and examples showing how collaborative relationships enable expertise to become useful in civic life in new ways.

3

Relationality in Practice

In Chapter 2, I presented a theory of relationality, focusing on why we should expect judgments of competence, trustworthiness, and likeability to influence people's decisions to engage in collaborative relationships. In this chapter, I examine whether the prospect of interacting with diverse thinkers in a collaborative setting actually brings these thoughts to mind. In those moments, do those who seek change express uncertainty about any of these aspects of relating to others and, if so, do these aspects differ depending upon the people and the context?

In addition, while competence, trustworthiness, and likeability are terms consistent with the language that scholars use, they are not necessarily the terms that people use in everyday language when faced with the prospect of a new collaborative relationship. Thus, another key goal of this chapter is to see how potential collaborators express uncertainty around "relating to me" and "relating to others" in their own words.

Having a tight grasp on people's own words is essential for understanding the situation as potential collaborators see it. Given that two of my hypotheses are about testing new ways of overcoming uncertainty about relationality to foster new collaborative relationships, it is not enough (for example) to say that someone is concerned that a potential collaborator is not likeable. That is an interesting observation, but is not actionable in and of itself because it is unclear how to put that into practice. In my experience, it leads to questions like: how exactly can that person demonstrate likeability? What should they be doing differently? It also brings to mind questions about whether all potential collaborators care about likeability and think about it in the same way, or whether some collaborators are perhaps more concerned that the potential collaborator will not be trustworthy, or some other element of relationality?

With these questions in mind, in this chapter I engage directly with a wide variety of people who are looking to make change in their communities: local policymakers, science museum directors, organizers, AmeriCorps program leaders, K-12 educators, and university-based researchers. The people I engage with (for reasons described in more detail later) would all value new collaborative relationships with diverse thinkers to advance their strategic decision-making. Yet for a variety of reasons, the desire remains unmet. My goal is to understand this situation in their own words.

First, I present results from a series of in-depth interviews that include people from all of these different groups. Here my aim is not to estimate the prevalence of each element of relationality within a population, or to attempt to establish causality. Rather, similar to Cramer's (2016) book that investigates how people in rural areas understand the world around them (and especially their political world), my goal here is to investigate how people understand their potential collaborative world. I seek to understand how people describe and think about the prospect of new collaborative relationships in their own words.

Afterward, I present results from two surveys that examine the prevalence of various relational concerns within different populations. One is a national survey of local policymakers. The second is a national survey of nonprofit practitioners who are program leaders within AmeriCorps. This diverse set of data is particularly interesting because it underscores a key point from Chapter 2: the elements of relationality people are most concerned about can differ.

IN-DEPTH INTERVIEWS

I conducted a series of in-depth interviews in order to hear a diverse set of decision-makers talk about the opportunity to engage in new collaborative relationships in their own words. Why do they see them as potentially important, and what, if any, sources of uncertainty do they have about engaging with others who bring diverse forms of expertise to problems they are addressing in their work?

I adopt a case study logic in which the goal is description, not establishing causality. Data from these interviews will not be able to show that certain concerns "caused" decision-making. Nor is my goal to achieve representativeness of the entire population of decision-makers who are looking to make change in their communities (rigorously defining and then sampling from that population would be a tremendous challenge in its own right). Instead, my goal is to provide a richer understanding of how people describe uncertainty about relating to diverse thinkers in real-life settings. I give people the space and freedom to express in their own words what the prospect of new collaborative relationships on problems they care about means to them. In short, the goal is depth, not breadth. And, in addition to being interesting in their own right, the interviews also help inform the design of national surveys discussed later in the chapter.

When designing my case selection strategy, I began with the theoretical expectations mentioned in Chapter 2: the importance of perceptions of competence, trustworthiness, and likeability. From there, my goal was to recruit a diverse sample that focused on achieving theoretical range (Yin 2003, Gerring 2017), which included people looking to make change in their community and who have various social group memberships that corresponded to different status-based stereotypes that I expected to be task-relevant (e.g., occupation, gender, and race). I also wanted variation in terms of prior experiences, as the research on "talking to strangers" (that I discussed in Chapter 2) finds that prior experience is one of the most powerful predictors of desire to interact with strangers (Sandstrom and Boothby 2020). Last, I also needed to focus on people who are working to make change in their community and would value the opportunity to engage with new diverse thinkers on the challenges they are facing. From a research design perspective, this last point is much easier said than done, as people's unmet desire to collaborate is generally invisible to outsiders.

Fortunately, given my position as president of research4impact, I was often in touch with people who fit all of these criteria. The reason is because, after the initial failure of the online platform in 2017 (that I described at the beginning of Chapter 1), we "reinvented" the organization in 2018 to offer hands-on matchmaking. This became what we refer to as research4impact 2.0. I describe how research4impact 2.0 works in more detail in Chapter 5, but for the present purpose, what matters is that because of this reinvented version of research4impact, I am routinely contacted by practitioners, policymakers, and researchers who I know have a baseline interest in new collaborative relationships that have not yet arisen.

Given this, I designed my case selection procedure as follows: for a period of time in 2020 (from spring to early summer), whenever someone

reached out to request a research4impact match and/or to get more information about how the matchmaking works, I also mentioned that I was
working on this book and asked if I could ask them a few extra questions
that were relevant to it. Almost everyone agreed. I also asked them if
there was someone else they would suggest I reach out to (who they knew
also had a baseline interest in new cross-sector connections). If they said
yes, I reached out to that person myself. Similar to Michener (2018), my
total number of cases was not predetermined, but instead I concluded the
interviews once they were yielding few new insights about the elements
of relationality that were sources of concern, at least within the set of
people interested in research4impact (i.e., once I had reached a point of
saturation; Small 2009).

Overall I interviewed 52 people: 17 were local elected officials (at
either the city, county, or town level), 26 worked at nonprofits in which
they either had experience interacting with researchers or had given it
some thought (the types of nonprofits included museums, schools, and
community-based organizations), and nine were researchers (all of whom
are in the social sciences). Of the 52, 50 percent were female, 78 percent
were non-Hispanic white, 94 percent were located in the United States,
and 23 percent reported that they themselves saw part of their professional identity as a matchmaker. This last attribute indicated significant
experience with cross-sector experiences, and were always people who
had been referred by others (rather than reaching out to research4impact
themselves). I was particularly interested in whether they might discuss
ways in which they overcome uncertainty about relationality in their
work.

These semi-structured interviews lasted between 30 and 60 minutes,
and I conducted all of them myself. They were semi-structured in the
sense that I began with an interview protocol, but also allowed the conversation to focus on areas and directions that my interviewees deemed
relevant. Everyone I spoke with had plenty to say on this topic! In fact,
in five cases, the respondents had so much they wanted to share that 60
minutes was not enough and they asked to schedule follow-up calls. One
other interesting note was that my respondents frequently told me that
they had never been asked about these kinds of topics before, especially
the questions that focused on counterfactuals about why seemingly beneficial connections have not already arisen.

A copy of my interview protocol appears in Appendix A. As I
mentioned earlier many of these calls began with an inquiry about
research4impact, and so I usually started the conversation by responding

to that directly. Then I would share a bit more about my goals and invite them to tell me even more about their work. Next I would ask them to talk about any prior experiences with collaborative relationships as well as unmet desire for new ones (the part about unmet desire provided space for them to talk about anything that they hadn't already shared based on the initial research4impact inquiry). The specific types of collaborative relationships I asked about (including goals, and also types of potential collaborators) depended upon what made sense for the context. If I was speaking with a local policymaker, for example, I might ask about collaborative conversations (i.e., informal collaboration) with researchers at local colleges and universities related to research that would inform policy. Or, if I was speaking with a researcher I might ask about collaborative conversations and/or formal projects (i.e., informal or formal collaboration) with nonprofit practitioners in their general area (e.g., if the person is an education researcher, I might ask about relationships with classroom teachers or informal science educators at a local science museum). And so on.

Next, I invited them to talk about the degree to which others reach out to them to initiate new collaborative relationships like this, as well as about the degree to which they reach out to others, including in both cases what they believe might give others pause about reaching out and also what might give them pause about reaching out as well. This was a key moment in which I was listening for uncertainty about elements of relationality that mattered to them.

I would also ask about their colleagues – the degree to which they knew if their colleagues engaged in similar kinds of cross-sector collaborative relationships and their goals and experiences. I explicitly probed whether they had heard their colleagues express stereotypes about others, and whether they agreed with those stereotypes. Asking people directly about stereotypes can sometimes lead to defensiveness, and so first asking about colleagues and using them as a benchmark provided an easier way to learn more about respondents' attitudes. This was another key moment in which I was listening for elements of relationality. I would also follow up and ask respondents to share any advice they would give to others who wanted to reach out to engage with either them or their colleagues, and especially if there was something others should know about how to approach them. This question was another (indirect) way to possibly measure stereotypes of diverse thinkers that they would value engagement with.

The interviews ended with an invitation for them to share any questions that they think I should have asked but didn't. I also invited the folks who had reached out with a research4impact inquiry to share the name and contact information of someone else that they think I should be talking to (and in many cases, my respondents offered to make an email connection for me).

In advance of the interviews, one concern I had was that my respondents may be susceptible to social desirability pressures. In particular, I was mindful that the mere fact that I am asking about these collaborative relationships (and even consider the science of collaboration to be a topic worthy of an entire book!) would signal that I think they are important and that respondents may be shy about sharing ways in which they and their colleagues are hesitant to and/or uninterested in engaging with certain types of potential collaborators. I was also mindful of my positionality, as a white male professor at a prestigious university and who happens to run a separate nonprofit organization with a mission to foster new collaborative relationships. I have feet planted in both the research and practice worlds, along with some markers of high status (Ridgeway 2001), and thus I worried that my own interest in fostering more collaborative relationships might lead respondents to share overly rosy views of them. Given all this, as much as possible, I tried to employ question-wording that legitimized positive and negative responses. I also deliberately provided opportunities to talk about colleagues, as talking about others provided a way for respondents to couch any self-referential comments in terms of norms if they wished to do so.

Overall, respondents shared a wealth of insight into their professional lives, including important and fascinating information about the substance of their work, the goals they would like to pursue via new collaborative relationships, their work history, organizational politics, broader politics, and many other topics. The totality of what they shared could form a book unto itself, yet for purposes of this chapter, I hone in on one topical area – the ways in which they expressed uncertainty about relationality in their own words. I organize this presentation in terms of elements of relationality, and thus group quotes that, to me, capture similar elements.

SOURCES OF UNCERTAINTY ABOUT RELATIONALITY MENTIONED DURING IN-DEPTH INTERVIEWS

A summary of the elements of relationality that my respondents mentioned appears in Figure 3.1. Two elements reflect uncertainty about whether the information that the other person will share is likely to be

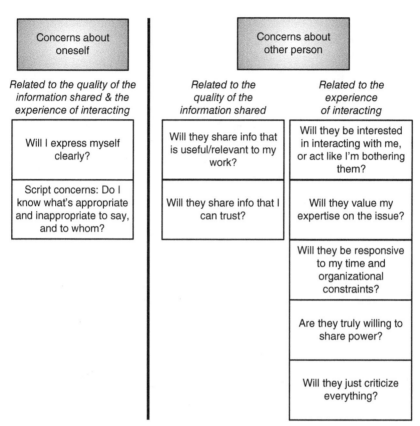

FIGURE 3.1 Summary of elements of relationality mentioned during in-depth interviews
Even when civic actors would value new collaborative relationships, they may be uncertain about whether potential collaborators will relate to them in ways they would like, and vice versa. This figure presents an overview of the elements of relationality that my interviewees expressed concern about.

useful or trustworthy. The remainder express various elements of concern about what the experience of interacting will be like. These interviews highlight how the aspect of warmth that Fiske et al. (2007) call "relationship development" (and what I have shorthand referred to as "likeability") can take many diverse forms.

In what follows, I describe each element and illustrate it using quotes from my interviews. I begin with concerns that interviewees expressed about themselves – whether they believed that they would be able to successfully relate to potential collaborators. Then, I share concerns that referred to whether potential collaborators would relate to them in ways that they would like.

Concerns about Oneself

During my interviews, several respondents expressed concern about their own competence during a potential new collaborative relationship. This might take a couple of different forms.

Will I Express Myself Clearly?

For instance, one education researcher who is now engaged in many collaborative relationships with teachers shared how, when he was starting out, he would just go to schools, hang out, and ask questions, and that "more often than not it led to a teacher asking: I have this problem – do you know how I might approach it? Do you know about research that might be helpful?" In response, I asked him what he had learned about why teachers would not cold contact a researcher – in other words, why might the extended period of "hanging out" be so important? He responded by relaying a self-competence concern that they had shared with him:

Often they don't really have a well-formed question. It's just a messy dilemma that they have ... when you can engage in conversation you can go back and forth. And it seems like too big or too messy to approach someone.

I also spoke with a public engagement practitioner whose job was to create workshops that brought together researchers and non-researchers who had a professional interest in what research says (e.g., people in the creative industry, community organizing, marine industries, local journalism, etc.). I asked her, essentially, why her workshops were necessary – what keeps these professionals from reaching out on their own? She responded:

Some people don't have much confidence after trying to do their own research in the past, or lack the confidence because in the past they find stuff locked behind paywalls, or it's too technical, or it's not exactly right/not exactly what they wanted. [And now they are] not feeling like they have the language to ask.

Script Concerns

The last part of the previous quote refers to what I would call script concerns – people not being sure about what is appropriate and inappropriate to say. These script concerns formed the large majority of the self-oriented sources of uncertainty about relationality that respondents expressed during my interviews.

For instance, a professor at an education school shared that most of his colleagues did not reach out to practitioners like teachers or museum directors to learn about their work or otherwise engage in new collaborative relationships. Some of it, he said, was a lack of time, but that wasn't everything. He then added:

For some of them, it's just a lack of familiarity with [the] lived experience of practitioners. Sounds weird from an education school ... but we do have professors who never taught or worked in the classroom ... they aren't familiar with the ways of a classroom or being in a museum. So it's uncertainty or lack of familiarity. It's almost easier for us to send a cold email to a professor in a School of Education at any institution far away, that also doesn't serve the immediate purpose of a research project, than it is to do that with a Museum Education Director nearby that they don't know.

This was a noteworthy response because the reasoning wasn't about not having experience per se, but instead that the lack of experience means that they don't feel like they know how to have these interactions in the first place.

Several other people I spoke with also echoed script concerns as one source of uncertainty about relationality that helped explain the lack of collaborative relationships. For example, a county legislator in Ohio, who identified a lack of communication between the local research universities and the county government, said:

So often you go to talk to [researchers who focus on evaluation] their first question is: What are we trying to learn? I don't know how to answer that. I need you to help me write the research question. I need to know if what I'm doing is working. Usually we know something is not working, and don't know how to examine the deeper question of why.

A program manager at a large environmental advocacy organization shared:

Take a challenge that a flood plain manager in Colorado in [organization] faces. They wouldn't know where to start to contact an academic. They will use language that conservationists use. They would frame their problem in a way that a consultant would know, but not a research question that an academic would hook onto.

Similarly, when I asked a different nonprofit leader if she would reach out to researchers on her own, even to those she may have met before, she said:

[I don't] have a lot of clarification how much detail I would have to do before reaching out. Wasn't sure if we needed a whole study design already done. I don't have experience creating that.

One final example of these script concerns I want to share came from a practitioner who was involved with training researchers for community-based research projects, and thus played a matchmaker role herself. These were funded projects that were supposed to involve the community, but one thing she found is that the imprecision around the use of the term "community" stopped many researchers dead in their tracks. As she put it:

[Researchers] would say: "I can't work with the community. What do I do? Go door to door? Put up flyers? Do a town hall?" We had to say: "They won't be terrifying to you! They are just like you." The language made it seem really big and scary. This came up in trainings. They can't do community engaged research because they had assumptions of what it meant.

Indeed, she described the nuts and bolts of one aspect of her work as follows:

I coached [a researcher] in how to facilitate meetings with community partners. She didn't know how to ask the questions she had – how to come up with the questions. It's not part of our training. She knew she had no idea what she was doing.

In addition to concerns about the script itself (i.e., what is appropriate and inappropriate to say), some script-related concerns reflected uncertainty about the most appropriate or inappropriate people to say it to – in other words, who is the right person to reach out to? For instance, one county legislator from New York, who has a large public research university in her county, said:

It may be a combination of the fact that no one in the system has really been using the college as a resource, and so no one has a pathway to get into it. No point of contact. Even a menu of options. I feel like this is something in which we haven't asked the questions, and on the academic side they may not know what we're working on or looking for, to say we could help you with that.

A practitioner who works at a science center used particularly colorful language to characterize barriers to interacting with researchers at local universities:

I don't know where the entry point is. It's a game of hot potato. Nothing is anyone's responsibility. Huge challenge. We've heard them use words like "fortress." Even being invited to campus and saying "I can't go there. I'm not welcome. *I don't even know where to park* [emphasis mine]."

A researcher at a large public research university, who has been involved with initiatives to partner with local community members, talked specifically about the feeling that keeps local nonprofit leaders away. They've expressed to her thoughts along these lines:

The university is a very elite space. For community members in many places there is a strict divide between the university and the town it's in. There is tension. Many people who feel like they are not welcome on campus.

Not feeling welcome likely reflects many different elements of relationality, including perceptions of how researchers at the university relate to them. Yet I include her quote under "script concerns" because she emphasized how the community members she engages with would not even know where to start – who would be the most appropriate person to start with? Then she added, "You really need people who are bridge-builders – people who actually see the divide." This sentiment is particularly important because implicit in it is the fact that in her experience most colleagues had not previously considered that "not feeling welcome" would even be a barrier to creating new collaborative relationships with local community leaders. Script concerns (and uncertainty about relationality more generally) are invisible to those who do not intentionally seek to understand and respond to it.

Concerns about Others

In my interviews, respondents mentioned several elements of relationality that referred to whether others would relate to them in ways that they would like. These concerns about others encompassed the information that they would share as well as what the experience of interacting would be like. I begin with concerns expressed about the information being shared. As it turns out, in my interviews, all of these information-based concerns were mentioned by practitioners and policymakers about researchers. I do not interpret that as meaning that the opposite situation never occurs, but instead it likely reflects that people from those groups made up the majority of my interviewees.

Will They Share Information That's Useful to My Work?
To begin, my respondents expressed concerns about whether the information shared would be useful and trustworthy. I should note that in none of these cases did people wholly dismiss the idea that interacting with researchers could yield beneficial information. For instance, none of the local policymakers I spoke with thought that research could not, in theory, be helpful to their work, and none of them said that about their

colleagues either. Instead what they expressed was uncertainty about it – that they would have concerns about any potential new collaborator.

For instance, a county legislator in upstate New York, located in a county with a well-known research university, shared the kind of skepticism that colleagues express about new interactions with local researchers:

> I think my colleagues would not even pose a research question. Like I would say: I wonder if there is research on coroners? I approach it as: this is a knowable thing, there has to be someone who knows this, and it's not me. They say: I've been doing this for 10–15 years, and I am the expert.

While some of my interviewees definitely expressed stereotypes about researchers (as I discuss later on), that was not the case here. Instead, the concern here was about whether the researchers would have anything useful to say. A county legislator from Ohio specifically made this distinction when I asked if her colleagues had any stereotypes about researchers:

> Some might, some might not. Less about the person, but about the content of the work. Less obvious the inherent value: What would it have to tell me?

When I asked a mayor in Ohio about how he would suggest that local researchers contact his office, the very first thing he emphasized was being explicit about communicating relevance, and not assuming that relevance would be obvious:

> First, have good ideas. I mean, that's true. In order for it to be relevant … gotta be relevant and reflective of real needs. I'm definitely a believer that good ideas rise to the top.

A high-level bureaucrat for a city in the northeast also identified concerns about how useful the information would be when discussing why he doesn't typically reach out to local researchers at colleges and universities located in his city:

> The calling you up and telling you what I need, will probably not be articulated very clearly. Not stated in a way that helps … identify the best researcher for this, and best techniques for this. It will be a long time for how they get to a project, or it will happen quickly but it might not be the most helpful thing. Output might be a 20 page paper but it's not the question you want to know the answer to and it's ultimately minimally helpful.

I also spoke with a person who does research and evaluation at a large environmental advocacy organization. She is a natural person, in theory, to want to interact with (university-based) researchers, yet also cited a concern about a lack of useful information:

Big concern is that their results won't be applicable ... whatever the smart person will show me, won't change how I plan my program or teach my program. ... That person would never know enough about [our issue] to know how we do things.

Are They Trustworthy?

Several other people mentioned that they would be concerned that any potential collaborator might not be trustworthy/share trustworthy information. As with the point about usefulness, no one explicitly stated that they knew for certain that they would receive untrustworthy information. Instead, they expressed uncertainty about it, and acknowledged that they would be concerned. They emphasized that trust is something that needs to be cultivated. For instance, a nonprofit practitioner talked bluntly about the hesitancy of initiating a new interaction with a stranger around the problems she's addressing in her work:

It's hard for people to walk out of their bubbles ... it's scary to cold call someone. I don't know you, and I don't trust you because I don't know you.

A county legislator from Ohio, who readily acknowledged ideological similarity between her and her stereotype of researchers at her local university, nevertheless cited trust as a concern:

This whole separation ... this is part of the challenge ... need to re-establish trust between policymakers and those academicians that, I don't know, seems like they lost some credibility. Instead of this independent source, it seems like academia wants to support a certain philosophy or certain party.

Another local policymaker, when I asked how researchers should reach out, also emphasized the need for trust-building. He acknowledged that a third party can help, especially on short notice, but then added that trust is something that is built up over time and also not something that, in his experience, researchers seem to know:

Quite frankly, I think, and it sounds so simplistic ... invite [policymakers] to your kitchen table. First thing ... red flag ... what do you want from me, what do you need? That's wrong, but that's what you're dealing with. They think you're going to want something in the end. You have to bring them in in a way that lets them understand how what you've done and how it can be helpful to them down the road. You have to gain the trust and gain the respect. Do it when you don't need them. Then when the time comes you almost have a partnership with them. You've given them a reason to be a part of it.

A researcher at a public university also emphasized the hesitancy that arises from a lack of trust, especially as it relates to engaging with marginalized communities in her city:

I believe one of the most important things that we as researchers can do is literature reviews. What people need is: What does the literature say about x,y,z? [Where I work] we had no infrastructure in place to let anyone know, in part because we were working with people disinclined to trust us ... yeah there was no system in place to enable the porous nature of that boundary. Not set up to do that.

Will They Be Interested in Interacting with Me, or Act Like I'm Bothering Them?

In addition to concerns about the information being shared, many respondents shared concerns about what the experience of interacting with a potential collaborator would be like. One interesting difference here is that when it came to relationality concerns about competence and trustworthiness, people often voiced these concerns in terms of the words themselves (i.e., they used the language of relevance, usefulness, and trust, as noted in the quotes shared earlier). Yet when they expressed uncertainty about the experience, they did not generally use the term "enjoyable" or "likeable." Instead, they used many other terms to capture what they expected the experience to be like.

One source of uncertainty was about whether the other person would be interested in interacting/view them as someone worth interacting with. For instance, an education researcher said that teachers he knows would never feel comfortable cold-contacting researchers at a nearby university because "They're intimidated to email – they feel like the professor will be busy and worry they'll be bothering them." Another practitioner who helps educators with curriculum development used the same "intimidated" language. She acknowledged that teachers are "curious about education researchers ... if there is a whole group that is researching this, then what are they finding? Can this influence what I'm doing?" But then added that they would never feel comfortable reaching out directly:

There is a tension. There is societal – it has to do with a value-laden judgment of roles. Education researchers are seen as more expert, more valued, more highly paid. Teachers are less so. They are intimidated. Even with the local university ... not sure who to reach out to ... each has a niche area of study.

An organizer told me the same thing about reaching out to political science professors. This organizer reads a lot of political science research, and during our conversation, it became clear that he was very familiar with much of the academic work on voter turnout and organizing strategy. He also lives near several universities with a vibrant cluster of researchers working on these topics, and told me that he would greatly value collaborative relationships so that the newest evidence could inform his work (and his expertise could inform their work as well). Yet he said he has never reached out:

Why don't I reach out to [nearby universities]? I think part of it is that I don't like to make an ask of someone's time unless I have something specific, generally thinking. And what am I going to say? "I was just wondering if you would like to talk about these ideas in general?" And send that to the entire [local university] listserv? There's a cultural norm against that. They'll respond: "Who's this crazy guy?" I guess I could do that, say "Is anyone interested in talking about this?" I guess if I had something more concrete maybe I would feel more comfortable reaching out, but I'm not there. I don't have something more specific. It's kinda weird to say: "Does anyone want to develop a friendship? Be an academic-practitioner friend?" That's a socially awkward thing to do. Even if it's illogical and we should just reach out to people … but it's an uncomfortable thing to do.

He admits there is a good reason for outreach, and in part his hesitation reflects some of the self-oriented concerns mentioned earlier (e.g., script concerns about who is most appropriate to reach out to), but the bulk of what makes him uncomfortable is the reaction that he imagines.[1] A leader of a different community-based organization, working in the health space, echoed a similar thought about being uncomfortable (and intertwined with concerns about self-competence):

I don't know what I would do without [a matchmaking organization like research4impact]. I have no idea who to reach out to, I'm not used to doing this kind of work. I don't really know anyone in this space. And even if I did I would feel awkward reaching out to them … what credibility do I have?

Some people I spoke with expressed a similar kind of concern about whether the other person would be interested in them. They said they would find it valuable to see potential collaborators take a relatively costly action to demonstrate that they are truly interested. For instance, one county legislator in Ohio lamented the lack of communication between her and her colleagues and the several research universities that were nearby. She perceived that as tied to a lack of interest among the researchers there. She then added that one way for researchers to demonstrate that they are interested in a collaborative relationship is to show up:

Sometimes just showing up is just the biggest part … why aren't they just in the local council meetings … so they can get a sense of what is happening … you can't influence policy from an ivory tower in a really helpful way … I look

---

[1] To be sure, one could also ask why the researchers at his local universities have never reached out to him, which would be a reasonable question to include if I had conducted in-depth interviews with one or more of those researchers.

forward to the day when there is a genuine interest in the university that deals
with social conditions of communities.

A town supervisor in upstate New York made a similar point about the
value of someone taking a costly action to demonstrate that they really
want to engage collaboratively with him:

I prefer a face-to-face conversation. I don't like phone. Would rather sit down at
my office. When a professor first contacted me [to ask about a dispute his town
was having with a solar energy company that wanted to build a solar farm] I
was hesitant. What's your interest in our town and what we're doing? If you're
willing to come [have a face-to-face conversation], now I know you're serious.
Something about that personal contact. Two professionals talking. That's a wonderful thing. We don't get enough of that.

Past experiences weigh heavily on people as well. For some practitioners and policymakers I spoke with, negative experiences in the past were
interpreted directly in terms of the stereotypes about researchers. They
were also invoked in service of the belief that researchers were uninterested in new connections. One practitioner who engages in matchmaking
said:

I connect researchers and industry, and [researchers] don't follow-up. The stereotypes just reinforce that. I do think the preconceptions matter. We only hear the
bad stuff, but not the good stuff.

A children's museum director talked about the hesitation his staff feels in
terms of a bad experience with a STEM researcher long ago:

They emailed a professor and that person never got back to them. Not casting
aspersions, but they inferred that because that one person didn't respond then
professors must not be interested.

An extension officer in upstate New York also talked about how one bad
experience feeds into the stereotypes of researchers as inaccessible:

[There are] natural places where it's super easy to rely on the research – on agriculture, invasive species, tick issues, anything that hits widespread public health
and agriculture, really critical things that drive food systems and economics. They
are really trusted with research. Also water quality – look to [our university] to
convene and provide unbiased information. [Yet] some execs reach out and get a
bad response, and that sours them from doing it again.

Another practitioner evoked researcher stereotypes, but in a different
way. He spoke to the question of whose evidence truly counts in collaborative relationships with researchers (c.f., Epstein 1995), and the concern that researchers may not be interested in engaging with practitioners

who are not focused on the right kind of evidence. Here he is talking specifically about public health practitioners who are qualitative in their orientation:

[Public health practitioners] focus on narrative description in terms of what is going on. For them it is very critical that the researcher should have an appreciation of their field, of their expertise, of their method, and should not force them to see numbers in the people. [There's a] stereotype that researchers are just very quantitative people and just see big numbers and not the people behind them. ... [They] see it as a dehumanization because researchers just care about what does the data show, what is the truth, and may not always be there to pick up the pieces of what that truth reveals.

Arguably this quote reflects two concerns – uncertainty that researchers may not be interested in interacting, and also that researchers may not value the expertise that practitioners bring to the issue. This latter point connects with the next element of relationality that I discuss.

Will They Value My Expertise on the Issue?
A common other-oriented concern that my interviewees expressed was that the potential collaborator would not value their expertise on the issue. To illustrate this point, I quote several people at length. I do so because I view all of them, in slightly different ways, as expressing concerns that the experience will not be enjoyable because they would effectively be interacting with someone who does not actually want to be collaborative.

Several of these concerns were expressed in terms of mindset. For instance, a county legislator from upstate New York expressed several sentiments along these lines:

There's a perception of research and experts that "their word is the final word" rather than "this is one more piece of information to throw into the mix." Researchers reinforce this perception by putting it that way too: "This is what I've discovered! Now let me tell you about it and how it applies all over the place."

She said a big concern for her and her colleagues is that they will be lectured at, along the lines of "I'm just going to tell you this, expect you to believe it and absorb it." She then added:

A big conversation around my area is around fracking, natural gas, the transition to green energy. [Local researchers] are coming to speak about why fracking, natural gas, and pipelines are not wanted in our community. It's not about opening a dialogue, but making it clear that this is unacceptable that we would even consider using carbon-based energy. And that is probably the reaction that most of my colleagues have with people who do research and work at colleges. Makes them be avoided ... no one likes being lectured at.

Many others expressed a similar sentiment about researchers. It is worth quoting several to give a flavor for the texture of these concerns, as I believe that in many cases the behavior they're describing is probably not intentional yet nonetheless is counterproductive from the perspective of fostering collaborative partnerships. For instance, here's what a county legislator in Ohio shared:

They come to the table much like elected officials, much like administrators ... they know everything ... not interested in something not on paper and backed up with facts. [Yet] just inventing the lightbulb isn't enough. If you want to effect change, you gotta bring people along with you.

A town supervisor from upstate New York used slightly more colorful language:

That's what's wrong with the colleges today. Teachers have no life experience other than a book. And they say: this is the way it is! That gets my goat going pretty good.

Many of the nonprofit practitioners I spoke with also echoed similar concerns. For instance, an education director at a museum, who is often approached by researchers who are interested in the impact of museum experiences on learning, spoke about his equivalent to "being lectured at," which is "being approached from a culture of knowing." He said that he was far more interested in a new collaborative relationship when it was clear that someone approached the topic from a culture of *learning* instead:

If a researcher says "I'm an expert in this and want to investigate it in your environment" then I'm not very interested. If instead they say "this is a thing that's driving me crazy, wouldn't it be interesting if we did x?" or "Have you ever noticed...?" These latter prompts are a conversation, versus a series of statements. When people use statements often it's interesting to them but not to the museum environment. It's about a culture of learning, openness, respect ... honoring that you're not just waiting for them to come in with answers. Or that they know things about your work that you need to know ... what they want you to know about your work ... power dynamic needs to be collegial, not just I have answers for you.

A different practitioner, who works on the evaluation team at a nonprofit, expressed a similar idea and was especially attuned to the methodological element:

A lot of methodologists say: It has to be an RCT [randomized controlled trial ... i.e., an experiment] and that's the only way it can be. What [nonprofits] need is not necessarily your preferred method, taking into account timing, capacity. Takes a certain skillset, flexible thinking that is not always there. It can be hard to make that leap. You need an ambassador and bridge the two kinds of worlds.

A practitioner who worked with an environmental NGO in the United States talked about how he can tell if he doesn't want to engage with a researcher:

Lack of empathy with wanting to learn about what others value. They respond when someone on my team disagrees with them with the attitude of: "Who are you to disagree with me? What credentials do you have as a staff member? In my pecking order you would be nothing. But of course we're not in that pecking order here ... we're in a different world ... dynamics about credentials and hierarchy that matter greatly in academia [don't] matter outside of it."

The researchers I interviewed expressed similar concerns, either in reference to themselves and/or colleagues. For instance, one researcher who studies urban planning and development contrasted what it is like to present at a city council meeting versus an academic meeting:

[It's] easier to just go to an academic conference and lecture for 10 minutes ... but if you go into a room filled with people who are skeptical and have strong opinions, you really have to be able to answer their questions ... can't blow them off. I think a lot of academics have a really hard time with plain-spoken questions from ordinary people. This weird idea that we're an elite profession but we have jobs with almost no accountability. One way to expose yourself to accountability is to be in a room with people who are happy to say you're wrong. You have to explain it to them ... not just provide a coefficient.

A sociologist who studies community-based environmental problems explained hesitation that stemmed from graduate training:

When you're in a PhD program you're given this lens of expert ... but you need some ability to allow for other forms of expertise to come in ... so you're not working as the one expert.

One practitioner who convenes teachers along with STEM (science, technology, engineering, and math) researchers to create new learning experiences for students shared how people from both sectors often share with him how they are uncertain about how others in the room will value their expertise. In response, now when he invites people, he makes sure they specifically know why they are being invited and why their expertise on the topic is valued:

What is important here is that if you understand why you are here ... your level of expertise is being taken seriously ... that will lead to something better ... trigger their sense of self and pride ... we need you! You bring something that no one else can. You bring something here and we need that role and this voice in this conversation. We need it in an unadulterated way. No need to prepare ... just be who you are. In this space this expertise is needed. Only together can we achieve what we need to achieve.

One way to characterize his strategy is that it entails assigning "roles" to the interaction, as he is essentially saying to each collaborator that their role is to bring their unique expertise to this task at hand. As it turns out, "role assignment" is a strategy that matchmakers can use when forging new collaborative relationships between diverse thinkers. I discuss "role assignment" in more detail in Chapter 5, when I describe the hands-on matchmaking model that we designed as part of the reinvented research4impact 2.0 (after the initial online platform did not work).

Another researcher at a large public university who has worked hard to create spaces that equally reflect contributions by the university and by community members (and especially from people of color and low-income people who have historically felt most alienated from the large public university in their backyard) emphasized that her colleagues often have a very narrow idea of expertise. She said:

You need to see the community as knowledge producers, and cultural wealth. We're not just letting them into our precious space. They are bringing gifts and knowledge that we need to know ourselves.

She also added something really important, which is that although researchers at her university may be used to having (and welcome having) their ideas challenged by colleagues, they are less used to it from community organizers and those who run small nonprofits outside the university. This lack of experience with having one's ideas and one's power challenged by racial minorities, those with less education, and/or those with a less prestigious occupation is new for many of them.

Will They Be Responsive to My Time and Organizational Constraints?

At the beginning of each interview, I made sure to ask my respondents how much time they had to talk. This might seem like a throwaway question, yet I would argue it reflects something more important. Here I was aiming to overcome one source of uncertainty that respondents may have about interacting with me: that I would not be responsive to, and respectful of, their time constraints. Echoing this point, in my interviews,

I found that uncertainty about whether a potential collaborator would be responsive to one's needs and constraints was another source of concern. This concern was that the interaction would not be enjoyable because a potential collaborator would not acknowledge and respect their time and/or pre-existing organizational constraints on decision-making.

For instance, a practitioner who works at an environmental organization cited a concern that researchers would not have "enough empathy that others have constraints on their time, and priorities." In addition, during our conversation, a nonprofit leader who leads youth civic education programs was reminded of his experience with a previous collaborative relationship with a researcher who did not seem to value the constraints of his program:

We were talking about targets of population that we work with ... we have an equity focus. Researchers were saying that to push equity agenda you have to work with all students, but with different types of curriculum for different students. But from the other side, we have limited resources, and so we need to limit. How do you make a decision if the researchers aren't thinking in a practical lens?

Another practitioner expressed a frequent concern she's heard from community groups she works with, which is that researchers may not always respect their time and also their autonomy:

[Community groups and K-12 schools] have learned that universities are not the best partners ... they are not always coordinated, they don't offer good points of exit, etc.

She then added that there is this sense of: "I need something from you right now, and it's a boon for you to be connected with me." These kinds of concerns take away from the enjoyment of the interaction, and she said in several cases, even if these groups and schools saw good reason to connect, the sense was: "I'm worried that it'll take away from what I'm doing. Sometimes we just gotta get it done." Having a sense that you need to engage on someone else's timeline does not make for an enjoyable experience.

Finally, I wish to share what two local policymakers told me, which also speaks to this concern about not being willing to respect organizational constraints in their decision-making. For the policymakers, this concern was not framed in terms of time but instead in terms of political realities. One county legislator in Ohio told me:

I think there's a purity issue ... academic papers and research are really black and white: the data affects outcomes or decision-making. Yet accountability is gray from beginning to end. I think academics have a level of distaste for this.

And a mayor in Ohio shared: "[We're] not gonna waste our time with ideological stuff with no basis in fact or practicality." At first blush, this comment sounds more like it's about not having useful or relevant information, yet he meant it in a similar way as the county legislator above, as a comment about whether the researcher would even be willing to talk through practicalities as they relate to leading the executive branch of a medium-sized city.

Are They Truly Willing to Share Power?

All of the foregoing concerns may apply (and were raised by my respondents) regardless of whether the goal of their potential new collaborative relationships was knowledge exchange or a more formal project. Yet there was one concern raised about the experience of interacting that applied in particular to the latter goal (e.g., a new coalition, a new research partnership). That was a concern about power-sharing. Recall that formal collaboration refers to projects in which collaborators share power in terms of ownership, decision-making authority, and accountability.

One researcher mentioned power-sharing when talking about his experiences in formal partnerships with educators at science museums. In particular, he shared with me the feedback that educators expressed to him afterward:

One other challenge that I learned while at the museum when we really tried to do partnership work with our educators and we tried to involve the educators as much as possible in the research process – sometimes even generating the research question itself, data collection, timelines, analysis, thinking about data analysis together – I learned from that which was a blind spot for me and also the other researchers ... we were inviting and asking practitioners to be part of the research process, but we as researchers weren't being part of the practice process. We were trying to be inclusive, but they were shouldering more of the burden than we as researchers. This came out in the debriefing, and it influenced how work was carried out going forward. You are asking people to play different roles at different times, and making sure equity in how these roles are dispersed ... it was revealing to me.

One of the practitioners I spoke with echoed a similar concern, which is that even when researchers are trying to increase a community's role in the research process, and thus challenge the status quo for how the research agenda gets set, they might ultimately fail if they do not formalize how power will be shared:

In the experience that I had ... when there weren't formal accountability structures what happened was that the status quo tended to persist. ... Unless we give shared power to people disrupting the status quo, the status quo will persist. [The] university controls all systems and processes and inherently has more power, even if the idea going into it is that they are going to share things equally. My interest in formal processes comes from baked-in cynicism … [the] tendency for the status quo to persist.

The blind spot to this issue seemed to be quite prevalent, even leading other community groups working on health equity issues to be wary of who's in charge: "the university has offered to take a leadership role, but you may lose stakeholders if the university takes a leadership role."

Last, one matchmaker I spoke with, who connects researchers with community-based organizations working to reduce health inequities, expressed this concern from the perspective of researchers:

Some [community-based organizations] are just really territorial. They don't want people to come in and take over part of what they're doing and maybe get some credit for it. They're just very … This is my thing and I don't want other people giving me lots of input and sharing this with you. Putting together these matches means you're giving up some ownership.

Will They Just Criticize Everything?

There is one final way that my interviewees expressed concerns about the experience of interacting. This was arguably the most blunt expression of a lack of enjoyment, and I include it separately because, to me, it is qualitatively different from just not valuing others' expertise. A county legislator in Ohio worried about new collaborative relationships with researchers because she thought they might just criticize everything legislators do:

I think the barrier to subjecting ourselves to academics is the fear that they'll learn it's all bullshit … that everything we do doesn't work, and then they'll say that we have to fix it. Knowing you could have a level of trust to have a constructive conversation and be vulnerable is really important … giving people access to how messed up it is … hard to open up to that.

This quote serves as an important reminder that collaborative relationships (even the most informal) do ask people to be vulnerable.

Open-Ended Interviews Summary

To briefly summarize, when asked about the possibility of new collaborative relationships with diverse thinkers that would inform strategic decision-making related to the challenges they are facing, my respondents collectively shared several ways in which they and their colleagues would be uncertain that potential collaborators would relate to them in ways they would like, and vice versa. Some of these elements of uncertainty reflected concerns about oneself, including the ability to express oneself clearly and also knowing what is appropriate and inappropriate to say. Other elements reflected concerns about others, including whether the information shared would be useful and whether the other person can be trusted. Concerns about others also referred to the experience of interacting, and represent ways in which people operationalize "will it be enjoyable?" in their own words. This includes concerns about whether the other person will be interested in interacting, will value their expertise on the issue, be responsive to time and organizational constraints, be truly willing to share power, and just criticize everything.

INVESTIGATING THE PREVALENCE OF RELATIONALITY ELEMENTS IN TWO POPULATIONS

The interviews provided an in-depth look at how a variety of local policymakers, nonprofit practitioners, and researchers seeking change in their community put relationality concerns in their own words. From a research perspective, the major benefit of the interviews is their depth. At the same time, I was also interested in getting a sense of how prevalent these concerns might be in certain well-defined populations.

To that end, I fielded two surveys that included closed-ended prompts based on the kind of language people shared in the interviews. The surveys do not cover every single type of civic actor that I interviewed, but they do provide diverse, national samples of two of the major types: local policymakers in the United States, and one type of nonprofit practitioner (AmeriCorps program leaders from across the United States). In each case, respondents were prompted to think about having a collaborative relationship with a researcher to discuss a challenge they were facing in their work. They were then asked to indicate which, if any, of a list of concerns they shared. The set of eight concerns listed was the same across both surveys.

Local Policymakers

First, I present results from the local policymakers survey. This was a national sample of local government officials collected by CivicPulse, a nonprofit organization that maintains a large database of local policymakers. The sample of respondents was randomly drawn from the population of policymakers in US local governments (i.e., township, municipality, and county governments) with at least 1,000 residents, and included top elected officials and governing board members. The survey took place from April 8 to May 24, 2021 and included 541 respondents.[2]

Parts of the survey, to be discussed in Chapter 5, asked about how often local policymakers engage in collaborative relationships with researchers in their local colleges and universities as well as if they would like to engage more or less than they currently do going forward (i.e., as a measure of whether there is an unmet desire to collaborate along these lines). Here, I focus on the part of the survey in which I provided respondents with "a list of possible concerns policymakers may have when interacting with university researchers" and then asked them to indicate which, if any, they have. They could respond yes or no. The concerns were phrased as follows, and (in the interest of minimizing survey time) were meant to be pithy ways of phrasing the ways in which respondents in my interviews talked about elements of relationality that they were uncertain about:

[Researchers] may not have domain-specific expertise
They may not have trustworthy information
They may not have practical information
They may not value my knowledge and experience as a policymaker
They may lecture me
They may use unfamiliar language
They may push a political agenda
They may just criticize everything I do

Figure 3.2 presents the percentage of policymakers who responded that they shared each of these concerns. While none were shared by a majority of local policymakers, some were clearly more prevalent than others. Concerns that researchers may push a political agenda (47.5 percent of respondents) and that they will not have practical information to share (34.1 percent) were the most prevalent. After that, there were three concerns that were equally prevalent: they may lack domain-specific knowledge (18.6 percent), won't share trustworthy information (18.6 percent), and won't value my knowledge and experience as a policymaker (17.8 percent). The other three concerns were quite rare.

---

[2] CivicPulse included survey weights to increase sample representativeness, and all results presented are weighted. The full text from the survey appears in Appendix B.

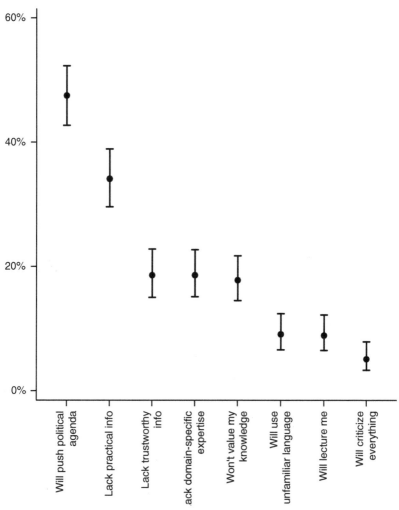

FIGURE 3.2 Local policymakers' concerns about interacting with local researchers

Figure displays weighed percentage who reported having the particular concern along with 95 percent confidence intervals (N = 541).

The difference in level of concern that the researcher may lack practical information and that the researcher may lack domain-specific expertise is worth underscoring. In existing research on competence judgments, we often talk about information in terms of being useful/relevant, and arguably both "having practical information" and "having domain-specific expertise" would count as being useful and might even be thought of as interchangeable. Yet the fact that policymakers are far more concerned about practicality underscores how, from their perspective, they are far from interchangeable. On average, researchers who attempt to communicate usefulness by appealing to domain-specific knowledge, without saying anything about how the information could be practically applied, are much less likely to demonstrate that they will relate to local policymakers in ways that they would like.

AmeriCorps Program Leaders

The second survey included a national sample of nonprofit practitioners. In partnership with America's Service Commissions (ASC), the national organization of state service commissions in the United States, Elizabeth Day and I conducted a survey of AmeriCorps state program leaders in June 2021 (Levine and Day 2023). These leaders run programs funded at least in part by AmeriCorps and that meet a wide variety of human needs in their communities: improving educational outcomes, reducing intergenerational poverty, providing financial education, leading community engagement opportunities, improving children's social-emotional learning, preserving natural habitats, and so on.

Overall, 285 leaders from AmeriCorps state programs completed our survey, which covered a wide variety of topics.[3] Relevant to the chapter here, the survey included this question: "Suppose you were presented with an opportunity to talk with a researcher in your region you've never met about challenges you are facing in your work. In advance of the interaction to what extent (if at all) would you have the following concerns?" Here, instead of only a yes or no response, respondents had space to express degree of concern using five response options from "extremely concerned" to "not at all concerned."

Table 3.1 lists the results in two ways, first looking at the percentage of respondents who reported being extremely or very concerned about each element of relationality, and then the percentage who reported being extremely, very, or somewhat concerned. As shown in the table, and as was the case with local policymakers, there was wide variation across the different elements. Program leaders' top two concerns reflected uncertainty about the quality of the information to be shared: whether researchers would have domain-specific expertise and whether they

---

[3] The results include survey weights that increase geographic representativeness of our sample.

TABLE 3.1 *Prevalence of relationality concerns among AmeriCorps program leaders*

	Percent of program leaders Extremely/Very concerned	Percent of program leaders Extremely/Very/Somewhat concerned
The researcher may not have domain-specific expertise	24.0	60.9
The researcher may not have practical information	22.8	50.6
The researcher may not value my knowledge and experience	13.8	31.5
The researcher may use unfamiliar language	11.6	30.4
The researcher may push a political agenda	9.3	24.2
The researcher may lecture me	6.3	17.1
The researcher may not have trustworthy information	5.8	21.5
The researcher may criticize me	6.2	14.6

Results are weighted percentages, and arranged in the order of decreasing level of "extremely/very/somewhat concerned"; $N = 285$

would have practical information to share. In addition, their third most frequent concern captured an aspect of what the experience of interacting would be like: whether the researchers would value their knowledge and expertise as AmeriCorps program leaders.

SUMMARY

Taken together, the evidence in this chapter underscores the fact that relationality can include many different elements about what it means to relate to someone else. And when I argue that people are uncertain about whether a potential collaborator will relate to them in ways they would like, and vice versa, that uncertainty captures a diverse array of concerns that are person- and context-specific.

Indeed, it is especially illuminating to compare the results from the two surveys. For instance, concern about whether researchers would share practical information was very prevalent among both local policymakers and AmeriCorps program leaders. In addition, concern about whether the researcher would value their knowledge and expertise was also frequently mentioned by both. Yet other relationality concerns were quite different. Local policymakers were far more likely to be concerned that the researcher would push a political agenda than the AmeriCorps program leaders. In addition, program leaders viewed "having practical information" and having "domain-specific information" as being largely equivalent, yet that was not the case for policymakers.

I return to this point about context specificity in Chapters 5 and 6, as it directly bears on the design of interventions for reducing uncertainty about relationality. For now, I close by recalling that the main overriding purpose of this chapter was to see if the prospect of new collaborative relationships with diverse thinkers would bring to mind relationality concerns that reflected the "building blocks" of competence and warmth mentioned in Chapter 2. It seems quite clearly that they can, and that people express them in many different ways. In that case, the next question is: do relationality concerns influence behavior? That's the question at the heart of the next two chapters.

4

The Link between Relationality and Collaborative Relationships

In this chapter, I return to the research4impact online platform mentioned at the beginning of the book. Hundreds of grassroots activists, nonprofit program leaders, deep canvassers, policymakers, and researchers built profiles, and we expected a buzz of new collaborative relationships. Yet that did not happen. Why might that be? While throughout the book I use that experience to motivate my discussion of many other examples of how expertise becomes useful in civic life, in this chapter I especially home in on the research4impact platform and what might have been missing.

This investigation picks up where Chapter 3 left off. There we saw how, when asked to consider the prospect of new collaborative relationships, people may be uncertain about whether potential collaborators who bring diverse forms of expertise to problems they are working on will relate to them in ways that they would like, and vice versa. Moreover, "relating to others" includes a combination of the information to be shared and the experience of interacting.

In this chapter, I argue that uncertainty about relationality can influence behavior and, more to the point, the problem with the research4impact online platform is that it did not take active steps to overcome this uncertainty. Thus, it produced a situation in which people who built profiles would have valued new collaborative relationships with others in the network (after all, that's why they created the profiles in the first place!), yet uncertainty about aspects of relationality gave them pause about who to engage with and how to engage with them.

To make this case, my goal is to compare the research4impact online platform as it existed with an unobserved counterfactual: what would have happened if everything was the same except that it institutionalized mechanisms for overcoming uncertainty about relationality? While it's impossible to realize this alternative world in practice, what I can do is try to find another organization that is similar in many respects except this one.

It turns out that one fits the bill: Catchafire. Catchafire is an organization that also has an online platform for creating new collaborative relationships between diverse thinkers who typically start off as strangers to one another and are working to improve communities that they care about. Yet it is different in one key respect: it's been quite successful.

In this chapter, I conduct a comparative case study to help unpack these divergent outcomes. My case comparison collectively demonstrates evidence in support of the information and interaction hypotheses from Chapter 2: that people's decisions to engage in new collaborative relationships depend upon the information to be shared and what the experience of interacting will be like.

COMPARATIVE CASE STUDY

My comparison between Catchafire and the research4impact online platform (which I refer to as "research4impact 1.0" for shorthand) is an example of a qualitative research design called a most-similar case study (Gerring 2017). A most-similar case study compares two or more cases that have different outcomes yet exhibit similar background conditions. The goal is to uncover a factor that differs between the two cases and that, based on theoretical grounds, we have good reason to believe would explain the divergent outcomes. My comparative case study will not yield a precise point estimate with a confidence interval, yet it will allow me to conclude that the lack of institutionalized mechanisms to overcome uncertainty about relationality is the probable cause.

Figure 4.1 provides an overview of the two cases. In what follows, I provide detailed descriptions of research4impact 1.0 and then Catchafire, focusing on the major attributes listed in the figure. The information about research4impact comes from my own experience as a co-founder and president of the organization. The information about Catchafire comes from their published annual impact reports, website, and several conversations with people who have used the site.

research4impact 1.0

First, I provide a brief history about the origin of research4impact 1.0 and its basic structure. The initial idea arose in September 2016, during

	CATCHAFIRE	RESEARCH4IMPACT 1.0 (Online platform from 2017)
Involves nonprofit practitioners and other professionals connecting	Yes	Yes
Participation is voluntary	Yes	Yes
Entails online platform with profiles and ability to reach out to others	Yes	Yes
Offers opportunities for both informal knowledge exchange & formal partnerships	Yes	Yes
Institutionalizes mechanisms to reduce uncertainty about relationality	Yes	No
Did it work?	Yes	No

FIGURE 4.1 Overview of case comparison

the annual meeting of a big political science conference. I happened to be attending the same business meeting as my two co-founders, Don Green and Jake Bowers. By that point, each of us individually had several ongoing collaborative relationships with non-researchers (including those who work in government, grassroots organizations, and campaigns). Some were informal and focused on knowledge exchange. In addition, each of us had conducted and published the results from several research partnerships.

It turned out that there was something else we shared in common. Increasingly, all three of us had colleagues from the research, practice, and/or policy worlds ask us for more details about how our collaborative relationships started and how they could do something like that themselves. These questions are understandable. The origin stories of cross-sector collaborative relationships are typically a mystery. Details are rarely shared in print (even when they entail research partnerships, the results of which do appear in print).[1] Even if the people approaching

---

[1] For more on this point, see Appendix C. There I cite the lack of origin stories appearing in print to help motivate the need for a detailed step-by-step guide for conducting research partnerships.

us intuitively knew interaction was an essential first step, their line of questioning aligned with the general argument of this book: they were uncertain how to engage.

During a meeting in the hallway after the business meeting, the three of us happened to strike up a conversation about the increasing frequency with which colleagues were approaching us with these kinds of questions. We all expressed a desire to make it easier for people to form these kinds of new collaborative relationships.

That initial conversation crystallized into plans for a workshop in late January 2017 entitled "Experiments in the Public Interest." While many of the "how do you start?" conversations that we had been having arose with people interested in both experimental and non-experimental work, we decided to focus on experiments at the beginning to narrow the scope a bit. This decision also reflected the substantially growing interest in research partnerships focused on experiments in political science, the discipline in which all three of us received our academic training (Butler 2019, Druckman and Green 2021, Levine 2021).

"Experiments in the Public Interest" took place on January 30, 2017, at the National Press Club in Washington, DC. One hundred and five people attended, almost entirely political scientists and non-profit practitioners, and the room was overflowing. I would characterize the room as filled with excitement and possibility as well as more than a little angst. President Trump had just been inaugurated, and many people in the room described their interest in new cross-sector collaborative relationships as a reflection of a desire to work differently than they had been. For them, Trump's election (which, rightly or wrongly, had been viewed as unlikely and a surprise by most people in the room) felt like a wake-up call. For the researchers in particular, many were motivated by a growing concern about anti-intellectualism. They wanted to be more intentional about challenging widespread academic detachment from the world. For the nonprofit practitioners, many expressed an even greater urgency to strengthen their empirical basis of what works.

The afternoon workshop entailed two hours of presentation and facilitated discussion, followed by a happy hour. Attendees sat at large round tables, and there was an initial round of introductions in which all 105 people stated their name, organization, and position. This was important so that people had a rough sense of who was there, and really underscored the diversity of problems that people in the room were addressing. We then had six flash talks in which pairs of researchers and practitioners/

policymakers discussed the goals and origin story of their work.[2] Next we had group discussions at each table to lift up people's interest in, but also questions about, how to start new collaborative relationships. Finally, we hosted a happy hour that was supposed to be one hour but lasted for two. The initial introductions, flash talks, and table-wide engagements had clearly greased the wheels of conversation!

As it turned out, during the planning stages, the workshop had morphed from a one-time event to a kick-off for what came to be known as research4impact 1.0. In large part, our change of thinking reflected nudging from our funder, who encouraged us to think about ways to institutionalize these connections for a broader set of people going forward. This encouragement was definitely pushing against an open door, as we saw while planning for the workshop that there were many people who wanted to attend but couldn't.

We decided that an online platform would be a way for people from the research, practice, and policy spaces to reveal their interest in new cross-sector collaborative relationships and connect with each other. Moreover, it could be used for a wide range of new connections, including formal collaboration (research partnerships that entailed experiments as well as partnerships that did not entail experiments) and informal collaboration oriented toward knowledge exchange. Ultimately, the LinkedIn-style online platform allowed people from these different communities to build searchable profiles that included a wide variety of collaboration-relevant information in response to closed-ended and open-ended questions. In advance of the launch, we also gathered feedback from a dozen people from across these spaces who tested the site to make sure that the profile text was useful and the site search feature was functional.

In the profiles, people could include their name, position, location(s) where their work takes place, whether they do experimental and/or non-experimental work, and their primary sector (government, nonprofit, academic, other). We also included a list of topics they work on (e.g., civic/political engagement, communication, public opinion, consumption/financial decisions, etc.). On top of this, there were large fill-in-the-blank spaces for the following information:

Past research
Past collaboration
Current work
Extra information

[2] All of our examples were research partnerships, just given the focus of this initial event.

The last two sections were the most forward-looking, and that's where people wrote about specific research questions they want to answer (e.g., "How can we increase voluntarism in our community?") and broad research areas they want to address (e.g., "I am open to collaboration in many areas related to political persuasion"). In many cases, people shared information relevant to research partnerships, though not always. Some were quite explicit about wanting knowledge exchange (e.g., a researcher who posted: "I'm happy to just offer advice or brainstorm with folks who are not yet sure what they want to do or if cooperation with an academic is a good idea. Please get in touch!"). There was also a place on the profiles for people to include a link to a personal website as well. Last, there was no charge to use the site.

In sum, the platform enabled people to curate highly personalized profiles with several open-ended opportunities to describe themselves and why they would be interested in new cross-sector connections. That said, once they joined the platform by creating a profile, people were on their own. It was easy to search profiles and use the platform to message others, and of course they knew that others in the network were at least in principle open to new cross-sector collaborative relationships (otherwise they would not have joined). Yet these new connections needed to be self-initiated, and there was no specific form letter and/or script suggestions to guide the process of reaching out to others.

From the perspective of profile creation, research4impact 1.0 was quickly a success. As I mentioned in the opening of Chapter 1, within the first ten months, 388 people built profiles, of which approximately two-thirds were academics and one-third were nonprofit practitioners (along with a small handful of people working in government). These were people who demonstrated that they saw good reason to connect with diverse thinkers around problems they were working on. In addition, while it's true that most people joined the network based on their work affiliation, engaging in cross-sector collaborative relationships was generally a voluntary activity and not a required part of their job description (thus the fact that they joined the network anyway suggests that a lack of organizational incentives was not greatly holding them back). Moreover, the content of the profiles was civic in orientation, in the sense of being oriented toward problems that affected broad communities they care about. Thus, we had observed close to 400 people who overcame several of the major barriers to voluntary civic engagement: they had demonstrated a certain degree of motivation as well as capacity and had taken advantage of an opportunity (Rosenstone and Hansen 1993, Verba et al. 1995).

We had every reason to believe that the growth of the network would lead to a flurry of new collaborative relationships. Yet it did not. By December 2017, only seven (!) people had initiated contact with someone else in the network. Of those, six were researchers. Almost zero nonprofit practitioners initiated a new collaborative relationship on the platform.

The winter of 2017–2018 had become a "do-or-die" moment for us. We were nearing the point where information in the profiles was starting to become outdated. The platform's continued relevance depended upon encouraging people to log in and update their current and desired work. The question was whether that was worth the trouble, or if we should simply shut it down.

Alternatively, another option would be to reach out to some of those who created profiles and ask them directly about why they weren't using it. Maybe we had missed something big when designing it. Or maybe the hesitation we were observing was due to other factors unrelated to the platform's design. Perhaps it really was time constraints, or simply a lack of interest (perhaps they were "collaboration-curious" but that was the extent of it).

I decided to pursue this outreach approach. I contacted some of those who had joined the platform by building a profile, yet had not initiated any new collaborative relationships. I focused on those who had attended our kick-off meeting (or, if they didn't attend, had expressed interest and regret for not attending) and also those that I had previously spoken with about the platform and thus already knew to some extent. Overall, over the course of several months, I reached out to 45 people, including 28 nonprofit practitioners and 17 researchers.

While I was intentional in who I reached out to, the interactions themselves were very informal. Sometimes they occurred over email, sometimes over the phone, sometimes in person with people I saw at conferences. At the time I was reaching out solely in my role as the head of a nonprofit organization, not as a researcher trying to systematically understand how to foster new collaborative relationships (unlike in my interviews in Chapter 3, where I specifically opened by saying that I was conducting research on this topic and writing this book, and solicited their consent prior to our conversation).

I had a vague sense that relationality-related concerns might be a source of hesitation (though I had not put the theoretical pieces together in my head quite yet), but I did not know for sure and I did not want to prime people. On top of that, I did not feel like I knew the right way to prime people even I had wanted to. I was uncertain how to ask about elements of relationality – I did not yet have the right language for what that might look like in this context. So, I wanted to provide the most general prompt possible and allow the conversation to flow from there.

When I reached out, I said that I wanted to get their feedback on the platform and their experiences with it. I also readily shared my main observation at the beginning of the conversations – the fact that hundreds of people had taken the time to join but very few had actually used it to reach out to others. I had hoped that naming that descriptive norm would make people comfortable sharing any sources of hesitation they had.

As it turned out, many responses referenced elements of relationality. In particular, practitioners I spoke with frequently doubted whether the researcher would really care about what they have to say. Some also expressed trustworthiness concerns, especially if they worked in areas that were explicitly under attack at that time (e.g., those who worked on reproductive rights). In other cases, both researchers and practitioners mentioned being under severe time constraints and concerned that it would take too much time to figure out how to engage and also how a collaborative relationship with a particular person would be useful to them at that moment (this latter concern spoke to questions about the helpfulness of the information that they, and the other person, would bring to the table). Many also expressed script concerns – being uncertain about the most effective way to convey their goals and expertise cross-sectorally. In short, from these brief and very informal interviews, I gleaned an early sense that uncertainty about relationality was an important barrier to new collaborative relationships, even among people who had already built profiles and articulated reasons in those profiles why engaging with diverse thinkers could be valuable to their work.

Catchafire

Catchafire was founded in 2009 to help nonprofit leaders effect change by connecting them with skilled volunteers. The practitioners in the network seek to improve their communities by conserving the environment, improving education, developing young people's skills, fighting for civil rights, helping people in poverty, and so much more. Yet resources are often very scarce and staff are stretched thin while also being asked to take on many tasks at once, some of which are outside their area of expertise.

That's why, just like research4impact 1.0, Catchafire created an online platform to make it easy for nonprofit practitioners to connect with volunteers who bring unique forms of expertise that are relevant to their goals and challenges. The volunteers help meet immediate organizational needs and also empower staff, and they typically start off as strangers to each other (I infer this latter point based on the existence of the platform – if people already knew each other, they would not need a separate platform like this). Moreover, the practitioners and the volunteers share a desire to improve the communities that they are part of as well as a recognition that bringing diverse expertise to improving those communities is extremely valuable.

Catchafire's online platform works as follows. Nonprofits populate it with listings that contain specific goals. The listings include a brief overview of the organization as well as contextual information about its work, mission, and the importance of the problems it is tackling and opportunities it is creating in the community. The goal is to communicate their impact and how, by working with them, volunteers can tangibly contribute to the impact themselves. If nonprofits want help with any part of the listing process along the way, Catchafire has a team of advisors that are available to offer advice. Once listings are up, then volunteers respond to them through the platform.

Nonprofits use Catchafire listings to advertise their desire for new collaborative relationships with one of two goals: informal collaborative conversations with volunteers oriented toward knowledge exchange and/ or formal collaborations that entail shared projects with volunteers. New collaborative relationships oriented toward knowledge exchange consist of one-hour phone calls that center pressing questions related to organizational strategy and how to move forward. These conversations broadly speak to the question "What works?" and may cover topics such as how to select the right database, use social media more effectively, build new partnerships for fundraising, or collect the data they need to better measure their impact. The practitioner and volunteer remain independent decision-makers, yet the one-hour conversation is useful for brainstorming and figuring out a few key steps about what to do next. They are premised on the idea that even a single one-hour conversation can inform collective action within the nonprofit going forward (along the indirect route I identified in Chapter 1). And these conversations also provide volunteers with the opportunity to learn about how their expertise is valuable in new ways and in new contexts.

Alternatively, the goal of these collaborative relationships may be to directly lead to new collective action in which the practitioner and volunteer work on a project together. These projects involve some degree of shared ownership, decision-making authority, and accountability, and may last several weeks or months. Projects vary widely and may entail co-creating new marketing campaigns, revamped websites, fundraising campaigns, and so on. Some projects are also a series of strategy sessions (perhaps related to marketing, succession planning, social media, and the like) in which diverse thinkers engage interactively over several weeks. These "facilitated strategy sessions" are ideal when a single one-hour call might not be enough.

Many practitioners do not pay to access the online platform. Instead, Catchafire relies on foundation partners who fund access for a list of nonprofits in their network (typically their grantees). Many of the foundations are community foundations that focus on building the capacity of small nonprofits located in a particular geographic area (e.g., the Boston metro region, the Atlanta metro region). Indeed, as we also experienced with research4impact 1.0, large well-resourced nonprofits tend to have the expertise they need in-house and are less likely to seek out cross-sector connections with strangers using platforms like this.

Even when "free," many practitioners still may not feel like they even have the time for a one-hour call (or more), and so there can be a gap between having access to the platform and using it (i.e., creating listings). As a result, Catchafire has started quantifying the value of the time spent. Over time, they've shifted their messaging away from saying that Catchafire would save time and instead started quantifying how the time nonprofits do spend fostering new collaborative relationships is worth it. For instance, they describe the formal projects in terms of money and hours that will be saved if they find a match via Catchafire versus how much it would cost to outsource it and/or complete the job on their own.

Catchafire has been quite successful. From their founding in 2010 through 2018, the number of matches steadily increased every year. During that period, 3,997 practitioners engaged in a new collaborative relationship with a volunteer, either for a single call or for a longer project. The total number of hours that volunteers donated was approximately 358,000. In 2018 alone, 1,243 practitioners matched for a call or project, and volunteers donated approximately 75,000 hours. By 2021, those numbers had increased more than threefold: 4,065 practitioners and approximately 245,000 hours donated.[3]

---

[3] Data come from the 2018 and 2021 annual impact reports published by Catchafire.

ANALYSIS

Echoing Figure 4.1, Catchafire and research4impact 1.0 are functionally similar in many ways. Both involve an online platform with profiles created by nonprofit practitioners,[4] in which new connections occur through the platform by one person directly reaching out to another, the use of the platform is voluntary, building profiles takes time, and the people involved typically start as strangers. Moreover, the reason why people join both platforms is to form new collaborative relationships that impact collective action either indirectly (via an informal knowledge exchange) or directly (by engaging in a formal shared project together). The civic actors involved in both networks want to improve communities they care about, and believe that engaging directly with others who bring distinct, task-relevant expertise is relevant for their strategic decision-making.

Yet despite these many similarities, the outcomes were drastically different. To put things simply, Catchafire has worked and research4impact 1.0 did not. So, in the spirit of a most-similar case study comparison, we need to ask: is there a key difference between them that is a likely cause of the different outcomes? This is where my theoretical guidance leads me to focus on relationality.

First, recall how research4impact 1.0 worked. In the profiles, people identified why they wanted new collaborative relationships, but in terms of deciding how to initiate new connections, they were on their own. When we designed the platform, our assumption was that, once people in the network knew others' substantive goals, and observed the fact that others had chosen to join the network in the first place, then they would feel comfortable reaching out. Thus, although research4impact 1.0 gave potential collaborators an opportunity to communicate why they wanted to form new collaborative relationships, it did not institutionalize mechanisms to actively assist them in how to do that.

In contrast, as it turns out, Catchafire's listing-creation process actively facilitates new collaborative relationships by institutionalizing mechanisms along these lines. These mechanisms reduce uncertainty about how potential collaborators will (and should) relate to each other, thus aiming to establish that they will relate to each other in ways that they would like. And as it turns out, these relationality-creating mechanisms speak

---

[4] Researchers and policymakers could also create profiles on the research4impact online platform, but here I am just focusing on what the two cases share in common: profiles created by nonprofit practitioners.

to many of the concerns that my interviewees expressed in Chapter 3.[5] In particular, the very structure of the listing-creation process and the listings themselves build in mechanisms to demonstrate that the experience of interacting will be enjoyable (by overcoming script concerns, uncertainty about time expectations, self-competence concerns, and concerns about whether the other person would value one's expertise) and that high-quality information will be shared (by overcoming trustworthiness concerns and self-competence concerns). I discuss each in turn.

Script Concerns

Similar to the research4impact 1.0 online platform, which included a list of collaboration topics, Catchafire provides a pre-set list of dozens of "call types" (topics for one-hour strategic conversations like organizational strategy, marketing strategy, social media, tech systems, etc.) and over 100 "project types" (categories of formal, clearly delineated projects that extend over time) that nonprofits can choose from. Yet on top of providing lists, Catchafire also provides examples of the (anonymous) text that previous practitioners have used to describe their needs. That text can be directly copied and pasted into one's own new listing. For instance, if nonprofits say that they want a conversation to talk about organizational strategy, then they are presented with examples of actual text from other successful organizational strategy requests. If someone isn't quite sure where to start they can use this text:[6]

I'd like some advice on the best way to start the strategic planning process. I was recently elected to a Board of Directors and asked to head the strategic planning committee.

Or if someone wants an example of a slightly more specific request, they can use this text:

My organization is shifting our programming to be virtual. I want to brainstorm some different ideas and directions our organization could go with to create new programs or adapt our existing ones.

These examples provide specific text of what to say to ensure one's goals are legible to the intended audience. They also legitimize that it's alright

---

[5] As a result, in what follows I use the same language that I used in Chapter 3 to label them, though I acknowledge that this was not always the language that I saw Catchafire use in the materials I reviewed or on its website.

[6] These quotes were taken directly from Catchafire's website, which I accessed on April 4, 2022.

to say it – that this is the type of (somewhat vague, or maybe ultra-specific) request that someone can make and expect to initiate a successful new collaborative relationship.

For the formal projects, Catchafire also includes a large amount of basic project language that is hard-coded into the template for each listing, including expected deliverables, reasons why nonprofits might need this type of project, and a project plan (who needs to do what and when). From there, nonprofits can then add more contextual information about their organization and the impact they are having. So for instance, one Catchafire project listing is called a "Survey Results Analysis," which is also akin to one type of project that researchers and practitioners in the research4impact 1.0 network might wish to partner on.[7] If a nonprofit wants to find a match for this purpose, it is not simply the case that they select it from the drop-down menu and then fill in the blanks with organization-specific information. Rather, the "Survey Results Analysis" listing option on the Catchafire website includes a hard-coded list of deliverables such as "Analysis of 1 set of survey data that is already at hand," a list of reasons why nonprofits might need this such as "You have distributed a survey to stakeholders and have survey results that need to be analyzed," and a four-step project plan with includes prep work (reviewing data), two rounds of analysis, and a final summary.

This additional information on the Catchafire pages for collaborative conversations and for projects provides a script that helps overcome any uncertainty that practitioners may have about what they need to say, and what is appropriate to say, upfront. It also provides a clear order of events for the script: first the practitioner writes the listing, and then volunteers respond. With the research4impact 1.0 platform, either person could initiate the interaction. In retrospect, it is possible that was too open-ended.

One final way in which Catchafire helps overcome script concerns is that it employs a team of advisors who are available to assist practitioners when they are creating new listings. This team reads listings after they are posted and will reach out to clarify things that are unclear, fix typos, and make sure practitioners have filled in all of the blanks. Ultimately, the success of each listing depends upon qualified and motivated volunteers choosing to respond via the online platform, but these advisors help ensure that listings clearly convey practitioners' needs in the first place.

---

[7] In the research4impact case, the data analysis may be a bit more involved than the standard Catchafire case. Thus in that case the benefit exchange is such that a researcher might offer to analyze administrative data pro bono and in return ask to use some of the data in a publishable paper.

Uncertainty about Time Expectations

A second type of relationality concern that Catchafire's online platform explicitly overcomes is about whether the potential collaborators will be responsive to each others' time constraints. One way that happens is by distinguishing one-hour calls as a separate activity unto themselves and explicitly labeling them as one hour. Another way is that each of the project listings provides an explicit time estimate for how long it is expected to take. For instance, the "Survey Results Analysis" project listing says that the deliverable should take 2–4 weeks, and so this is common knowledge upfront for both nonprofits and volunteers. On top of that, for nonprofit practitioners who are thinking about creating a new listing, Catchafire also tells them to "expect to spend approximately 1–3 hours managing this project."

Self-Competence Concerns

Volunteers may be uncertain about the value of their expertise – a feeling of "Am I really an expert in this?" Often people are uncertain about whether what they know can really be helpful to others in very different contexts. To be sure, some people are overconfident, but in many cases, part of the process of making expertise useful in civic life entails connecting dots anew.

With that in mind, Catchafire actively aims to overcome self-competence concerns by identifying ways in which knowledge in one context may be useful in another and then conveying that possibility to volunteers. After they create accounts, volunteers receive emails that contain Catchafire-created videos communicating the value of their skills. The videos have titles like "Your skills are invaluable to nonprofits" and then provide specific examples of how skills can be helpful. For instance, one thing they focus on is how baseline skills such as technical knowledge or marketing skills that volunteers may take for granted in their day-to-day jobs can be transformative for nonprofits that do not have someone on staff with those skills.

Trustworthiness Concerns

Nonprofits may be uncertain about whether they can trust the volunteers, and that's especially the case if they need to share data or other sensitive information about organizational strategy, fundraising, and so on. Here,

Catchafire helps overcome concerns about this element of relationality by giving practitioners tools to help verify trustworthiness, including testimonials from previous Catchafire projects, examples of work produced from those projects, and examples of nondisclosure agreements (NDAs) that they can use if they are sharing data (along with informing them about the importance of NDAs if they are new to using them). I should note that the research4impact 1.0 profiles had a specific spot for past collaborations, which in part gets at a similar idea, but did not have a space for testimonials from others.

Will They Value My Expertise?

Testimonials from others also help with overcoming practitioners' concerns that a volunteer may not value their expertise. Another way is to interact directly. For one-hour conversations, this is the core of the engagement, and if everyone's expertise is not being valued, then the collaborative relationship has a natural end point. Yet for possible longer-term projects, Catchafire normalizes the idea that practitioners should have a brief initial conversation with volunteers who are interested, in part to get a sense of what it is like to engage interactively with them – how comfortable they feel around the other person, if the other person is pleasant, if the other person is responsive (or alternatively dismissive) of considerations raised, and so on. The practitioner (and the volunteer as well) can easily make these judgments prior to committing to working together. Moreover, this step is hard-coded into the information that Catchafire shares with practitioners who are just getting started using the platform and then again when they post new project listings.

CONCLUSION

Comparing research4impact 1.0 and Catchafire reinforces something important about how expertise becomes useful in civic life: it happens through collaborative relationships that people value and feel comfortable engaging in. Successfully doing that requires establishing relationality, which the Catchafire online platform facilitates in five explicit ways. Overall, this case comparison provides evidence consistent with the information and interaction hypotheses in Chapter 2. To be sure, it does not permit tests of each hypothesis individually, yet taken in totality (and when combined with considerations raised in the in-depth interviews from Chapter 3), we see evidence that attributes of the information shared and the experience of interacting both matter for potential collaborators.

All of that said, one might still look at my case comparison and be tempted to identify other differences between the research4impact 1.0 and Catchafire online platforms that I did not discuss in detail. Maybe what really matters is that research4impact involved researchers, and those kinds of connections simply entail unique barriers? I address that possibility directly in Chapter 5, where I discuss the introduction of an intervention to overcome relationality uncertainty in that context.

5

Surfacing and Meeting Unmet Desire for New Collaborative Relationships

Expertise matters in civic life when we share it with others, yet new collaborative relationships that people would value do not always arise on their own for a variety of reasons mentioned in Chapters 3 and 4. In this chapter, I turn from explaining the barriers to testing new ways to overcome them.

With that in mind, this chapter has three main goals. First, I test the two intervention hypotheses from Chapter 2. To do so, I examine two ways of creating collaborative relationships anew: (1) introducing third parties (i.e., "matchmakers") who actively connect people who would remain disconnected if left to their own devices (and in the process help ensure that they relate to each other in ways that each would like), and (2) having potential collaborators directly provide information that overcomes uncertainty about relationality. These are by no means the only types of interventions that can establish relationality in situations where uncertainty exists, but I focus on them because they are quite common and also relatively accessible for implementing anew.[1]

---

[1] For instance, the Catchafire online platform discussed in Chapter 4 would be another type of intervention. One interesting question for future research would be to investigate how people who seek to create new collaborative relationships decide which intervention is the right one for them. On several occasions I've had people reach out who are interested in creating new collaborative relationships between researchers and non-researchers, and during the conversation I'll share details about my experience with research4impact 1.0 (the online platform, as described in Chapter 4) and then the introduction of hands-on matchmaking as research4impact 2.0 (described later in this chapter). A common follow-up question I receive is about whether there are ways to automate the process – essentially an alternative online platform that could be more successful, as opposed to implementing relatively labor-intensive hands-on matchmaking. My answer is always to start from the

A key premise of testing the impact of these interventions is that there exists at least some unmet desire for collaborative relationships that people would value (otherwise, designing potential interventions to meet it would not make sense). Thus, along the way in this chapter, there is a second goal, which is to provide data showing several situations in which unmet desire arises. I do not intend to make global, overarching claims about its prevalence throughout all of civic life – those claims are not tenable for a variety of reasons I discuss at the end of the chapter – but instead I describe many examples in which unmet desire arises among a diverse set of people who seek change, including nonprofit practitioners, researchers, and local policymakers. Lastly, the third goal is to take stock of the impact of these new collaborative relationships between diverse thinkers, showing how they facilitate expertise becoming useful in civic life in new ways.

I organize the chapter as follows. I begin by discussing third parties, including several examples of organizations engaged in active matchmaking for their members and then a detailed case comparison between research4impact 2.0 and its online platform predecessor. Second, I discuss the strategy of directly communicating relationality to meet unmet desire. Next, I present three further examples of unmet desire, two in the context of local policymaking and one among early-career neuroscientists. Last, I provide a summary of the chapter's wide range of findings along with brief comments about the difficulty of making global statements about the prevalence of unmet desire (and instead why such assessments need to be context-specific). Woven throughout the chapter, and especially when discussing the strategies of using third parties and directly communicating relationality, are several studies and other data showing the impact of connecting people with diverse forms of expertise.

THIRD PARTIES: SEVERAL EXAMPLES

Research on persuasion (Lupia and McCubbins 1998), research translation (Dobbins et al. 2009, McGinty et al. 2019), and boundary spanners

---

theoretical principles that matter – how one can feasibly, and successfully, ensure that strangers feel comfortable interacting with each other. Later in this chapter I discuss why, once we realized that the research4impact online platform was not working, our attention turned to hands-on matchmaking as opposed to (for example) substantially revamping our platform so that it mimicked the structure of Catchafire.

(Bednarek et al. 2018) emphasize how third parties can vouch for the credibility of speakers and also connect people who are otherwise disconnected. Examples of such third parties in civic life – oriented toward building new connections among people who seek change in communities they care about – abound. I begin my discussion of third parties by describing a few.

One example is the Commons Social Change Library, based in Australia. It describes itself on its website as an "online collection of education resources on campaign strategy, community organizing, digital campaigning, communications and media, working effectively in groups, fundraising, diversity and inclusion and much more." One of the most distinctive features of the site is that, in addition to including resources that people can access and read, it also employs librarians who help groups identify what they can share and how to share it, and then also actively broker new connections with other organizations that they do not currently know.

Another example of an active third-party matchmaker is the Climate Advocacy Lab, based in the United States, a nonprofit organization that includes an extensive library of online resources for the climate organizers, activists, and researchers in its network. It, too, employs staff members to broker new connections between people in the network.

A third example is the Research-to-Policy Collaboration (RPC), a model that supports lawmakers by connecting them with researchers who share interests (Crowley et al. 2021). The goal is to strengthen the use of research evidence in policy on a wide variety of issues, such as substance use, child welfare, workforce development, and many others. RPC staff connect researchers with deep understanding of these issues in a way that meets the cadence of policymaking – recognizing that policymakers' needs continually shift and that the usefulness of research depends upon both its rapid availability and the ability of policymakers and their staff to engage in back-and-forth collaborative relationships with researchers. Importantly, the RPC model was created precisely because its developers knew that these collaborative relationships often don't start (and weren't starting) on their own.

Hall (2022) describes another example of the critical role that third parties play in facilitating new collaborative relationships, in this case within transnational advocacy networks. Her focus is the Online Progressive Engagement Network (OPEN), a nonprofit organization that supports digital campaigning groups in over 19 countries around the world. A critical part of OPEN is that it hires "network architects" whose job involves, first, knowing what strategies its members are pursuing, and then second, actively brokering new connections between members when knowledge exchange would be valuable. Typically, these connections are brokered online, though the network architects also organize face-to-face meetings to deepen relationships and make people more comfortable engaging with each other.

The very existence of network architects is premised on the idea that new connections do not happen on their own. Even if people in the network would value engaging with others (because campaign tactics and strategies that work in one place may work in another), OPEN has found that matchmaking is critical. The network architects connect people who already know each other but may not be aware of what they can learn from each other. They also connect people who do not already know each other, also in order to share knowledge and build new connections that will inform strategic decision-making. Both are important, even in a network like this one in which activists are part of the same sector and already have a common language to describe what they do.

The final example I highlight upfront is CHAIN: Contact, Help, Advice, and Information Network (Russell et al. 2004). CHAIN is an online resource run by the National Health Service in the UK for people working in health care who have an interest in learning about and adopting evidence-based medicine. And as it turns out, CHAIN experienced similar early failures as the research4impact 1.0 online platform. Russell et al. write:

The originators of CHAIN initially saw the network as a tool for people interested in evidence based health care to make connections themselves. As the network has developed, however, the role of staff in brokering the contact between members has become increasingly prominent. (2)

All of the foregoing examples illustrate part of my argument, which is that third parties are important for creating collaborative relationships between diverse thinkers because potentially valuable connections do not always happen on their own. In what follows, I go further and use a case study to show the impact of implementing third-party matchmaking where it does not currently exist. Akin to the comparison in Chapter 4, this case study provides analytic leverage to understand what happens when a wide variety of background conditions are held constant.[2]

While individuals can certainly act as third-party matchmakers – a point that I return to in Chapter 6 – my case study focuses on an organization. Relative to any single individual, organizations arguably are likely to have an easier time identifying opportunities and overcoming uncertainty about relationality across a wider set of people, as well as setting new norms about what is possible. In addition, my focus on organizations also underscores the importance of an oft-neglected part of civic life within the research literature: the meso-level (Han and Barnett-Loro 2018). Meso-level analyses focus on the strategies that organizations pursue to realize collective aims, such as (in this case) institutionalizing procedures for creating new collaborative relationships between people with diverse forms of expertise.

THIRD PARTIES: THE CASE OF RESEARCH4IMPACT 2.0

The example I focus on is matchmaking that was implemented as part of research4impact 2.0. Recall from Chapter 4 that the initial version of research4impact – version 1.0 – was an online platform on which 388 researchers and nonprofit practitioners (and a smattering of local policymakers) created online profiles, yet almost no one reached out to anyone else. Also recall that in my informal interviews with people who joined the platform but did not use it, they expressed several concerns that stemmed from the same sources of uncertainty about relationality that interviewees and survey respondents shared in Chapter 3: script concerns, concerns about whether others would value their knowledge, uncertainty about the value and trustworthiness of information that specific people would share, and concerns about the time and expectations required to engage successfully. It was clear from these informal interviews that the online platform itself did not provide enough relational glue to overcome these concerns. While offering opportunities is important for those seeking new collaboration, this example underscores how it needs to be the right kind of opportunity – one that takes seriously the

---

[2] While matchmaking sometimes has the connotation of new *romantic* relationships, the research4impact 1.0 evidence from Chapter 4 along with the examples in this chapter suggest that at least some civic actors would find it beneficial in the realm of new *collaborative* relationships.

ways in which people want potential collaborators to relate to them, and vice versa.

Based on these interviews, in 2018, Don, Jake, and I[3] decided to launch what came to be known as *research4impact 2.0*, which would entail hands-on matchmaking. Our decision to offer hands-on matchmaking was guided by theoretical considerations – our belief about the most effective and feasible way to ensure that people in our network could relate to each other in ways that they would like. While we considered the possibility of revising our online platform to more closely mimic the structure of Catchafire's platform discussed in Chapter 4 (which connected nonprofit practitioners and skilled volunteers), ultimately we concluded based on my informal interviews that a hands-on approach would likely be more successful.[4]

With the decision in hand, I decided to develop and implement a process called Research Impact Through Matchmaking (RITM) (Levine 2020a).[5] RITM was premised on the general idea that hands-on matchmaking can be important for creating new collaborative relationships between strangers. But it also went beyond that because simply introducing people to each other only addresses some of the types of relationality concerns that might prevent successful new collaborative relationships from forming. Indeed, while it may be common to think about a matchmaker as simply a person who makes an introduction, the research4impact 1.0 experience suggests that how the match is made (i.e., how relationality is established) matters. Thus, I designed RITM to include methods that would more directly overcome several sources of uncertainty about relationality.

Here I describe the RITM method and then my experience implementing it as part of research4impact 2.0. I present it in detail because I believe it is important to be clear about what, exactly, the matchmaker is doing – what kind of information is being gathered from potential collaborators and then how the matchmaker is taking that information and using it to reduce uncertainty about relationality. My goal in presenting RITM is not to argue that it is the *only* way to conduct hands-on matchmaking with diverse thinkers. Instead, I treat it as a case study of a reasonable

---

[3] Don Green, Jake Bowers, and I were the three co-founders of research4impact.
[4] The key point is that the best relationality-creating intervention is likely to vary, and the decision about its structure should be guided by considerations about what forms of uncertainty about relationality exist and how to effectively overcome them.
[5] My description of RITM here expands upon the content in the original paper that introduced it (Levine 2020a).

way to do so given the information about researchers and practitioners I had gathered from those who built profiles on the research4impact 1.0 online platform (and then to examine RITM's impact and compare it to the inaction observed on the platform).

The RITM process begins when a requester (i.e., a researcher, practitioner, or policymaker) reaches out to research4impact to indicate that they are looking for a cross-sector collaborative relationship that does not yet exist – in other words, there is unmet desire. Once initiated, it includes two main steps: (1) defining the scope and (2) making the connection.

Step 1: Defining the Scope

In this first step of RITM, the matchmaker engages in a "scope call" with the requester to learn about their work and expertise, and about why they are looking for a new collaborative relationship (i.e., what kind of diverse expertise would be helpful for the goals and/or challenges they are facing in their work). Defining the scope entails learning enough so that their request may be characterized in a way that simultaneously captures the voice of the person making it while also being stated in terms that appeal to the intended audience. Crucially, given that these collaborative relationships are voluntary, scope calls entail articulating both why requesters would value engagement as well as why potential collaborators should want to engage with them. They also entail surfacing any hesitations that requesters themselves may have about engaging in new collaborative relationships, perhaps about the information to be shared and/or the experience of interacting (i.e., the two broad types of concerns about others described in Figure 3.1).

In some cases, requesters already have a well-formed question that is likely to appeal to an intended audience. For example, in 2021, a practitioner who runs an organization working to increase year-round voter engagement reached out to research4impact. Her organization had pioneered a new app that provides up-to-date information to keep voters informed about issues they care about and how legislation related to those issues is progressing. The app sends alerts when Congress will be voting on these issues and then makes it easy to share their opinion directly with their representative's office. Afterward, the app tracks how the representative votes as well as the outcomes of bills.

One measure of the app's impact is the number of people who use it. Yet the leader of this organization reached out because her theory of change entailed not only spurring more ongoing activity, but also higher voter turnout. Her theory of change was that greater engagement with the business of legislating would also increase voter turnout during midterms, primaries, and other nonpresidential elections. She was looking to engage with a researcher to first talk about what would be involved with measuring impact in these ways – how feasible would it be to link behavior on the app with voter turnout data, how much would it cost to do so, and how long would it take. This would be a collaborative conversation to think through key strategic decisions regarding how best to conceptualize and measure impact. She was also open to a longer-term partnership to study the impact of the app on nonpresidential voter turnout.

I mention this example in detail because it shows how defining the scope can sometimes occur quite quickly, which was the case for several reasons here. One is that the practitioner had a single, clearly defined goal in mind that would be legible and feasible from the perspective of many researchers. She wanted to answer the question: how does engagement with the app affect voter turnout? Her question was posed in a way that matches the structure that researchers are looking for with new projects. They need an outcome measure that varies and one or a set of measurable variables that might explain that outcome. In this case, all of this information was clearly stated right from the beginning. Her outcome of interest was voter turnout, which is also an outcome of interest for many researchers. Her "independent variable" was engagement with the app – while that is not necessarily something that researchers have studied before (after all, that's what made the app innovative!), it was a very concrete independent variable.

In addition, it was clear why both parties should want to speak to the other person (i.e., a "benefit exchange" could be clearly identified). During their interaction, the researcher would share details about ways to systematically measure the voter turnout impact of the app, which would benefit the practitioner. And the practitioner would share what her organization had learned so far about who participates and how they participate, which would be interesting and novel information for any researcher who studies topics related to voter engagement (and thus could shape the researcher's ideas about gaps in the literature, new research projects, and so on). If the initial conversation went well and they decided to formally partner on a research project, then both stood to gain from that as well. The practitioner could use data from a systematic study of impact to adjust the app's design, apply for future funding, and for personal gratification to know that her theory of change is working. The researcher could use the data to advance scientific understanding and write a publishable paper.

The upshot is that in this case, defining the scope was relatively straightforward: the practitioner's goal was clear, it was stated in a way that was likely to appeal to people from her intended audience, and it was easy to articulate a benefit exchange. The matchmaker's job is relatively easy here, yet still important. Even if the practitioner can easily answer the questions, she may not know that these are the only questions that need to be answered – a situation of not knowing what you don't know. Indeed, during the scope call, the practitioner specifically mentioned having unclear expectations. She said that she reached out to research4impact instead of trying to contact researchers on her own in part because it wouldn't be clear which researchers to contact, but also because she wasn't sure how much detail needed to be worked out in advance of contacting them. Thus, it helped to engage with a third-party matchmaker to be certain about what information needed to be known and shared upfront and what could remain unknown and worked out at a later date (i.e., it helped to engage to reduce uncertainty about relationality). In this case, a key part of the scope call was clarifying these expectations about the new collaborative relationship.

In other cases, defining the scope may be more involved, which also means that the matchmaker is arguably even more valuable. This can occur under several situations. One is that requesters may have a general topic of interest on which they would like to engage rather than a specific question they would like to answer. Another is when the benefit exchange is not immediately clear. For instance, a researcher may say that they study workers' rights and would love to engage with practitioners who are working on this issue. That's a great starting point, but also requires digging a bit deeper to define the scope in ways that would appeal to the intended audience. What kinds of workers' rights organizations is the researcher interested in engaging with – unions, advocacy organizations that aren't unions, something else? Why should these practitioners want to engage – that is, what specific knowledge does the researcher have that they are likely to find valuable? And what question needs to be answered – is the goal knowledge exchange, or a more formal research partnership, or possibly both?

Another example where defining the scope is more involved is when the language that one person uses to describe their work needs to be translated into what would make sense to the intended audience. For instance, suppose a nonprofit practitioner works with an organization that hosts events to foster greater cross-cultural exchange within a community. The practitioner wants to connect with a researcher to talk about how to measure impact. In this case, the relevant keyword could be focused on a researcher who studies "cross-cultural exchange," but that may seem overly narrow only because researchers use different terms such as "social capital" or "civic engagement" to describe their work. Using the latter terms when conducting matchmaking is more likely to be successful with the intended audience.

Another key goal when defining the scope is to ensure that the requester can "see themselves" in the language being used. This is why scope calls also entail re-stating the requester's goal and the reasoning for using any alternative language, and then also inviting the requester to share ways in which the revised language is either inaccurate or correct (Levine 2020a). Deliberately inviting people to comment on inaccuracies, as opposed to asking something like "Does this sound ok?" helps legitimize the possibility that they may have concerns and that it is alright to raise them.

To summarize, defining the scope is the first part of RITM. This process involves several ways in which third parties work to reduce uncertainty about relationality between potential collaborators:

- Clarify the intended audience for a given request.
- Ensure that the requester's goal uses language likely to resonate with the intended audience.
- Articulate a benefit exchange (i.e., be able to answer the question: "Why should someone from the intended audience want to engage in a new collaborative relationship with you oriented toward that goal?).
- Surface any hesitations that the requester has about interacting with potential collaborators.

Step 2: Making the Connection

After defining the scope, the second step of RITM entails the matchmaker locating a match and making a connection. The methods for locating a match can take many different forms, and I describe two that we've used as part of research4impact 2.0 in the next section. For now, though, I skip ahead of the process of finding a match and focus on facilitating the connection after a match has been found. The key challenge when a third party connects two strangers who bring diverse, task-relevant forms of expertise to a problem is the same as I've identified throughout the book: each party may be uncertain that the other person will relate to them in ways that they would like, and vice versa. Some of that uncertainty can be surfaced and addressed during the scope call itself, as noted in the previous section. Yet making the connection is also another key moment for overcoming as much uncertainty about relationality as possible.

As a general matter, being intentional about how to make the connection is important because people typically think about and plan what they are going to say and ask in advance of a task-related meeting (Vorauer et al. 2009, Loyd et al. 2013). Thus, the content communicated to all parties when the connection is made can help steer this pre-meeting elaboration in ways that grease the wheels of conversation, so to speak.

In the case of RITM, this means facilitating new connections (e.g., writing emails) in ways that aim to overcome forms of uncertainty about relationality that are likely to matter to potential collaborators, either because they came up during the scope call and/or because I had reason to expect them to matter given prior experiences and the interviews in Chapter 3. In particular, I was focused on hesitations stemming from script concerns, concerns about whether potential collaborators would value their knowledge, concerns about the helpfulness and trustworthiness of the information shared, and concerns about the time required to engage successfully. To be sure, I would not expect that facilitation could completely overcome all of these concerns in every circumstance, but at the very least, I expected a few techniques would be broadly helpful.

In particular, RITM facilitation uses three main techniques: state each person's unique expertise, frame the conversation as a mutually beneficial learning opportunity, and re-state the goal of the conversation. First, stating each person's unique expertise is an example of "role assignment," which is akin to giving each new collaborator a discrete "role" for the conversation.[6] In this case, having a matchmaker explicitly name each collaborator's unique task-relevant expertise increases the likelihood that people fully share it (and others value it) during the conversation (Stasser

---

[6] Recall how "role assignment" echoes a technique mentioned by one of my interviewees in Chapter 3.

et al. 1995). As Sunstein and Hastie (2015:112) wrote in their book on how to improve group decision-making: "If a group wants to obtain the information that its members hold, all group members should be told [in advance] that members have different, and relevant, information to contribute."

Role assignment is especially helpful given the likelihood that potential collaborators unconsciously form status-based stereotypes, in which they may not recognize or value the expertise that each other brings to the task because of their social characteristics (Ridgeway 2001; see Chapter 2 for more details). By making task-relevant expertise common knowledge, it helps to both legitimize each person's expertise (thus aiming to overcome uncertainty about whether one has useful information to share, and also uncertainty about the trustworthiness of others' information) and also greases the wheels of conversation by providing a topic to ask each other about (thus aiming to overcome script concerns about what is appropriate to say).

The second technique is to frame the conversation as a mutually beneficial learning opportunity. The main idea here is that it is important that each collaborator sees a benefit from the interaction (or what I labeled earlier as a "benefit exchange") and that one way to achieve that is to ensure that collaborators view diverse forms of expertise as "an important resource for learning how best to accomplish [their] core work" (Ely and Thomas 2001:266). Role assignment helps achieve that goal, yet one way to further reinforce this way of thinking is to explicitly frame the interaction as a mutual learning opportunity. Galinsky et al. (2015), in their paper summarizing research on how to realize the benefits of diversity for group decision-making, argue that leaders can frame an interaction in this way by emphasizing how both people will "learn a lot" and "enjoy talking to one another" when making the connection. I employed this technique to help overcome relational concerns about whether the other person would care to learn about one's own task-relevant expertise.

The third technique is to re-state the goal of the conversation. This ensures that it is common knowledge: all collaborators know it, and know that others know it. In addition to role assignment, this technique further helps grease the wheels of conversation by providing a natural starting point as well as a clear metric for evaluating the conversation afterward. It also helps overcome concerns about time constraints by reducing the time needed to make sure the purpose and topic of the new collaborative relationship are clear from the beginning.

General Applicability of the RITM Process

To summarize, the RITM matchmaking process has two main steps: establishing the scope and making the connection. The steps and techniques involved may be used by any third party seeking to build new collaborative relationships between diverse thinkers, whether that third party is a single individual acting alone or an organization that wants to institutionalize matchmaking for forming new connections.

That said, the specific questions to ask during the scope call, and the kinds of roles that need to be "assigned" when making the connection, must be tailored to the ways that potential collaborators want others to relate to them (and vice versa) during the interaction. For instance, based on the survey of local policymakers in Chapter 3, a third party applying RITM to create new collaborative relationships between them and researchers would want to pay particular attention to establishing the non-partisan credentials of the researchers and also the practical knowledge of what they know when engaging in role assignment (and ensure that the researchers know how to share information in a non-partisan way as well; see Pielke 2007). Or, to echo the AmeriCorps program leaders survey also from Chapter 3, creating new collaborative relationships between them and researchers would involve paying attention to domain-specific expertise and practical information to be shared. Stepping back, the general point is that the techniques apply broadly, even though the specific implementation of them will vary considerably.

Last, it is also worth underscoring that while the RITM steps apply to collaborative relationships with both informal and formal collaboration goals, the fact that they focus on facilitating the initial match means that they are arguably only necessary *and* sufficient for success when the goal is matchmaking to create new knowledge exchange.[7] That's because when the goal is a formal partnership,[8] initial knowledge exchange is necessary but not sufficient for a new partnership to arise and be successful. Formal partnerships extend over time and their success depends upon

---

[7] Assuming, of course, that collaborators really do value each other's knowledge.

[8] Recall that the key distinction between collaborative relationships oriented toward knowledge exchange (informal collaboration) as opposed to formal partnerships (formal collaboration) is the degree of interdependence between collaborators. Knowledge exchange in and of itself entails relatively little interdependence, whereas formal partnerships entail projects with shared ownership, decision-making authority, and accountability, and thus far more interdependence.

not only overcoming uncertainty about relationality, but also a variety of other steps such as securing funding, training staff, completing new written agreements, achieving organizational buy-in, disseminating results, and so on. There can be a lot of variety in the precise steps involved, and they will vary depending upon the types of collaborators and the nature of the project. The steps involved with two nonprofit practitioners engaged as coalition partners for the first time are going to be different than a researcher and a government agency working together on a new initiative (for instance, the former does not need university institutional review board approval; the latter may entail extensive government approvals). The point is that it is hard to create one single facilitation method (i.e., "how-to guide") that applies across the full range of possible formal partnerships that diverse thinkers may wish to create. All of that said, I suspect one type of formal partnership that many readers of this book may be interested in is a new research project. Thus, in Appendix C, I include a full step-by-step guide for the initial knowledge exchange and what's needed afterward when the goal is to create new research partnerships.

Aside: The Impact of Knowledge Exchange on Strategic Decision-Making (Evidence from a Field Experiment)

Before I discuss the implementation and impact of RITM as part of research4impact 2.0, here I address a question that frequently arises when talking about collaborative relationships in civic life oriented toward knowledge exchange. I have found that when I highlight the possibility, and value, of new knowledge exchange as a goal unto itself between people who do not know each other, the potential impact on strategic decision-making is not always apparent. Back-and-forth interaction with the goal of knowledge exchange does not quite feel like "collaboration" to many people – indeed, as I discussed in Chapter 1, what comes to mind when people think about collaboration is far more often *formal* projects – and that can raise questions about how much a collaborative conversation could really matter.

With that concern in mind, here I present results from a randomized controlled trial that tests the impact of knowledge exchange on strategic decision-making in civic life. In particular, I tested whether the most fundamental interactive vehicle for knowledge exchange (a single collaborative conversation) could influence behavior in a meaningful way. And my baseline comparison would be a common way that people think about knowledge exchange that does not entail being collaborative: written dissemination.

Thus, I designed a study to compare what happens when decision-makers receive written disseminated information containing task-relevant expertise, versus what happens when they receive that same written disseminated information along with interactive knowledge exchange: a conversation to talk through how to apply the information in their particular context. For this study, I partnered with a nonprofit organization that conducts multi-day workshops around the world to train practitioners how to design and lead issue awareness campaigns in their local communities (the full details are described in Levine 2021b). The specifics of each campaign vary, but they are all related to increasing environmental sustainability. For instance, one workshop in Kitale, Kenya, included nonprofit practitioners who were learning how to lead campaigns that would persuade farmers in their local communities to shift from mono-cropping and toward more sustainable farming techniques. In another workshop outside Hanoi, Vietnam, participants were nonprofit practitioners who wanted to create awareness campaigns to persuade pig farmers in their local communities to start using living bio-beds as opposed to directing all waste to local waterways.

While the workshops trained participants to lead issue awareness campaigns on their own after the workshop was over, doing so was entirely voluntary and my partner organization knew that many participants did not ultimately do so for a variety of reasons. One reason was that, although the training was quite comprehensive, there were still important decisions that participants would have to make to successfully implement a campaign in their local community.

That observation motivated the design for our research study. We randomly assigned participants from four workshops in different countries to receive post-workshop follow-up in one of two forms. One half of attendees received an email from the workshop leader with actionable information that would be helpful as they faced key decision points designing and conducting their own issue awareness campaign. This technical information included quantitative and qualitative techniques for learning about the campaign's intended audience in advance, such as choosing which community members to interview and how to randomly select people from local markets and public squares to complete audience assessment surveys. It addressed stumbling blocks that my partner organization knew participants in the past had experienced, but that unfortunately they did not have time to cover during the main workshop.

The other half of attendees received those same written materials as well as a 30-minute Skype conversation with the workshop leader to talk through how they would apply this technical information in their particular context. The conversation introduced no new technical information above and beyond the written materials. It was only a back-and-forth interaction about how the participant could apply the techniques in their local community.

Note that the conversation is a good example of a collaborative relationship that aims to *indirectly* influence collective action. It is a collaborative relationship in the sense that it entails people with diverse forms of expertise (the workshop leader with expertise in how to design issue awareness campaigns, and the workshop participant with expertise in the local community where the campaign would be implemented) sharing what they know in order to come to a better understanding of how the technical knowledge and local place-based knowledge could be used to design the most effective issue awareness campaign. Its aim is indirect influence given that the workshop leader would not be partnering directly with participants to create the campaigns, but instead would be strategizing with them as they decide how to do so on their own. And it would indirectly influence collective action in the sense that, if participants chose to move forward, they would be working with one or more colleagues from their organization to implement it.[9]

Then, a few weeks later, all participants received a personalized email from the workshop leader inviting them to ask any questions about the materials (including offering to speak about them if that would be easier or more helpful than email). This ensured that all participants received at least some personalized contact from the workshop leader after the workshop had ended, regardless of whether they had been randomly assigned to receive the 30-minute Skype conversation. We thus held that aspect constant for everyone.

The key outcome measure of our study was behavioral: whether or not workshop participants chose to conduct an issue awareness campaign within two months of the workshop. The differences were striking, as shown in Figure 5.1. Among those who received only the written follow-up materials, 12.0 percent chose to conduct a campaign. Yet

[9] All of that said, one key difference between these collaborative relationships and most of the others I study in this book is that the workshop leader and the participant already know each other. They are not strangers. Thus, my goal in describing this example is not to suggest that it precisely mirrors the context of the examples from the rest of the book, but simply that it is a systematic test of the impact of knowledge exchange on decision-making in civic life.

	Received Only Written Disseminated Information	Received Written Disseminated Information + Engaged in Collaborative Conversation about It
Number of Workshop Participants	25	34
Number of Participants who Received Conversation	–	28 (82.4%)
Number of Participants who Conducted Issue Awareness Campaign	3 (12.0%)	20 (59.0%)
	Intent-to-Treat Estimate: 47.0 percentage points *(p < 0.00)* Complier Average Causal Effect: 57.0 percentage points *(p < 0.00)*	

FIGURE 5.1 Impact of knowledge exchange on decision-making
This is adapted from Levine 2021(b), Table 1. See that paper for more details on study procedure, including why the number of participants assigned to the two groups differed. In addition, the second row refers to the fact that, for a variety of reasons unrelated to the study itself (discussed in the paper), the workshop leader was unable to reach some participants who were supposed to receive a collaborative conversation.

among those who had received the written materials as well as the conversation to talk through how the participant would apply them in the local context, 59.0 percent had chosen to do so. Whether measured relative to everyone assigned to receive the conversation (the "intent-to-treat estimate") or relative to only those for whom the conversation actually took place (the "complier average causal effect"), the impact of knowledge exchange was substantively meaningful and statistically significant.[10] In addition, survey evidence from the study can help explain this behavioral difference. There was no evidence that those who had the conversation knew more about the technical material. Rather, the difference was in efficacy – those who had had the collaborative conversation were more likely to say that they personally felt capable of conducting an issue awareness campaign.

Two takeaways are worth noting. First, this study demonstrates that the power of knowledge exchange to indirectly influence collective action is potentially substantial. While there may sometimes be a good reason for diverse thinkers to want to engage in more formal partnerships,

---

[10] See estimates in Figure 5.1. P-values reported in Figure 5.1 are two-tailed, with estimates produced using randomization inference.

collaborative relationships solely focused on knowledge exchange can also greatly impact strategic decision-making. That's why, as I noted in Chapter 1, it is important that we explicitly distinguish and legitimize both goals of collaborative relationships in civic life. It is also why, when I am surfacing unmet desire for new collaborative relationships (as I will describe via several examples in the rest of this chapter), I am often very explicit about offering and legitimizing knowledge exchange as a worthy goal in and of itself.

The second takeaway from our study is that it demonstrates one of the key points I mentioned at the beginning of the book: using expertise in civic life is rarely a situation of plug-and-play. Instead what's needed is back-and-forth interaction to think about how the expertise would apply in a given context. The study results clearly demonstrate this point with respect to the technical information that workshop participants received. Thus, when I argue that collaborative relationships that people would value in civic life do not arise on their own, it means that we are missing key opportunities for using expertise to solve community problems.

Back to RITM: Testing the Introduction of a Third Party

I now return to talking about Research Impact Through Matchmaking (RITM), and how I implemented it in two ways as part of research4impact 2.0 (the "two ways" here refer to two ways of making a match, which I mentioned I had done earlier in the chapter). The first way was targeted toward practitioner-oriented email lists. In early 2018, I posted an announcement to five practitioner-oriented email lists inviting them to "learn about research that can help solve some of your organization's trickiest problems." I posted only once on four of the email lists and twice on the fifth email list (once in early 2018 and then a second posting in late 2018). I chose to advertise via these lists because, relative to cold emails from a relatively unknown organization at the time, I thought that my audience would be more likely to view the opportunity as trustworthy.

In the posts, I described research4impact as a global network of researchers with expertise on a wide variety of social and behavioral science research. When practitioners clicked to learn more about the opportunity, they were taken to a sign-up page that listed specific ways that a new collaborative relationship with a researcher could be helpful. The page invited people to respond who were looking for knowledge exchange and/or a more formal research partnership:

[Researchers] can tell you about relevant research that'll help track your impact in the world and to funders, develop the right measures and programs to achieve your goals, find the right data for your purpose, use data more efficiently and effectively, and so on. They can also give you a brief overview of a wide literature (because no one has time to read all that!).

You'll have short, high-impact personalized conversations. In addition, sometimes these conversations lead to longer-term research collaborations.

To make the implementation of research4impact 2.0 as comparable as possible to the research4impact 1.0 online platform, I made sure that all of the lists were composed of the same kinds of practitioners that had built profiles. This meant that they all work at nonprofits with a public interest mission (i.e., citizen groups; Berry 1999). They included program leaders, grassroots advocates, and organizers who are tackling a wide variety of issues related to the health of democracy and the social determinants of health: poor health care, low education, gun violence, climate change, low political engagement, traffic congestion, poor working conditions, and so on. And they are all involved in building a healthier public square, by fostering participation in the political process among people who are currently inactive and/or by boosting people's capacity and opportunity for more meaningful civic and political participation.

Practitioners expressed initial interest via a sign-up form online. From there, I implemented RITM by defining the scope. In most cases, this entailed a phone call, though sometimes the initial information in the form/email was sufficiently complete that it was possible to define the scope over email. Next, my process for finding matches was very targeted. I used my own network to locate a researcher who would likely be a good match, reached out to that person directly, and then asked them if they would like to be connected. If they said yes, I used the RITM techniques of role assignment, framing, and re-stating the goal when making a connection.

As in Chapter 4, my research design is an example of a most-similar case comparison (Gerring 2017), in which many of the background conditions comparing the research4impact 1.0 online platform with RITM-based research4impact 2.0 hands-on matchmaking are held constant (i.e., research4impact is the organization involved and the new collaborative relationships to be formed entail connecting the same kinds of nonprofit practitioners with researchers[11]). Yet as I'll describe

---

[11] In the online platform, researchers could reach out to practitioners as well as vice versa. Yet for purposes of the comparison here, I am only focused on practitioner-initiated collaborative relationships.

more later, the outcomes were quite different – the opportunity to take part in hands-on matchmaking led to far more new practitioner-initiated collaborative relationships than the do-it-yourself online platform. Given the presence of many similarities, yet a different outcome, the goal of a most-similar case study is to identify a factor that differs between the two cases and that we have theoretically grounded reason to believe is likely to explain the divergent outcomes. In this case, given the way in which RITM is specifically designed to overcome uncertainty about relationality, and the link between that and decisions to engage in new collaborative relationships, it seems reasonable to believe that the introduction of a third-party matchmaker can explain the divergence.

Results from research4impact 2.0

In total, I received 55 requests in response to these posts in 2018. Recall that the initial formation of research4impact was premised on the possibility of unmet desire – that there were practitioners (and researchers and policymakers) who would value new cross-sector collaborative relationships, yet these relationships did not always form on their own. The lack of engagement with the online platform called that starting premise into question. However, the responses to these email list postings suggest otherwise. They show that there was indeed a group of practitioners who valued new cross-sector connections. Similar to Catchafire, I observed they were interested in taking advantage of the right opportunity that presented itself, one that was intentional about overcoming several of the major sources of uncertainty about relationality.

Echoing this point, at the end of the scope calls, I asked most of these 55 people if they would have reached out to researchers on their own instead of responding to the research4impact opportunity. Yet, just like my interviewees from Chapter 3, the answer was consistently no. Sometimes they would immediately cite relational concerns to explain why not. In other cases, they would say it's because they wouldn't know who to reach out to. Though even in this latter case, I found that when I probed deeper to understand why exactly "not knowing who to reach out to" was such a barrier, the underlying reasons were often a combination of limited time and also relational concerns that added a lot of uncertainty to the process of finding people and reaching out to them. It's worth noting that, although researchers have very accessible public profiles with contact information, those profiles do not typically indicate if they welcome unprompted contact from practitioners, or what they see as the practical implications of their work that they would be open to sharing, and so on. Thus, while in theory it's entirely possible for practitioners (or anyone) to reach out to them, it is not surprising that they do not when publicly available information does not explicitly overcome these forms of uncertainty about relationality.[12]

Table 5.1 lists the four major types of requests during these scope calls: to receive an overview of a large research literature, to make an immediate evidence-based decision, to gain ideas about how to measure impact, and to collaborate with a researcher on a new project. While this dataset is surely not representative of all practitioners that could benefit from a new collaborative relationship with a researcher (it would be difficult to reliably define this population), it does provide a window into what kinds of unmet desire for collaborative relationships already existed. To my knowledge, descriptive data along these lines have not been previously collected.

The overwhelming majority of practitioners who responded were looking for a collaborative conversation to gain an overview of a large research literature that would inform their strategic decision-making. These were cases in which they were facing new goals or challenges in their work and believed that insights from the research literature could inform the path forward. New collaborative relationships with a researcher could indirectly influence the collective paid and/or volunteer work that they were doing as part of their organization.

For instance, one person who responded was a program leader for an environmental advocacy organization in the United States. The organization engages members of the public to write personalized comments during public comment periods when new environmental regulations are under consideration. Personalized comments can be really impactful, but they are also quite time-intensive relative to other forms of voluntary engagement like signing a form letter. So, in this case, the practitioner was looking to gain a brief overview of what the research literature says on how to persuade people to take meaningful, personalized actions like this (as opposed to relatively low-cost actions like making a small donation, signing a petition, or submitting a form letter).

---

[12] To be sure, many researchers may truly not want any unprompted outreach along these lines. Yet in my experience, there are many who would welcome it, yet one would not know that just from reading their publicly available websites.

This collaborative discussion, in turn, informed their outreach strategy to potential commenters.

Another request for an overview of a research literature came from a grassroots advocate who worked with a nonprofit organization that promoted biking in Wellington, New Zealand. She was looking for more effective ways to persuade people to use bikes, both for environmental reasons and also as a response to terrible traffic in the city core, and wanted an overview of what the research says about how to encourage people to use alternative forms of transportation instead of personal cars. The collaborative conversation identified several possibilities from past research, and she and the researcher talked through what would be most feasible in her area/given her budget. A third practitioner worked with a nonprofit that was tackling loneliness among older adults in the UK. She was looking for an overview of what the research literature says about how to encourage strangers to talk to one another in general and, in particular, if there is any work along those lines targeting older adults who live alone in nonurban areas. Here, the interaction informed volunteer recruitment as well as outreach to their target population.

The second most common type of request from practitioners who reached out to research4impact for matchmaking was to discuss ways of measuring the impact of their programs. This type of request would occur in situations where the organization has a theory of change about the impact it seeks to have, yet current data collection was not capturing it as directly as possible. The collaborative conversations covered both what to consider measuring as well as how to do so.

For instance, a program leader in Toronto working to improve school performance was running an after-school program that sought to strengthen children's social-emotional skills. One way to measure the impact of a program like that is to measure *output*: how many children attend the program, how old they are, how long they attend, what their performance is during the program, and so on. That is relatively easy information to collect, yet the organization's theory of change is to actually improve school performance, which requires longitudinal data collection over time as well as data that originates outside the program itself. And so the practitioner was looking to have a conversation with a researcher about what the range of feasible measures would be, and also tips about how to collect the data (and especially what kinds of hurdles or difficulties to anticipate in advance, such as concerns about attrition). Another example came from an organization based in London that saw lack of information as a major barrier to voter turnout and political trust. The organization ran a website that provides information about polling locations and candidates. It had been relatively easy to measure website traffic, yet it was much harder to measure what the organization's theory of change called for: downstream behavioral implications. A leader of the organization was looking to engage with a researcher to better understand how to measure these broader consequences.

Practitioners who wanted to talk about how to measure impact, either for internal reasons and/or possibly given external requirements from funders, knew they needed to be collecting different types of data but did not have a good sense of what was possible. At least in the short run, a collaborative conversation would be helpful to fill that gap. This was another example in which a new collaborative relationship with a researcher was not (at least at first) oriented toward the goal of a formal partnership. Instead, it would help inform the collective work that the practitioner was doing in their organization.

A third type of request shown in Figure 5.1 was relatively uncommon – there were a small number of practitioners who were looking for a collaborative conversation with a researcher to inform an immediate evidence-based decision. In these types of requests, timing was critical and the conversation would discuss research findings that would be directly applied in a new context in the very near future. For instance, one practitioner was about to implement a get-out-the-vote drive to increase voter turnout among racial minorities in Washington, DC. She wanted to speak with a researcher to learn about which messages had been studied in similar efforts in the past and that she could directly implement with volunteers in her organization. The conversation directly influenced the script that this leader employed during canvasser training. Another request came from a practitioner who worked for a large volunteer-based organization focused on climate change. He was conducting a membership survey that would measure political ideology, and wanted to speak with a researcher about the best ways to do so. During their conversation they worked out the question-wording for this upcoming survey.

Some of the practitioners with these first three goals were open to the possibility of a more formal collaboration with a researcher, but that was not their immediate goal. The fourth type of request, however, was different. This included several practitioners who knew from the beginning that they were interested in partnering on a research project. For instance, one practitioner ran an organization that trains other organizers, and was looking to partner with a researcher to evaluate the impact of its training. Another practitioner was working on election reform in the United States, and wanted to partner with a researcher to study the impact of particular types of election reforms on turnout and candidate extremity. New collaborative relationships that began with the goal of a research partnership promised to directly influence collective action, as they led to a practitioner and researcher collectively working together on this new project.

Stepping back, the four types of requests that I received from practitioners also align with previous studies about the ways in which decision-makers use research evidence in practice and policy. Goal 3 (to make an immediate evidence-based decision) aimed for an "instrumental use" of research, in which research-based expertise would immediately inform a practice or policy decision. Past work finds that instrumental use of research is quite rare (Bogenschneider and Corbett 2010) and the distribution of my requests is consistent with that finding. Goals 1 and 2 (to receive an overview of a large research literature; to gain ideas about how to measure impact) aimed for "conceptual use" of research evidence. In these cases, the practitioners' main goal when engaging with the researcher was to inform their conceptual understanding of the issue they were addressing in their work and the best ways of moving forward, but the research would not immediately inform a decision. The main difference between these two goals was whether the issue they were facing was specifically tied to impact assessment strategies versus if it referred to deepening understanding and informing strategic planning more generally.[13] Last, it is also worth noting how the range of goals in Table 5.1 echoes the two main types of collaborative relationships that Catchafire created as well, as described in Chapter 4. Catchafire, too, gave nonprofit practitioners the opportunity to create short-term collaborative relationships focused on knowledge exchange as well as longer-term collaborative relationships that entailed new projects with shared ownership, decision-making authority, and formal accountability between the parties involved.

---

[13] I should add that it is possible that practitioners expressing Goals 1 and 2 had in mind an entirely different use of research evidence: political. Political use of research evidence entails using it to help justify pre-existing positions or decisions, and/or to build a coalition of support for a course of action (Bogenschneider and Corbett 2010). That did not seem to be the case given the nature of my scope calls, but it is possible nonetheless.

TABLE 5.1 *Goals of nonprofit practitioners (based on responses to email list postings during part of 2018)*

Goal 1: to discuss an overview of a large research literature	33
Goal 2: to gain ideas about how to measure impact	9
Goal 3: to make an immediate evidence-based decision	3
Goal 4: to collaborate with a researcher on a new project	13

Data come from initial outreach in 2018 to practitioner email lists; total number of respondents was 55, though numbers in table do not total 55 because some practitioners stated multiple goals. Collaborative relationships oriented toward goals 1–3 were focused on knowledge exchange that would indirectly influence collective action that the practitioners were involved with. Collaborative relationships oriented toward goal 4 were focused on partnering directly with researchers on new projects.

Of the 55 initial requests, I initiated a new collaborative relationship for 42 of them. For the other 13, 12 people decided to delay either after their initial inquiry and/or after our scope conversation, and there was one person that I could not find a suitable match for. Of those 42, 37 connected with their matches, and five misconnected.

What about impact? By and large, did RITM produce collaborative relationships that met the requesters' initial goals? To investigate that, I measured success relative to their goals in the way most consistent with why they reached out in the first place. I followed up to ask the requester if the connection provided information that was useful for addressing the challenges they identified (or, to echo this book's title, if they were exposed to expertise that, through an interactive back-and-forth, was useful for addressing the civic challenges they were tackling). This measure of goal attainment is a meaningful, but also sufficiently broad, question that could apply to all types of requests. In addition, in cases where they were interested in a formal collaboration (Goal 4), I gathered information on whether they decided to launch a new research partnership. I also offered to share a step-by-step guide for forming new partnerships (see Appendix C) and/or talk further if that would be helpful. Throughout, I was mindful of the fact that the path from initial connection to a formal project entails several steps beyond the initial relationship-building – it can also entail securing funding, training staff, completing new written agreements, achieving organizational buy-in, and so on. Moreover, there are a variety of reasons why people may learn valuable information that helps them decide that now is not a good time or that this particular partner is not the right partner (Levine 2021).[14]

With these measures in mind, I followed up with the 37 requesters who received matches within a few weeks of the initial match. 86.5 percent (32 of 37) responded and said that the connection was helpful and, in particular, surfaced new information and understandings that would inform their strategic decision-making going forward. This included one person who initially said that the connection was not helpful and requested a different match, and then found the second match to be helpful. Several also shared that they had interacted multiple times. The other five people did not respond to my email follow-up. Lastly, 63.6 percent of those interested in a formal research partnership decided to launch one.

Overall, comparing the inactivity on the research4impact 1.0 online platform with the 55 requests in response to the email list postings and the hands-on matchmaking as part of research4impact 2.0, these results provide a good first test of what happens when a third party is introduced in a situation where there appears to be unmet desire yet uncertainty about relationality is also present. In the language of most-similar case comparison (Gerring 2017), it is a theoretically grounded factor that can help explain the divergent outcome. These results also respond to the possibility I raised at the end of Chapter 4, which is that perhaps the different outcomes between the Catchafire online platform and the research4impact online platform did not reflect anything about relationality but instead perhaps reflected something about collaborative relationships with *researchers*. This initial set of results suggests that's not the case.

The initial round of outreach in 2018 along with the process of individually locating matches was sustainable for a short period of time as a voluntary organization run by people with other full-time jobs. Yet by the beginning of 2019, we needed to streamline some aspects of the process, especially the process for locating a match. That's why we shifted to a model in which we relied on unprompted requests from researchers

---

[14] The knowledge exchange may be incredibly fruitful, yet there can be a variety of other reasons (e.g., lack of organizational buy-in, lack of funding, lack of staff, and changing external circumstances) why a new project does not ultimately arise. For an overview of the steps involved with one type of formal collaboration – that which entails researchers and practitioners working together on a new research project – see Appendix C.

and nonprofit practitioners as opposed to crafting new email list postings. We also began advertising these requests to our entire network via
a newsletter. Each request was published in the form of a short "blurb"
in the newsletter, and we invited people to email us in response to these
blurbs and then we would make the match. We shared blurbs on social
media as well. Overall, these innovations retained the two major steps
of RITM (having a scope conversation with a requester and making a
match), yet changed the technology for recruiting requests and locating
matches.

Between 2019 and 2021, 96 researchers and nonprofit practitioners
reached out to research4impact stating that they were interested in a new
collaborative relationship. We implemented RITM with each of them. This
includes 50 researchers and 46 nonprofit practitioners. Of these 96, six
decided to delay after the scope call revealed some unanswered questions,
and so in total we published requests in the newsletter from 90 people.

Because multiple people could respond to each blurb in the newsletter, this new method often produced more than just one match per
person. In total, these blurbs led to the creation of 160 new collaborative relationships during this time, with the number sharply increasing
in 2021 as the team of matchmakers expanded.[15] Researcher-initiated
requests were matched with an average number of 1.51 practitioners,
and practitioner-initiated requests were matched with an average of
2.09 researchers. There were four requests that produced no matches.

Table 5.2 includes data on the 90 requests' goals, using close adapta-
tions of the four categories from Table 5.1 (adapted to acknowledge that
by this time, requesters were both practitioners looking for researchers
and vice versa). The first thing to note is that the total number adds up
to much higher than 90. This is because by this point (relative to the
requests from 2018), we had many more people who expressed their
goals as looking for knowledge exchange and also possibly interested
in a formal research partnership. They are coded in Table 5.2 as being
interested in an informal collaboration first in order to learn about a
broad area and expand their understanding of the problem they were
working on, as well as a new formal partnership later on depending

---

[15] Overall, from 2018 to the end of 2021, research4impact 2.0 initiated 308 new collaborative relationships between researchers and practitioners, and researchers and
policymakers. This included those from the initial round of outreach in 2018, the
newsletter-arranged matches from 2019 to 2021, and then several other special projects
that occurred outside of these two methods (and whose results are not presented here).

TABLE 5.2 *Goals of research4impact requesters (based on unprompted requests to the organization from 2019 to 2021)*

Goal 1: to learn about expertise on a general topic	73
Goal 2: to gain ideas about how to measure impact	10
Goal 3: to make an immediate evidence-based decision	0
Goal 4: to initiate a new formal collaboration	60

Data come from requests to research4impact from 2019 to 2021; total number of requesters was 90. Numbers in the table are greater than 90 because several researchers and practitioners had requests with multiple goals.

upon the outcome of the initial knowledge exchange (i.e., they count as interested in goals 1 and 4 or goals 2 and 4). In addition, given the fact that by this time we had established a reputation for careful match-making that was not instantaneous, it is perhaps not surprising that zero requests were tied to an immediate evidence-based decision. RITM (especially when applied between people who start off as strangers) is generally not set up for highly time-sensitive requests.

As before, I reached out to requesters afterward to assess the impact of the new collaborative relationship in terms of goal attainment (i.e., a subjective assessment of whether it provided actionable information that was useful for the challenge in their work they identified when they initially reached out). Of the 86 people who had requests published in the newsletter and generated at least one match, 77 responded and said that it was (and often with detailed responses about precisely how it was useful and how they had interacted more than once). The others did not respond to my follow-up note. Thus, at the very least, a con-servative estimate would be an 89.5 percent success rate for third-party matchmaking during this time. Lastly, among those who were possibly interested in a formal partnership, I also asked if they had launched one. 55.8 percent said that they had.

Overall, there are several takeaways from the research4impact 2.0 experience. At one level, it demonstrates specific ways in which practi-tioners and researchers value new collaborative relationships with each other. And for those who are specifically interested in the use of research evidence, it provides important new descriptive data about the ways in which nonprofit practitioners value research-based expertise. Stepping back, it also provides evidence of the general phenomenon of unmet desire – if new collaborative relationships that people would value always arose on their own, research4impact 2.0 and matchmaking procedures like RITM would be unnecessary.[16] Last, this experience supports one of the two major intervention hypotheses from Chapter 2: third parties can create opportunities that overcome uncertainty about relationality and surface and meet the unmet desire, and as a result create new pathways for expertise to be useful in civic life.[17]

DIRECTLY COMMUNICATING RELATIONALITY

The other major intervention hypothesis in Chapter 2 was that people with diverse forms of expertise are more likely to engage in collaborative relationships when potential collaborators directly provide information that overcomes uncertainty about relationality. To test this, I partnered with a national civic association in the United States in early 2019.[18]

The organization's mission is to raise awareness, and engagement, around climate change. The organization has a national-level paid staff along with hundreds of volunteer-led chapters covering almost every congressional district in the country. Each chapter is led by one or more group leaders. Each year, staff in the national office survey these group leaders to assess their needs and top challenges, and at the beginning of 2019, one of the biggest challenges they were facing was how to increase volunteer commitment. Group leaders from across the country had been observing substantial rises in people interested in joining the organization after the Trump Administration pulled out of the Paris climate agreement. People would show up for a meeting or two, often quite fired up and motivated, yet group leaders needed to translate that interest and motivation into sustained climate action that went beyond just attending

---

[16] Echoing a point from earlier in the chapter, one could argue that perhaps this interpretation is not correct given that there could be people who would value a new collaborative relationship yet do not have the capacity to find the right person. That is certainly possible, yet what I found when some of my initial requesters reported "not having capacity to find the right person" is that they were not referring to the time needed to actually write emails per se, but instead the time required to figure out what to say, how to word the email, communicate expectations, and so on. In other words, finding the right person requires having the time to overcome uncertainty about relationality.

[17] There is also a related, yet distinct, question that arises: what is the causal impact of RITM as the matchmaking method, as compared with other matchmaking methods that vary particular elements? To investigate this question, one could conduct a randomized controlled trial with a well-defined baseline comparison. I have not yet conducted such a study (and also carefully considered what the baseline comparison group should entail), yet it is a fruitful area for future research.

[18] The content in this section is largely drawn from a study reported in Levine (2020b).

meetings. Having more volunteers is great, so long as there are established pathways through which they can build commitment to the organization in ways that are meaningful to them and also aligned with the strategic goals of the organization. Group leaders expressed an acute, and widespread, need to learn about what works yet also lamented that they did not have a lot of time to invest in achieving that goal.

Mindful of these survey results, my organizational partner and I came to the conclusion that group leaders might value the opportunity for a collaborative conversation with a researcher who has expertise on voluntarism and could talk through evidence-based strategies that might be effective. At the same time, the staff member I was working with also identified two forms of hesitation (i.e., two sources of uncertainty about elements of relationality) that she believed would be salient when group leaders were offered this opportunity. One is a concern that the researcher would not value group leaders' expertise related to the history, political context, and organizational constraints in their chapters (all of which would affect the success of any new strategy for improving volunteer commitment). The second concern reflected the fact that because they felt so busy group leaders would need to know that any time invested would be worth it. It was imperative that time was used efficiently. Last, from talking with many group leaders, she also knew that they were not already in touch with researchers to talk about this, and did not believe they would be likely to reach out on their own to establish new collaborative relationships.

Based on these considerations, my partner and I worked together to design outreach to all group leaders that would offer an opportunity to speak about research on voluntarism relevant to them. In addition, given our conversations about the possible sources of concern, we also varied the content of the outreach to see if directly communicating relationality would increase take-up rates. All 456 group leaders were randomly assigned to receive one of four messages, as shown in Figure 5.2. The control group received a baseline message, reproduced in Figure 5.2a.

Other group leaders received one of three treatment group messages. Each of these treatment groups received the same control group message along with an extra paragraph immediately above the "Interested?" paragraph. One of them was designed to reduce uncertainty about whether the collaborative relationship would be a good use of time. I call this the "efficiently share what they know" paragraph, and it read as follows (with the full email text appearing in Figure 5.2b):

5.2a: Email text from control group

Hello [Group Leader],

We wanted to start off the new year with an exciting opportunity for our group leaders!

Want to strengthen your volunteer base as we gear up to [build awareness of climate change and one possible response to it]?

If so, you're in luck! We're partnering with [matchmaking organization], allowing any interested group leader to talk to an expert about the latest techniques for volunteer engagement, and how you can apply them in your chapter.

[Matchmaking organization] connects organizations with social scientists eager to share research on how to recruit new volunteers and further engage existing ones. They've already connected over 40 volunteers and staff with researchers from across the country.

Interested? Just send a quick note to [email address] by this [date] if you wish to take part.

Include your name, email address, and a one-line note saying you're interested. Then [individual associated with matchmaking organization] will respond to schedule a 30 minute phone conversation at a time that's convenient for you.

Your participation in this opportunity can help [climate organization] improve its training and operations as we gear up for supporting our volunteers throughout the country in this critical year ahead.

Thank you for all you do,

[Director of volunteer engagement for climate organization]

5.2b: Email text from "Efficiently share what they know" group
(Includes all text from control group email + addition of the "Previous participants..." paragraph)

Hello [Group Leader],

We wanted to start off the new year with an exciting opportunity for our group leaders!

Want to strengthen your volunteer base as we gear up to [build awareness of climate change and one possible response to it]?

If so, you're in luck! We're partnering with [matchmaking organization], allowing any interested group leader to talk to an expert about the latest techniques for volunteer engagement, and how you can apply them in your chapter.

[Matchmaking organization] connects organizations with social scientists eager to share research on how to recruit new volunteers and further engage existing ones. They've already connected over 40 volunteers and staff with researchers from across the country.

Previous participants reported that it was an extremely efficient experience. The researchers acknowledged that folks are busy and don't have time to keep up on all the latest research they might wish to. So the name of the game is *efficiency–they provide a concentrated dose of "news you can use".*

Interested? Just send a quick note to [email address] by this [date] if you wish to take part.

Include your name, email address, and a one-line note saying you're interested. Then [individual associated with matchmaking organization] will respond to schedule a 30 minute phone conversation at a time that's convenient for you.

Your participation in this opportunity can help [climate organization] improve its training and operations as we gear up for supporting our volunteers throughout the country in this critical year ahead.

Thank you for all you do,

[Director of volunteer engagement for climate organization]

FIGURE 5.2 Email text from study that tested impact of directly communicating relationality

5.2c: Email text from "Value others' expertise" group
(Includes all text from control group email + addition of the "Previous participants..." paragraph)

Hello [Group Leader],

We wanted to start off the new year with an exciting opportunity for our group leaders!

Want to strengthen your volunteer base as we gear up to [build awareness of climate change and one possible response to it]?

If so, you're in luck! We're partnering with [matchmaking organization], allowing any interested group leader to talk to an expert about the latest techniques for volunteer engagement, and how you can apply them in your chapter.

[Matchmaking organization] connects organizations with social scientists eager to share research on how to recruit new volunteers and further engage existing ones. They've already connected over 40 volunteers and staff with researchers from across the country.

Previous participants reported that it was an extremely pleasant and affirming experience. They said that the researchers they spoke with were kind, respectful, genuinely interested in their work, and very clearly wanted to learn about their organizations.

Interested?Just send a quick note to [email address] by this [date] if you wish to take part.

Include your name, email address, and a one-line note saying you're interested. Then [individual associated with matchmaking organization] will respond to schedule a 30 minute phone conversation at a time that's convenient for you.

Your participation in this opportunity can help [climate organization] improve its training and operations as we gear up for supporting our volunteers throughout the country in this critical year ahead.

Thank you for all you do,

[Director of volunteer engagement for climate organization]

5.2d: Email text from "More details about information shared" group
(Includes all text from control group email + addition of the "Previous participants..." paragraph)

Hello [Group Leader],

We wanted to start off the new year with an exciting opportunity for our group leaders!

Want to strengthen your volunteer base as we gear up to [build awareness of climate change and one possible response to it]?

If so, you're in luck! We're partnering with [matchmaking organization], allowing any interested group leader to talk to an expert about the latest techniques for volunteer engagement, and how you can apply them in your chapter.

[Matchmaking organization] connects organizations with social scientists eager to share research on how to recruit new volunteers and further engage existing ones. They've already connected over 40 volunteers and staff with researchers from across the country.

Previous participants reported that it was an extremely informative experience. The researchers shared a wide variety of new techniques for providing emotional support to volunteers (such as using legitimation rhetoric, memory heuristics, and self-disclosure). They also shared many techniques for deepening volunteers' commitment to a cause (such as new ways of eliciting commitments, providing reasons, and citing social proof).

Interested? Just send a quick note to [email address] by this [date] if you wish to take part.

Include your name, email address, and a one-line note saying you're interested. Then [individual associated with matchmaking organization] will respond to schedule a 30 minute phone conversation at a time that's convenient for you.

Your participation in this opportunity can help [climate organization] improve its training and operations as we gear up for supporting our volunteers throughout the country in this critical year ahead.

Thank you for all you do,

[Director of volunteer engagement for climate organization]

FIGURE 5.2 (cont.)

Previous participants reported that it was an extremely efficient experience. The researchers acknowledged that folks are busy and don't have time to keep up on all the latest research they might wish to. So the name of the game is efficiency – they provide a concentrated dose of "news you can use."

Note the key framing here is similar to what Catchafire (from Chapter 4) employs. Our goal was to avoid a negative framing along the lines of "it won't take much time" and instead emphasize the return on investment – how any time spent would be worth it.

Another treatment group paragraph was designed to reduce uncertainty about whether the collaborative relationship would be truly collaborative as opposed to a one-way monologue of sorts. I call this the "value others' expertise" paragraph, and it read as follows (with the full email text appearing in Figure 5.2c):

Previous participants reported that it was an extremely pleasant and affirming experience. They said that the researchers they spoke with were kind, respectful, genuinely interested in their work, and very clearly wanted to learn about their organizations.

Note that both of these extra paragraphs provided information to directly overcome uncertainty about relationality tied to the two elements that my organizational partner believed would matter to group leaders. Last, we were mindful that both of the relationality groups entailed adding more information to the baseline control group message, and thus it would be possible that any differences in response rates we observed could be explained by the addition of extra information (rather than the content of that extra information). As a result, the study also included a fourth group that received a paragraph with more details on the kind of information that would be shared. I call this the "more details about information shared" paragraph, and it read as follows (with the full email text appearing in Figure 5.2d):

Previous participants reported that it was an extremely informative experience. The researchers shared a wide variety of new techniques for providing emotional support to volunteers (such as using legitimation rhetoric, memory heuristics, and self-disclosure). They also shared many techniques for deepening volunteers' commitment to a cause (such as new ways of eliciting commitments, providing reasons, and citing social proof).

In sum, group leaders were randomly assigned to receive one of four outreach emails. My partner distributed them in January 2019. There was only one round of emailing, with no follow-up reminders, and group leaders had one week to respond. To streamline the matching process, and because of my own personal knowledge on research related to voluntarism, all respondents were matched with me. The main hypothesis was that directly providing language to overcome uncertainty about relationality (i.e., either the "efficient" paragraph or the "value others" paragraph) would increase the demand for new collaborative relationships relative to only receiving the baseline message. I did not expect that the paragraph with "more details about information shared" would affect take-up rates.

This experiment is a reasonable test of the intervention hypothesis about what happens when potential collaborators provide information to directly communicate relationality. Yet it's worth emphasizing that the only reason we were able to design relationality treatments that I expected to be effective is because of my organizational partner's rich knowledge of group leaders' needs and also sources of concern. A core prerequisite (and challenge) of implementing the direct communication strategy is that potential collaborators need to have enough information about the elements of relationality that each other is likely to be uncertain about. It is unlikely, for instance, that a relationality treatment that added language emphasizing how much the researcher would provide trustworthy information would have impacted behavior very much, as my organizational partner had no reason to believe that group leaders doubted the trustworthiness of information that researchers would provide (unlike, for example, one of the top concerns that local policymakers expressed in the survey results from Chapter 3).

I should also note that, as we were discussing the theory and format of the relationality language, my organizational partner commented (unprompted!) on how it is unusual to be so explicit about these relational elements when engaging in new interpersonal contexts. Her comment very much echoed the research cited in Chapter 2 about how, in new interpersonal settings, we tend to focus far more on whether we are competently presenting what we know (akin to the "control" and "more details" groups in this experiment) and less on how we will relate to others in ways that they would like.

Figure 5.3 reports the results from our email outreach. It shows the proportion of group leaders receiving each of the four emails who chose to connect. In total, 10.5 percent of group leaders (48 of 456) chose to do so. In other words, as a result of this outreach, I initiated 48 new collaborative relationships with volunteer group leaders from across the United States to share an overview of research on volunteer commitment and

Experimental Condition	Percentage of Group Leaders Choosing to Engage in New Collaborative Relationship with Researcher
Control group	6.2%
"Efficiently share what they know" group	17.3%
"Value others' expertise" group	13.9%
"More details about information shared" group	5.1%

FIGURE 5.3   Impact of directly communicating relationality on formation of new collaborative relationships

talk through how they could apply it in their particular setting. As in the case of the responses to the research4impact hands-on matchmaking, the mere fact of responses (and what my organizational partner described as a fantastic overall response rate to a single email) provides evidence of unmet desire.

The breakdown in response rates by email script was as follows: 6.2 percent in the control group chose to connect, as compared with 5.1 percent in the "more details" group, 13.9 percent in the "value others" group, and 17.3 percent in the "efficient" group. Difference-in-proportions tests revealed that each of the relationality treatments increased group leaders' desire to engage in a new collaborative relationship with a researcher ($p = 0.05$ comparing "value others" with "control," $p = 0.01$ comparing "efficiency" with "control").[19] In contrast, there was no evidence that adding "more details" affected take-up ($p = 0.71$). In sum, these results provide evidence in support of one of the intervention hypotheses: directly communicating information that overcomes uncertainty about relationality can increase people's desire for new collaborative relationships with diverse thinkers.

---

[19] All tests are two-tailed, and are robust to randomization inference (see Levine 2020b for more details). There were 113 people in the Control group, 118 in the "More Details" group, 115 in the "Value Others" group, and 110 in the "Efficient" group.

My initial conversations with group leaders who responded lasted between 30 and 60 minutes and took place in January and February 2019. Group leaders shared their historical, political, and place-based expertise and I shared a few key insights from the behavioral and organizational literatures relevant to voluntarism. Together we talked through how these insights could inform group strategy going forward.

To assess the impact of these conversations, at the end of the calls, I asked if I could follow-up in the spring. Forty-four of the 48 people I spoke with welcomed this follow-up to see how things were going (the other four said they would prefer to reach out to me when they are ready). I sent these follow-up emails in April 2019. Of those 44, 34 responded (77.3 percent) and 10 did not. Of those 34, 24 wrote in their response that they had already put the techniques we talked about into practice and spoke positively of their impact (in other words, this includes 70.6 percent of those who responded, and over half (54.5 percent) of everyone I initially spoke with). One group leader from Raleigh, North Carolina, who took an especially data-driven approach, even shared that her group had experienced a 129 percent increase in activity relative to the prior year (Levine 2019). Overall, this study provided further evidence of how expertise can become useful in civic life via new collaborative relationships.

OTHER EXAMPLES OF UNMET DESIRE (AMONG LOCAL
POLICYMAKERS AND EARLY-CAREER
NEUROSCIENTISTS)

One reason my organizational partner in the previous study was interested in collaborating with me was because she knew that group leaders in her organization were struggling with how to increase volunteer commitment. She also knew that many would welcome research evidence that could help toward this goal, and that the timing of our outreach in January would be reasonable (as group leaders historically had extra capacity for new initiatives at that time of year, after the November/ December holiday season but well before the organization's big annual events in spring/summer). Another reason she was interested in partnering with me was that, as I mentioned earlier, she knew that new collaborative relationships between group leaders and researchers were unlikely to form on their own. In other words, from her perspective, the possibility that group leaders had unmet desire for new collaborative relationships made a lot of sense. And she was persuaded that our outreach could help surface and meet it.[20]

I highlight this point because, in addition to the research4impact 2.0 experience, it underscores the importance of being intentional about surfacing unmet desire for new collaborative relationships (and then, having chosen to do so, creating opportunities to meet that unmet desire in a way that is accessible and overcomes uncertainty about relationality). In the remainder of this chapter, I present three other examples of being intentional about surfacing unmet desire, this time involving local policymakers and early-career neuroscientists.

New Collaborative Relationships at the Beginning of the Covid Pandemic

The first example comes from March 2020, near the beginning of the Covid-19 pandemic. I worked at Cornell University in Ithaca, New York, at the time. Mindful of the highly decentralized public health system in the United States, my Cornell colleague Elizabeth Day and I suspected that there were many county policymakers near us who were facing unprecedented challenges in their work and in which research might be helpful. We were eager to learn more about their experiences and also eager to help if we could.

We decided to reach out unprompted to several county policymakers in upstate New York, near where Cornell is located. We identified our combined expertise in child and family policy and research translation (along with our connection to research4impact), and then offered to have a conversation to share research that would be helpful to whatever policy challenges they were facing. Responses soon poured in, as quoted in Levine 2022 (27):

One county executive was trying to figure out how to provide childcare for first responders. Childcare centers were ordered closed, but first responders could not stay home to watch their kids, and so she needed systematic research on other options. A second local policymaker watched as her county's offices shuttered

---

[20] As a point of comparison, at no time during our planning did my organizational partner suggest either of these two other possibilities: sending an email alerting group leaders to the fact that voluntarism research exists and could be helpful for the challenges they are facing and/or sending an email like that and suggesting that they could reach out themselves to talk to a researcher in this area about it. Indeed, if either of these possibilities strikes readers as strange, then it underscores my general point about the existence of unmet desire and how that desire can remain unmet without intentional methods for surfacing and meeting it.

and work moved online; she needed research on how other local leaders had used mobile vans to provide necessary services to rural residents without internet. Another county official sought to design a high-quality survey to elicit frank responses from municipal leaders about COVID-related challenges. In this case, she needed to discuss the fundamentals of survey design and implementation with an expert.

Moreover, it turned out that the outreach we had conducted and the conversations we were having were quite unusual. During each of these conversations, policymakers revealed that no one had reached out to them like this, yet such engagement would be quite beneficial even when there isn't a public health crisis occurring. They also revealed that they hadn't tried to contact researchers themselves. In other words, we were observing evidence of unmet desire to collaborate among these local policymakers.

Survey Evidence of Unmet Desire among Local Policymakers Nationwide

In spring 2021, I conducted a nationwide survey to see if our experiences uncovering unmet desire in upstate New York near the beginning of the Covid-19 pandemic might just be the tip of the iceberg. This was the local policymaker survey that I briefly discussed in Chapter 3. It included a national sample of local government officials, randomly drawn from the population of policymakers in US local governments (i.e., township, municipality, and county governments) with at least 1,000 residents, and included top elected officials and governing board members. The survey occurred from April 8 to May 24, 2021, and included 541 respondents.[21] Appendix B includes all question-wording for the results presented herein.[22]

I proceeded in two parts. First, I measured the prevalence of prior collaborative relationships over the past year, including how often policymakers interacted with researchers from colleges and universities in their region and whether any of these researchers had contacted them unprompted to talk about policy challenges they are facing. Then, I asked two closed-ended questions that measured unmet desire: how much policymakers would like to be in touch with

[21] Again, the survey was conducted by the organization CivicPulse. All results are weighted to increase sample representativeness.
[22] See Appendix B for supplementary analyses not presented in the main text.

local researchers to talk about policy issues, and also if they are open to local researchers reaching out unprompted to talk about research related to policy issues they are facing. I also included an open-ended question that invited respondents to volunteer topics that they would like to engage on.

In addition, I measured several political and demographic attributes. For instance, past work on policymakers' research use finds that those who are younger, women, and Democrats are more likely to use research in their work (Hird 2005:142–143), and so we also might expect to observe unmet desire more frequently among policymakers with these characteristics. In addition, those with prior relevant experience engaging with researchers (Weiss and Bucuvalas 1980:131) may want more interaction in the future. Last, those with pre-existing attitudes that American colleges and universities produce research that benefits society (i.e., those who espouse a more pro-science view) may also be more interested in interacting with researchers anew.[23]

Figure 5.4 displays the prevalence of prior interaction with local researchers. I present the data for all policymakers and then broken down by several of the individual attributes mentioned above.[24] Panel A displays the percentage of policymakers who had any collaborative exchange with local researchers in the past year (even just once over the entire year). One-quarter (26.5 percent) reported having at least one interaction.[25] Looking at subgroups, while there are clear differences based on some attributes, one overall finding is that *for every subgroup* shown less than half had any interaction. That's the case regardless of party, gender, and age. Panel B shows that the experience of receiving unprompted outreach is even less common: approximately one-fifth (21.8 percent) were contacted by local researchers over the past year, and that number reached no higher than 40 percent for any subgroup.

In addition, as shown in Appendix B, it turns out that non-local researchers are not substituting for local researchers. And more generally, in the absence of collaborative relationships with researchers, other sources of information are more dominant (other government officials in one's area, grassroots/community leaders, and business leaders are the

---

[23] This attitudinal assessment was measured in an entirely different part of the survey from the unmet desire questions. See Appendix B for more details.

[24] The coding of each of these variables is discussed in Appendix B.

[25] See Appendix B for evidence that this was not a reflection of the acute circumstances of the pandemic.

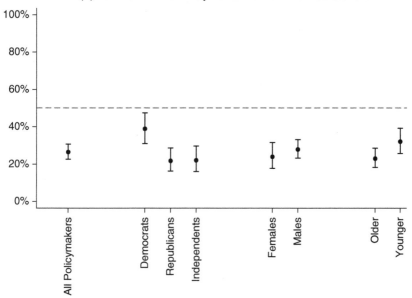

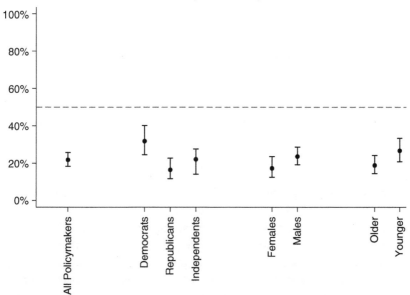

FIGURE 5.4 Local policymakers' prior interactions
Panel A (N = 541) shows percentage who had any interaction with a local researcher over the past year.
Panel B (N = 541) shows percentage who were contacted unprompted by a local researcher the past year.
Weighted means are marked along with 95 percent confidence intervals.

top three). These other sources have important policy-relevant information, but this information is unlikely to be a perfect substitute for the scientific research that researchers would share.

Next, Figure 5.5 displays the two measures of unmet desire: the percentage of policymakers who want more contact with local researchers than they currently have and also the percentage who welcome unprompted outreach. I present each of them for all respondents and then broken down by the same attributes of interest as in Figure 5.4. I also present breakdowns based on whether they interacted with local researchers or not over the past year, and also whether they believed that (in general) American colleges and universities produce research that benefits society (i.e., whether they espouse a pro-science attitude or not).

Unmet desire is widespread. As shown in Panel A, 57.0 percent of respondents said that they would like more contact with local researchers than they currently have. Looking at subgroups, while there are differences based on some attributes, *for every subgroup*, at least 50 percent of respondents wanted more collaboration than they currently have. Panel B shows that the willingness to be contacted unprompted to talk about research that may be helpful for policy issues they are facing is even more widespread. 77.6 percent of local policymakers said yes to this question, and in every subgroup, approximately three-quarters or more of respondents said yes as well.

One may be tempted to conclude that some of these closed-ended survey responses are cheap talk – maybe local policymakers are just saying they want to interact more with researchers because they know that a researcher is conducting the survey. Setting aside the question of why policymakers would choose to engage in cheap talk on this topic (it's not clear that engaging with local researchers is socially desirable per se), there is a good reason to believe that many of these responses are genuine. To see why, note that I also gave respondents an open-ended opportunity to write about a topic they would like to speak about with local researchers. Answering this question arguably requires more effort than a simple closed-ended response, and thus may be less subject to cheap talk. I found that 182 legislators took the time to write something (30 percent of all respondents). Among those who wanted more interaction with researchers than they currently have, 45 percent volunteered a topic. Among those who said that they welcome cold contact from local researchers, 37 percent volunteered one. While these percentages are certainly not as high as those in Figure 5.5, they nevertheless suggest substantial unmet desire for new collaborative relationships within this population.

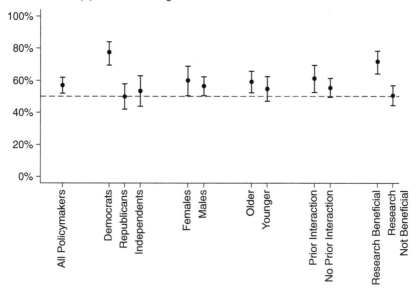

(A) Percent Wanting More Interaction with Local Researchers

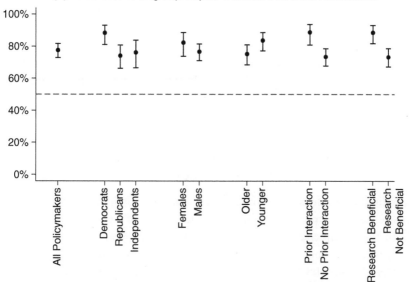

(B) Percent Welcoming Unprompted Outreach from Local Researchers

FIGURE 5.5 Local policymakers' unmet desire for new collaborative relationships with researchers

Panel A (*N* = 538) shows percentage of local policymakers who said they want either "a lot more" or "somewhat more" contact with local researchers than they have now.

Panel B (*N* = 539) shows percentage open to local researchers contacting them unprompted. Weighted means are marked along with 95 percent confidence intervals.

Appendix B displays the full list of topics policymakers shared along with the (unweighted) frequencies. The modal topic was a general desire to have more relationships with researchers to inform policy design, understand the nature of problems, and/or persuade colleagues. This is consistent with previous research finding that policymakers value interacting with researchers to "provide 'outside the square thinking' to expand their horizons and to enliven and inspire them" and not only to talk about a specific topic (Haynes et al. 2011:572). Among those who volunteered specific policy issues, the following were the most frequently mentioned: housing, environmental issues, economic development, land use/planning, functioning of local government, jobs/workforce, public health, roads/transportation/traffic, policing/public safety, energy, and broadband access. This list echoes Anzia's (2021) argument about how the functions of local government are mostly different from the national level. Arguably six of these topics – economic development, land use, housing, the functioning of local government, roads/transportation/traffic, and broadband access – directly reflect local concerns and the provision of local services. The others – environmental issues, energy, jobs/workforce, public health, and policing/public safety – also relate to the provision of local services though had direct substantive connections to prominent national debates at the time of the survey. These data underscore how the local agenda is both somewhat distinct and somewhat overlapping with national-level politics.

Survey Evidence of Unmet Desire among Early Career Neuroscientists

The final example comes from a survey conducted with early-career neuroscientists.[26] Similar to the survey of local policymakers, we asked about both their frequency of interaction over the past year and their degree of desired interaction going forward, with people who bring diverse forms of task-relevant expertise to the kinds of topics they are working

---

[26] I conducted this survey along with Lomax Boyd, Debra Mathews, and Jeff Kahn (colleagues at Johns Hopkins University). We collected responses from December 2022 to February 2023. The overwhelming majority of respondents (over 80 percent) were graduate students, postdoctoral fellows, or assistant professors, all of whom would be considered early-career neuroscientists. The remainder of the respondents identified as staff/senior faculty/other.

on. In this case that included three types of non-scientist organizations, described to respondents as follows:[27]

- Civic organizations (service organizations in which volunteers work together to solve a problem in their local community)
- Disease advocacy groups (organizations that aim to influence government or policy-making regarding a particular disease/condition)
- Educational organizations outside of their own, including formal educational organizations such as schools or informal educational organizations such as museums and community centers

We collected data from 97 respondents, including those at my home institution of Johns Hopkins (46 percent) as well as 10 peer institutions

---

[27] The introduction to this body of questions reads as follows:

"Next, we are going to ask you about your recent interactions with three types of non-scientist organization:

- Civic organizations (service organizations in which volunteers work together to solve a problem in their local community)
- Disease advocacy groups (organizations that aim to influence government or policy-making regarding a particular disease/condition)
- Educational organizations outside of your own, including formal (schools) or informal (museums, community centers) educational organizations.

Some neuroscientists are regularly in touch with non-scientists to talk about research-relevant topics, whereas others are not at all."

The questions about prior experiences read as follows (with parallel structure for disease advocacy groups/educational organizations):

"Over the past year, on average how often have you interacted with members of a civic organization to talk about neuroscience research that may be relevant to their mission? By 'civic organization,' we mean an organization in which volunteers work together to solve a problem in the local community."

- More than once or twice a month
- Once or twice a month
- Once or twice during the year
- Never

The percentage of respondents reporting "Never" is presented in the main text.

The unmet desire question followed that, and read (again, with parallel structure for disease advocacy groups/educational organizations):

"Looking ahead, how much would you like to interact with civic organizations?"

- A lot more than now
- Somewhat more than now
- The same as now
- Somewhat less than now
- A lot less than now

The percentage of respondents reporting either "A lot more than now" or "Somewhat more than now" is presented in the main text.

(54 percent). Ours was a convenience sample – we shared the link with program leaders at these institutions, asked them to distribute it, and then collected responses from those who responded. Thus, I do not claim that the results are representative of a well-defined population of neuroscientists, but instead present them as proof of concept to illustrate how university-based leaders (in both STEM and non-STEM fields) can assess the prevalence of unmet desire for collaboration with diverse thinkers.

Overall, we found substantial evidence of unmet desire:

- 73.9 percent of respondents said that they had no interaction with members of a civic organization over the past year to talk about neuroscience research that may be relevant to their mission. Yet 75.8 percent of respondents said that they would like more interaction going forward.
- 81.5 percent of respondents said they had no interaction with members of a disease advocacy group over the past year to talk about neuroscience research that may be relevant to their mission. Yet 63.7 percent of respondents said that they would like more interaction going forward.
- 34.8 percent of respondents said they had no interaction with members of an educational organization outside their home institution over the past year to talk about neuroscience research that may be relevant to their mission. Yet 64.5 percent of respondents said they would like more interaction going forward.

In addition, we found that respondents expressed a broad yet highly variable set of hesitancies about the possibility of interacting with new civic organizations, disease advocacy groups, and educational organizations.[28]

---

[28] The question read as follows:
"Below is a list of possible concerns neuroscientists may have when interacting with civic, disease advocacy, educational, and other organizations to talk about neuroscience research that may be relevant to their mission. Which of the following are concerns for you? (Check all that apply)"

- They may use unfamiliar language.
- I will not be able to provide practical information to them.
- They may see me as out of touch.
- I do not have time outside my current responsibilities (research, grant writing, and teaching).
- Their lived experiences won't relate to my work at all.
- I do not have the skills to engage with these issues.
- Most of my work cannot be shared prior to publication.
- I will be targeted be certain groups that I do not want to engage with (e.g., research animal activists).

This pattern underscores a key result from Chapter 3: uncertainty about relationality can refer to many different elements. What it means to relate to someone else, and what sources of uncertainty about relating to others may arise, will vary across people and across new potential collaborators.

CAN WE ASSESS THE PREVALENCE OF UNMET DESIRE?

To summarize, several key findings emerge from this chapter. First, we need to be intentional about surfacing unmet desire for new collaborative relationships in civic life. Second, utilizing third parties and directly communicating relationality are two valuable interventions. Taken together, these findings can underpin several actionable strategies for those looking to break down silos and create new relationships. I discuss those strategies in detail in the next and final chapter of the book.

Before doing so, here I wish to address several topics that often arise when people first learn about the possibility of unmet desire and the need to surface and meet it. The first is a question about prevalence: how common are collaborative relationships that people would value, yet that do not arise on their own? How do we assess the prevalence of unmet desire more broadly?

It turns out that answering this question in a transparent way – in a way that makes clear the assumptions underlying the answer – is more difficult than it may initially appear. Indeed, throughout this chapter, I have deliberately avoided making global statements about

- They may not value my knowledge and experience as a neuroscientist.
- They could misinterpret my work.
- They may not see me as having practical information to share.
- Other (please specify): _____

The variation in responses was broad and no single hesitancy was shared by more than a fifth of respondents. The five most frequent concerns were that they would be targeted by certain groups they don't want to engage with, they don't have the time outside their current responsibilities, they would not be able to provide practical information to these organizations, that leaders of these organizations would not see them as having practical information to share, and that organizations may misinterpret their work.

Last, it is worth underscoring that the list of possible concerns we chose to ask about was (in part) different from the list that was presented to local policymakers and AmeriCorps program leaders in Chapter 3, and is also different from the types of hesitancies that we aimed to overcome in the email-based field experiment presented earlier in this chapter. Here, we chose this list because we knew (based on conversations with neuroscience program leaders) that this list of concerns would make sense for this audience.

the prevalence of unmet desire in civic life for precisely that reason. Instead, I've reported instances of it in response to six interventions:

- Among nonprofit practitioners responding to research4impact matchmaking advertisements on email lists in 2018
- Among researchers and nonprofit practitioners who learned about the research4impact matchmaking opportunity via word-of-mouth from 2019 to 2021
- Among volunteer group leaders in a large climate organization who responded to a single email offering matchmaking with a researcher
- Among local policymakers who responded to an email at the beginning of the Covid-19 pandemic
- Among local policymakers who responded to several closed- and open-ended survey questions
- Among early-career neuroscientists who responded to a survey

There are several steps involved with making transparent statements about the prevalence of unmet desire. First, it requires specifying a well-defined population: who wants new collaborative relationships? It then requires specifying a target population: with whom do they want these new collaborative relationships? Last, it requires specifying a time period – prevalence over a week, a month, a season, or what? The examples above all differed along each of these dimensions.

The key point is that there is no single way to measure the prevalence of unmet desire. Instead, there are many possible sources of it that matter in a given context, and so any measures of or claims about prevalence need to be relative to those contextual factors.

This fact also underscores why comparability is challenging, as any claims about prevalence are likely to vary along several dimensions. For instance, in this chapter's results, upon first blush, there is seemingly a wide difference between the 57.0 percent and 77.6 percent of local policymakers who indicated unmet desire in the national survey (or, even the 30 percent who indicated unmet desire and wrote about a particular topic that they would like to engage with researchers on), as compared with 10.5 percent of volunteer group leaders who responded to the single outreach email. Yet the group leaders only had one moment in time to respond, whereas the policymakers "only" had to indicate if they are interested and if they had a particular topic that they wanted to talk about.

It's entirely possible that if we conducted follow-up emails to the volunteer group leaders over several months, the proportion responding would have been much higher. Or if instead of offering new collaborative relationships with researchers, we offered new collaborative relationships with volunteer leaders from other non-climate-related organizations who are facing similar volunteer commitment challenges. This latter group of people would also have diverse forms of expertise, and it is entirely possible that the desire to interact with them would be unmet in much the same way as it is with researchers. In addition, with respect to the local policymakers in the survey, it is unlikely that each of them would respond to new outreach at any particular moment in time (though as I noted earlier, this is not because we should consider their survey responses cheap talk, but instead because not every moment in time will be equally convenient). And lastly with research4impact, once we stopped doing outreach and instead relied on word of mouth, the timing of requests was entirely up to those who knew about us and had the time and interest at a particular moment. Taken together, what these examples underscore is that, because the prevalence of unmet desire is such a multi-dimensional topic, it is also the case that comparing prevalence across populations is more difficult than it may initially appear.

A final question about unmet desire that often arises is about assessment – is there a lot or a little? Here again it is important to be transparent about what these judgments depend upon, which is a combination of expectations and values. For instance, when we conducted outreach to volunteer climate group leaders, my organizational partner's initial expectation was that we would be highly unlikely to get a response rate greater than 10 percent. This wasn't because she was skeptical that unmet desire existed, but instead it simply reflected the fact that she did not want to bombard people with emails and so we were only going to send one email with no follow-up. When 10.5 percent responded and that single email led to 48 new collaborative relationships, she was quite pleased and considered the outreach a success.[29] Or, when we shifted

---

[29] I, too, was pleased with the overall response rate. In addition, I was also interested in the fact that we observed differences across messages in the hypothesized direction. This example underscores a key feature of research partnerships like this. Partners need to agree on the scope of the project, yet they may also enter into that agreement with different priorities in mind. Arguably, my partner was most interested in whether the volunteer group leaders learned helpful new information and were able to increase volunteer commitment (and thus ultimately create more pressure for climate policy action). I, too, cared about that, but I also had research goals in mind and thus it was critical that we set up the outreach in a way that varied the messages in theoretically relevant ways. I discuss this point about the existence of both overlapping and differential goals in research partnerships in more detail in Appendix C.

research4impact away from direct outreach on email lists and instead focused on word of mouth, our assessment about the unmet desire we observed (i.e., the number of people reaching out with matchmaking requests) became based on whether that number increased as more people heard about us. The general point is that no single benchmark is necessarily the correct one – rather, the key is to be transparent about the one that is chosen.

In short, based on the empirical findings in this chapter, I think it is reasonable to conclude that unmet desire for collaborative relationships is an important (and oft-overlooked) phenomenon in civic life. That said, I do not claim that it is ubiquitous across people, time, and place. The key is that anytime those who seek change need to strategize anew and work with others, especially if they begin as strangers, there is the possibility for unmet desire in one form or another. For civic actors themselves and/ or organizational leaders who work with them, these are moments to think about how best to surface and meet it. In the final chapter, I discuss several ways to do so.

6

Moving Forward

How to "Collaborate Now!"

Collaborative relationships are a fundamental feature of civic life. They help people who seek change strategize about how to pursue their goals, and can either indirectly or directly influence collective action in service of those pursuits.

While many researchers have identified both normative and empirical reasons why collaborative relationships between diverse thinkers are important for civic life, we know much less about the core phenomenon revealed by the research4impact online platform described at the beginning of Chapter 1: why collaborative relationships that people would value may never arise in the first place. Having time and organizational incentives (or, at the very least, not having organizational disincentives) are important. Yet even people with all of these may still be hesitant to connect. The hesitation stems from the fact that new collaborative relationships often entail interactions between strangers, and strangers can be uncertain about whether others are likely to relate to them in ways they would like, and whether they will successfully relate to others.

Thus, to foster new collaborative relationships, we need to first acknowledge that unmet desire may exist and be able to characterize it. Then we need to establish ways to overcome any uncertainty about relationality that is contributing to it being unmet.

In this book, I've proposed and tested two new types of interventions to surface and meet people's unmet desire to collaborate. One is using third parties, which may be organizations or individuals. Another is having potential collaborators directly communicate relationality. Taken together, these are arguably best thought of as possibilities – ways that can help overcome barriers to new collaborative relationships that people would value.

145

With all of that in mind, this chapter picks up on a point I mentioned at the end of Chapter 1. One of the main goals of this book is to produce what Stokes (1997) labels use-inspired basic research. The *basic research* part focuses on advancing scientific understanding of the conditions under which diverse thinkers choose to interact with each other. That was my main goal in Chapters 2 to 5. In Chapter 5, I also discussed the *use* part to some extent, as the empirical results informed the design of the impactful hands-on matchmaking implemented as research4impact 2.0. In this final chapter, I go a step further toward unpacking possible uses of the results by identifying concrete ways to put them into practice. When people see new informal and/or formal collaboration as essential to achieving their personal and organizational goals, and it's not happening on its own, how can they move forward? How can they foster valuable new collaborative relationships?

THREE STRATEGIES FOR CREATING NEW COLLABORATIVE RELATIONSHIPS

Suppose we have reason to believe that a set of civic actors has unmet desire for new collaborative relationships, then what should we do? What strategies can we use to make expertise more useful in these moments? These were the questions that Jake, Don, and I faced when it became clear at the end of 2017 that the research4impact online platform was not working and we had to decide what to do instead. We knew based on our prior conversations with researchers, nonprofit practitioners, and policymakers that there was demand for new cross-sector collaboration, but also that the online platform had not been enough for them to form on their own. And so the question we faced was how to meet that unmet desire. Here I describe three possible ways that we considered responding.[1]

Individual Third Parties

One possibility was that we continued doing what we were already doing prior to starting the online platform, which is to make connections

---

[1] To echo a point from Chapter 5, this set of possibilities was by no means inclusive of all possible responses. For example, we also could have substantially revamped our online platform in ways similar to Catchafire's platform discussed in Chapter 4. Yet given the feedback I had received from my informal interviews with research4impact platform users (discussed in Chapter 4), the possibilities discussed here were the ones we considered most strongly.

ourselves. Individual matchmaking can be a powerful way to overcome relationality concerns, but it is also limited to individual networks – to those who know us and feel comfortable reaching out to us, and also to potential matches that we know and feel comfortable reaching out to ourselves. On top of that, relying on individual matchmakers advantages some people (those in our networks) and disadvantages others (those not in our networks), and that would be true for any individual matchmaker. The threat is that the rich just get richer – those with high social capital to begin with are easily able to acquire more, whereas those without are further locked out. This kind of outcome would also go against the spirit of new collaborative relationships between diverse thinkers in the first place, as often the goal is to democratize access to technical and contextual expertise that is either not readily available or not otherwise at the table.

All of that said, the major potential benefit of the individual third-party approach is its decentralized nature – in theory, anyone can engage in matchmaking in the form that we are talking about, and thus anyone can unlock expertise in their networks and create new opportunities for diverse thinkers to help solve problems. Thus, to the extent that we try to realize the benefits of this approach, and minimize the potential drawbacks, it is especially important that a wide range of people with diverse networks are involved.

"Self-Service"

A second option is what I call the self-service strategy: we could encourage people to initiate their own new connections. Recall from Chapter 2 that we would expect that people who initiate new collaborative relationships on their own are likely to emphasize competence over warmth (Wojciszke 1994, Kumar and Epley 2018). This means they are more likely to focus on whether they are clearly communicating why they want to connect (i.e., their substantive goals) and less likely to explicitly communicate how they will aim to relate to their intended audience. Now, given the empirical results from Chapters 4 and 5, if we encouraged individuals to reach out themselves, we would make sure to highlight how they need to make sure they are relating to others in the way that they expect, including overcoming uncertainty about relationality.

Yet even with an expanded appreciation of relationality, there are two major challenges with implementing the self-service approach. One is that potential collaborators need to have (or at least believe that they have) sufficient knowledge about the elements of relationality that their intended audience cares the most about. The interview and survey evidence from Chapter 3 underscore how "relating to others" can take on many different forms, including the information to be shared and what the experience of interacting will be like. My goal in that chapter was to demonstrate that these elements matter when people consider engaging in new collaborative relationships, but it doesn't tell us which elements people may be uncertain about in any particular context and for any particular potential collaborator. The survey data from local policymakers and AmeriCorps program in that chapter underscore this point: the specific elements of concern may vary across potential collaborators.

In addition, recall that the main evidence I have in support of this strategy – the idea that potential collaborators can communicate relationality directly – comes from the field experiment I conducted in partnership with the climate organization in Chapter 5. In that study, I was only able to construct what I expected would be effective messages to reduce uncertainty about relationality because I was partnering with a staff member who had insight into what group leaders' concerns about interacting with a researcher were likely to be. But even on top of that, we also needed to know that reaching out by email (as opposed to telephone, or waiting until the national in-person conference that happens once a year) would be a reasonable medium for relating to our intended audience, and also that it was perfectly fine that all messages were in English as opposed to translated into other languages. All of this again underscores how one challenge with the self-service approach is that it requires sufficient background knowledge to be effective.

The other major challenge reflects the role of status-based stereotypes (Ridgeway 2001). Recall that status-based stereotypes can drive a wedge between whether someone has expertise and whether that expertise is socially recognized. New potential collaborators quickly and unconsciously form these stereotypes about each other. As a result, their judgments about others are based not on what the person actually knows about the task at hand, but instead on a combination of the person's salient social group memberships, and the shared cultural beliefs about the kind of task-relevant knowledge someone with those memberships is likely to have. Those who are members of social groups associated with low status are likely to have a much harder time initiating new collaborative relationships and having their task-relevant expertise being taken seriously.

Consider what happened during the Flint Water Crisis, a public health emergency that began in 2014 when the drinking water in Flint, Michigan, became contaminated with lead and other bacteria. As the crisis unfolded, residents (often mothers in particular) started bringing forth direct evidence of contaminated tap water and health problems such as hair loss and rashes to local authorities. Yet their expertise was repeatedly challenged. As Pauli (2019:143) writes, "Residents found their claims about the water and their own bodies dismissed as hyperbolic, uninformed, paranoiac." He also specifically identified the role of status-based stereotypes tied to their race and gender, which led officials to dismiss them for both lacking technical knowledge and also because they supposedly "didn't know how to think" (144) about technical topics like environmental contamination and water quality:

Activists were keenly aware that their race and gender affected whether their knowledge was recognized as legitimate.... In many ways, the core of the struggle for clean water ... was a struggle by residents to be taken seriously as knowers – by officials, by the media, even by fellow residents. (145–146)

Pauli's characterization of how their expertise was challenged because this was a technical topic in particular underscores a key point about status-based stereotypes: they are context-dependent and tied to what society views as important for success in a given task domain (c.f., Eagly and Karau 2002).

The existence of status-based stereotypes, and the prevalence of situations like what Flint residents faced, may lead those who are disadvantaged by such stereotypes to not feel comfortable initiating a new collaborative relationship and/or employing relationality language in the first place. They may doubt that their task-relevant expertise will be taken seriously by a potential collaborator, and on top of that, they may believe that employing relationality language will further feed into status-based stereotypes that undermine their credibility.

The upshot, which is akin to something I mentioned in Chapter 5, is that directly communicating relationality is a *potentially* effective approach given that relational information is so often left unsaid, but it is not without challenges. People can reach out themselves when they have reason to believe that others want to engage and when they feel certain about the elements of relationality that matter to themselves and their potential collaborator. Yet at the same time, this strategy is not always easy to implement, and it is also likely the case that not everyone will have an equal ability to implement this strategy. Similar to the strategy of individual third parties for matchmaking, there is a real threat here that relying too much on self-service will also produce a rich-get-richer phenomenon, as those who already have access to more information and/or are already more likely to have their expertise viewed as more useful will be strongly advantaged.

Organizational Third Parties

A third actionable strategy for reducing uncertainty about relationality entails third-party organizations as matchmakers. Here the focus moves away from what individuals can do and instead asks what kinds of opportunities and norms can be institutionalized at an organizational level. This is the strategy that Jake, Don, and I chose when we launched the hands-on matchmaking as research4impact 2.0.

One of the major benefits of third-party organizations is that they can arguably create a much wider network than any single individual. They also tend to have institutionalized mechanisms for data collection and are better positioned to gather more information about the context-specific relationality concerns (and prior experiences) from that broader network. In addition, third-party organizations are more likely to advertise themselves as doing this kind of work in a way that single individuals may not. Among people who do not already have access to individual matchmakers in their network, they may feel more comfortable reaching out to an organization rather than an individual they do not already know. Organizations also tend to have an easier time creating new norms. Their mere existence can create descriptive norms ("connecting with diverse thinkers around community problems is something that many other people do") and also injunctive norms ("connecting with diverse thinkers around community problems is something you should consider doing, as otherwise this organization would not exist").

All of that said, third-party organizations have potential drawbacks as well. As with individuals, no single organization can ever meet all of the need or create enough opportunities. In this sense, I agree with Butler (2019:374), who wrote about the value but also limitation of a single organization for fostering new collaborative relationships between civic actors like research4impact: "Research4impact is a development that will have a positive impact on the field; however, unless we are more proactive, we will miss many opportunities. We simply cannot wait for research4impact to find partners for us."

One way to overcome this capacity-related concern is to make match-making a higher priority within existing organizations that are already devoted to bridging diverse forms of expertise. For example, Scholars Strategy Network is a voluntary federation in the United States with local chapters across the country that aim to increase the role of research in the policymaking process. Chapter members are local researchers, and historically their emphasis was on creating and disseminating policy briefs that summarized research findings for (often local) policymakers. Similar to research4impact, one could describe the organization's goal at a broad level as bringing diverse forms of expertise to bear on complex problems in communities across the country. Starting in 2020, national staff began encouraging chapter leaders to engage in matchmaking as well, in order to more actively build new collaborative relationships between researchers and other civic leaders and community members (Levine and Mulligan 2020). Given the federated structure of the organization, this initiative arguably leveraged the benefits of both the organizational third-party strategy and also the individual third-party strategy. It entailed cultivating matchmaking capacity among individual chapter leaders, thus creating many potential new third-party matchmakers who all have diverse networks across the country (and themselves are quite diverse) and are situated within an organization devoted to this purpose.

In addition to the capacity-related concern, there is one other potential limitation to third-party organizations, which echoes the point about democratic agency mentioned in Chapter 1. Those who have written about the importance of new collaborative relationships as a key element of democratic citizenship also emphasize the empowerment associated with initiating them ourselves. For instance, Allen (2003:161) writes that an "ease with strangers expresses a sense of freedom and empowerment" and that "the more fearful we citizens are of speaking to strangers, the more we are docile children and not prospective presidents ... the more we are subjects, not citizens." For Allen, a comfort level with speaking with strangers is essential for a sense of freedom and for the health of our democratic fabric. Based on this, one could argue that encouraging others to initiate new collaborative relationships with diverse thinkers is an important part of the process unto itself. To the extent that people are not presently engaging in that way, then perhaps we need to find ways to provide new opportunities, incentives, and encouragement for people to practice initiating them on their own (and encourage people to practice relational responses when others reach out to them) rather than build new organizations for this purpose.

Two Caveats to These Strategies

I've discussed three actionable strategies for initiating new collaborative relationships in ways that overcome uncertainty about relationality: individual third parties, self-service, and organizational third parties. Each of them can be successful, yet each also entails limitations. My own belief is that among them there is no *a priori* single best way to encourage the formation of new collaborative relationships in civic life. Instead, we should work to create new policies and opportunities that encourage all of them to take root.

All of that said, before moving on, it is important to identify two important caveats. One is that, throughout the book and especially in this last chapter, my implicit assumption has been that more collaborative relationships are normatively desirable. This assumption reflects the wide range of private and public benefits that I identified in Chapter 1 (i.e., the ways in which those who seek change can use collaborative relationships to strengthen strategic problem-solving, enhance democratic agency, and establish broader norms of connection). Yet maintaining this assumption means taking potential collaborators at their word that the problems they are addressing, and the strategies they are developing, are "good." As a general matter, this is an assumption that we should interrogate. While systematically evaluating what counts as a normatively desirable collaborative relationship is beyond the scope of this book, I agree with Peter Levine (2022) that we should judge those engaged in collective action by whether they aim to justly relate to others outside their group. That is a reasonable basis on which to evaluate whether particular types of new collaborative relationships in civic life are normatively desirable or not.

The second caveat follows from the first. We should acknowledge that, even when relationality is assured and new collaborative relationships between diverse thinkers arise, truly solving many problems that affect an entire community of people requires far more than that, such as political pressure, good leadership, and sufficient resources to implement the strategies that collaborators decide are best. Acknowledging this point is not meant to take away from the overall conclusions of this book, or the idea that new collaborative relationships can aid strategic decision-making in valuable ways. But these points do serve as a helpful reminder of key assumptions that may not always hold and that help to realistically situate the role of collaborative relationships in civic life.

THE UNMET DESIRE SURVEY: A TOOL FOR
IMPLEMENTING THIRD-PARTY STRATEGIES

The previous section discusses three actionable strategies for creating new collaborative relationships. Two of them involve third parties actively engaged in matchmaking, either as single individuals and/or as part of organizations. Yet even once a decision is made to pursue matchmaking via a third-party strategy, the question of what to do next – how to actually implement matchmaking – immediately arises. Thus, in this section, I describe a tool to guide implementation that is highly flexible and may be applied to a broad set of contexts.

I developed this tool after receiving several inquiries from organizational leaders who were uncertain about how to proceed. Their entry point to the topic of this book was typically a recognition that new collaboration was important for achieving their goals, but they were uncertain what to do next. The tool helps get from here to there, so to speak, and it directly builds off the main arguments in this book: the idea that collaboration may have informal and/or formal goals, that either way new collaborative relationships are needed to start with, that these new relationships are voluntary and often entail interaction between strangers, and that strangers may be uncertain how to relate to each other.

In some cases, the people who reached out had already read about the "Research Impact Through Matchmaking" (RITM) method I employed as part of the research4impact 2.0 (Levine 2020a; also see description of it in Chapter 5). Yet they were uncertain about its applicability if the potential collaborators were not researchers and the collaborative relationship was not about achieving research impact per se. They also acknowledged that the two major steps of RITM – having scope conversations and facilitating a match – were helpful when someone else had already initiated the process, yet they were looking for more guidance about how to proceed when they were initiating it anew. In addition, they were uncertain how to think about logistics: when is the best time to initiate matchmaking, and who should do it? Last, they were looking for further guidance on how to structure scope conversations – that is, what short set of questions would apply broadly and also yield the necessary information for matchmaking?

All of these considerations ultimately led me to develop this new tool called an *unmet desire survey*. It is useful anytime an individual and/or organizational leader has reason to believe that there is an unmet desire to collaborate in their network or within their organization, whether that involves researchers or not. The tool's design is inspired by several of the examples described in this book, including the surveys of local policy-makers and AmeriCorps program leaders in Chapters 3 and 5, and also the first stage ("defining the scope") of RITM that I implemented as part of research4impact 2.0.[2]

Unmet desire surveys measure the reasons people may want to interact with diverse thinkers as well as any sources of concern they have about doing so. In particular, the surveys involve posing questions that gather detailed information about decision-makers' goals and challenges, the kinds of diverse thinkers they would like to be collaborating with as they strategize about how to meet those goals and overcome those challenges, and the kinds of hesitancies that they have about interacting with those people. As is common throughout this book, they are especially help-ful for situations in which new collaboration is voluntary and potential collaborators may not know each other, though they can provide useful information even in the absence of those conditions being satisfied.

The information gathered by these surveys then provides good reason to engage in matchmaking, thereby actively creating the new collaborative relationships that people reveal would be most beneficial to them. Note how this process has a distinct democratic quality to it, as unmet desire surveys are premised on the idea that, when asked, decision-makers can identify the kinds of collaborative relationships that would be most helpful to them.

In what follows, I first describe the background conditions that should be met before a third party decides to conduct an unmet desire survey. I then describe the content of the survey along with several examples of question-wording.

Background Conditions That Should Be Satisfied

The ideal timing for an unmet desire survey depends upon four back-ground conditions being met.

1) One is able to state a clear rationale for why new collaboration is needed, and a recognition that it is not happening on its own.

The first condition is that the survey designer is able to state a clear rationale for why new collaboration is needed and also why there is

---

[2] One example of an unmet desire survey, and in particular how it can be used within the federal government to aid implementation of the 2018 Foundations for Evidence-Based Policymaking Act, is here: https://fas.org/publication/how-unmet-desire-surveys-can-advance-learning-agendas-and-strengthen-evidence-based/ (Accessed October 9, 2023).

reason to believe that unmet desire exists. The part about clear rationale may seem self-evident, yet it's important to acknowledge upfront because if instead what's truly needed to tackle pressing challenges is only more money and/or more staff, then an unmet desire survey that surfaces opportunity for new collaboration will likely not be valuable (though see one caveat to this point in Policy Recommendation 1 later in this chapter).

The second part – that there is reason to believe that unmet desire exists – may stem from a general belief that people in one's organization or network are interested in new collaboration (and/or would be interested if presented with the opportunity), but that the necessary collaborative relationships are not arising on their own for a variety of reasons. Sources of interest may reflect a desire to improve the effectiveness of one's practice, policy, and/or more general understanding of a problem. They may also come from a new threat, opportunity, merger, and/or funding opportunity. Having a general sense of what shape the desire might take is important because it affects how the questions in the survey are worded.

I should underscore that the very act of asking people to report their desire to collaborate can expand their sense of what's possible beyond what they had previously considered. For instance, fielding an unmet desire survey can itself spark new interest, as it is possible that survey respondents may not have given much thought to the way in which certain kinds of new collaborative relationships would be beneficial for their work, but have no trouble doing so when asked the question (and/or being asked the question may prompt a conversation with the interviewer about possibilities they had not considered or perceived as legitimate before). In addition, by explicitly asking about less-resource-intensive forms of collaboration such as knowledge exchange, the survey can also "reduce" the sense that there is no time for new collaborative relationships.[3] Overall, regardless of whether desire already exists or arises as a result of the survey, it still meets the definition of *unmet desire* if people

---

[3] Stepping back, this possibility highlights how the decision to field an unmet desire survey and offer follow-up matchmaking may help overcome several barriers to new collaborative relationships all at once. Doing so may spark new interest among survey respondents, reduce perceptions of resource constraints, provide new incentives (by demonstrating that this is a valued and valuable use of time), and surface important information needed to overcome uncertainty about relationality. In short, the major factors identified in Figure 1.1 that influence decisions to participate in new collaborative relationships in civic life – interest, resources, organizational incentives, relationality, and opportunity – can all be affected by the decision of organizational leaders to proactively field an unmet desire survey.

are unlikely to act upon it on their own. In that case, we end up in the same place – there are new collaborative relationships that people would value, yet are not arising on their own.[4]

2) One can decide which decision-makers to prioritize.

This second condition is that the survey designer can decide who to target. The term "survey" often connotes an instrument administered via a random sampling procedure in order to make statements about a well-defined population. Unmet desire surveys can certainly be used to make statements about a population (i.e., they can gather information that informs transparent statements of the prevalence of unmet desire within a population, along the lines I mentioned at the end of Chapter 5). Yet typically their primary purpose is more targeted. The reason for this targeting is that conducting these surveys is not costless, and there is a good reason not to seek a random sample of decision-makers from a population but instead target those who are likely to have unmet desire as well as the authority and time to engage in knowledge exchange and/or a new formal collaboration in the near future. That said, unmet desire surveys can be continuously fielded (or fielded in a staggered way) with different members of one's organization or one's network, as the timing will work for some and not others, and thus reach a broader set of people as time goes on.

3) One has a plan for implementing the survey's results.

Unmet desire surveys are impactful to the extent that they surface actual unmet desire along with information needed for meeting it afterward via matchmaking. Thus, one of the most important background conditions that should be met is that the decision to field the survey is accompanied by a plan for conducting follow-up matchmaking.

4) One has the right people to field the survey

The person conducting the survey should be someone with whom the respondents feel comfortable discussing their needs and also

---

[4] As noted in Chapter 1, throughout this book, I have defined unmet desire in terms of collaborative relationships that people would value (i.e., having desire), yet remained largely agnostic about the origin of that desire. A thorough study of the possible sources of desire is beyond the present scope. Instead, the key point is that so long as desire remains unmet – that is, even if they hadn't thought about it beforehand, they would still not initiate new collaborative relationships on their own – then the unmet desire survey and follow-up matchmaking presented herein are useful.

TABLE 6.1 *Unmet desire survey questionnaire*

Type of question	Examples of question-wording
Question 1: Why collaborate?	Is there information about other programs/organizations/ experiences that would help achieve your goals/improve the effectiveness of your work/overcome challenges? What kinds of people have that information and would be helpful to connect with?

Question 2:
Goals/resources for
  the collaborative
  relationship
	Would you be looking for informal collaboration (oriented toward knowledge exchange) and/or formal collaboration (oriented toward projects with shared ownership, decision-making authority, and accountability)? What resources (human/financial/ technical/etc.) do you believe are needed for your goals? Are they already available or, if not, where might they come from?

Question 3: Uncertainty about relationality	What hesitations (perhaps due to prior experiences, lack of explicit permission, stereotypes, and so on) do you have about interacting with them? What hesitations do you think they might have about interacting with you?
Question 4: Counterfactuals	Why do you think these connections don't already exist?

someone who is able to effectively facilitate matchmaking. This includes having authority and also perceived credibility (ability and trustworthiness), both among the survey respondents and also the people who they might be connected with. Within certain organizational contexts, it may make the most sense to have a team of people to conduct the unmet desire survey, especially given varying levels of credibility and also varying networks that would facilitate new matchmaking.

The Questionnaire

Unmet desire surveys need not be very long, yet ideally they are conducted conversationally as opposed to in written form. That facilitates follow-up questions and further information gathering as needed, which is especially helpful if respondents have not been asked questions like this in the past. Table 6.1 provides an overview of the core questions. Questions 1 and 2 tap into substantive goals, including attributes of current work and collaboration goals (informal and/or formal).[5] Question 3 measures uncertainty about relationality from multiple perspectives (i.e., how people want others to relate to them; whether they perceive that they can successfully relate to others that they would like to). Question 4 is an opportunity for the respondent to highlight anything important to them that may have been missed by the earlier questions (e.g., any other barriers or hesitations they have about engaging). This last question can also surface important information about respondents' previous experiences, such as the kinds of previous collaborative relationships they've engaged in, what has worked well, what's been challenging, and so on.

At one level, unmet desire surveys are very straightforward to conduct, and they are also very flexible. Yet what makes them especially useful can also make them challenging to conduct, as these questions are unusual and may be difficult for respondents to answer in the abstract. The key is that the question-wording must be tailored so that it resonates with respondents, matches the context, and provides actionable information for follow-up matchmaking. In particular, the results need to be useful for identifying the kinds of people who would make good matches and also the best way of facilitating those matches anew (i.e., when the survey reveals concerns, then that suggests the kind of information that must be conveyed to new collaborators in order to overcome uncertainty).

Examples

Here I provide several examples of each of the questions. First, Table 6.2 provides examples of Question 1 – several ways to inquire about the kinds of goals or challenges that decision-makers are facing and whether new collaborative relationships with certain types of diverse thinkers would be helpful. These examples underscore how the specific question wording should vary depending upon the context. For instance, the first example in Table 6.2 directs AmeriCorps program leaders to think about engaging with a researcher on program evaluation challenges. An alternative version of this question could inquire about connecting with a researcher on challenges other than program evaluation, or could instead focus on connecting with fellow program leaders around program evaluation challenges, or something else altogether. Which goal

---

[5] In Chapter 1 I noted that, in practice, there are often degrees of formality. Survey designers may thus wish to inquire directly about formal collaboration that entails all three attributes noted in Table 6.1, or perhaps only some subset.

TABLE 6.2 *Examples of wording for Question 1 in an unmet desire survey**

Decision-makers	Possible Question 1 wording
AmeriCorps program leaders are facing program evaluation challenges	"Are there challenges related to conducting program evaluation that you're facing in which it would be helpful to speak with a researcher?"
Local policymakers are facing myriad policy challenges	"Are there policy challenges you're facing in which you would like to be in touch with researchers who work at colleges and universities in your region?"
Climate organizers are looking to cultivate more committed volunteers	"We know that many organizers are seeing an influx of new volunteers and wanting to strengthen their volunteer base. Are you in those shoes, and would it be helpful to engage with a researcher to learn about the latest techniques for generating volunteer commitment and how you can apply them?"
Agency staff in the federal government	"How does the success of your program relate to what is happening elsewhere? Is there information about other programs within the government and/ or outside organizations that would help improve the effectiveness of your work? What kinds of people from these other agencies/organizations would be helpful to connect with?"
Neuroscientists who are deciding what research topics to pursue	"Would you be interested in interacting with disease advocacy groups – organizations that aim to influence government or policymaking regarding a particular disease – to talk about how neuroscience research may be relevant to their mission?"

* Some of these examples come from actual unmet desire surveys that have been fielded, whereas others are examples of questions that could be asked of particular types of decision-makers and are based on examples presented in this book.

or challenge to focus on, and which types of diverse thinkers to ask about, depends upon what the survey designer knows about the nature of unmet desire along with what kinds of matchmaking are feasible given their network. Either way, the general point is that Question 1 should include enough specificity so that it resonates with respondents and the information gained from the responses will be actionable for matchmaking.

Question 2 may be implemented almost word-for-word as mentioned in the previous section, and thus I do not provide any more details about it here. While the terms "informal collaboration" and "formal collaboration" may not be familiar to many decision-makers, the descriptions in parentheses are clarifying. The part of Question 2 focused on resources should also be tailored depending upon what goals are mentioned (i.e., the range of resources needed for formal collaboration will be much wider than what is needed for informal collaboration).

Question 3, just like Question 1, should be tailored for the context. When designing Question 3, one of the major decisions entails what types of response options to offer. The response options should cover the most common sources of concern that respondents are likely to have about interacting with the diverse thinkers mentioned in Question 1. This list will vary. For instance, here is the list that I provided to local policymakers in the survey discussed in Chapters 3 and 5. The context here was an unmet desire survey that asked local policymakers if there were policy challenges they were facing in which it would be helpful to connect with local researchers:

Here is the list of possible concerns policymakers may have when interacting with university researchers. Which of the following might you have when interacting with university researchers?

- *They may not have domain-specific expertise.*
- *They may not have trustworthy information.*
- *They may not have practical information.*
- *They may not value my knowledge and experience as a policymaker.*
- *They may lecture me.*
- *They may use unfamiliar language.*
- *They may push a political agenda.*
- *They may just criticize everything I do.*

Other decision-makers may share some of these concerns, or not. For instance, practitioners embedded in an organizational bureaucracy may be very hesitant to engage with diverse thinkers outside their organization due to concerns about authority. Researchers may be hesitant to engage with civic organizations or advocacy groups because they may worry that these organizations will misinterpret their work. The general point is that, as with Question 1, the precise question-wording should match the context and what the survey designer knows in advance about the kinds of concerns that respondents may have.

Last, whereas Questions 1–3 are mostly forward-looking, Question 4 asks respondents to look backward and reflect upon why these collaborative relationships do not already exist. It can capture information that may have been missed by the earlier questions yet may be relevant for any new matchmaking. Sometimes the answer is that it simply was not needed in the past (this echoes the point mentioned earlier that unmet desire often arises when decision-makers are facing novel challenges or goals), whereas other times responses to this question can yield important historical information that is important to keep in mind when conducting matchmaking anew.

Follow-Up by Making the Connection

Unmet desire surveys yield actionable information about the kinds of collaborative relationships that decision-makers would value, often with people they do not already know. They are a tool to prompt people to reflect upon and share any unmet desire, and "establish the scope" of what is needed for creating new collaborative relationships between people with diverse forms of expertise. Armed with this information, the next step is to locate a match and make a connection that meets collaboration goals and also overcomes any uncertainty about relationality expressed in the survey. With respect to locating a match, two possible methods are conducting targeted outreach to individuals or using organizational distribution channels such as social media or a newsletter.

Then, when making the connection, the three techniques that I described in Chapter 5 (in the discussion of the RITM matchmaking method) are useful: (1) state each person's unique expertise (also known as "role assignment"), (2) frame the conversation as a mutually beneficial learning opportunity, and (3) re-state the goal of the conversation. The specific text that is used to implement these techniques will depend upon what is learned in the survey. For instance, suppose an unmet desire survey with AmeriCorps program leaders reveals a desire to engage with researchers around how to measure the impact of their programs, yet also concern around whether researchers are likely to share practical information. In that case, the ideal match would be a researcher whom the matchmaker knows has the requisite substantive expertise and is also able to share that knowledge in a way that is practical. When stating each person's unique expertise, the matchmaker would want to explicitly emphasize how the researcher brings relevant expertise and will share that expertise in a way that emphasizes its practical relevance. The researcher (and the matchmaker) may know that she will share research-based insights about measuring program impact that are highly practical, yet the point is that the program leader is initially uncertain about that.

That is why explicitly mentioning this point when making the connection is essential.

In summary, the unmet desire survey is a tool that individuals and organizational leaders can use to help implement third-party matchmaking. It is useful for any situation in which those who seek change in civic life would value new collaborative relationships with diverse thinkers, yet such relationships are not arising on their own. And, while individuals engaged in the "self-service" matchmaking strategy (described in the previous section) may be unlikely to conduct new unmet desire surveys themselves, they can potentially use the results of pre-existing ones to inform their approach. For instance, researchers who want to initiate new collaborative relationships with local policymakers can use the results from the unmet desire survey in Chapter 3 and make sure to emphasize their non-partisan motivations, practical information, and desire to learn from the policymakers when they first reach out to and interact with them.

POLICY IMPLICATIONS

Having discussed three actionable strategies for building new collaborative relationships and a tool that is useful for implementing the two third-party approaches, here I describe policies that create the conditions for their more frequent use. These policies increase opportunities for forging new collaborative relationships in a way that reduces uncertainty about relationality in general, and that apply broadly to a wide array of potential collaborators (e.g., they would apply to collaborative relationships that include researchers, practitioners, and policymakers, and they would also apply to those between diverse thinkers who do not have those identities).

Policy Recommendation 1: What Organizational Leaders Can Do

The first policy applies to those who lead organizations such as universities, government agencies, nonprofits, and foundations. Many leaders recognize the importance of collaboration between diverse thinkers to tackle civic challenges and advance organizational priorities. Yet recognizing that new collaboration is important in the abstract is not equivalent to actively creating the conditions for new collaborative relationships to arise, especially if these relationships are voluntary and between people in different organizations, agencies, and/or sectors who do not already know each other.

To create the conditions for these new collaborative relationships to thrive, organizational leaders need to actively pose the question "What kind of new collaboration do we need to achieve our goals?" and then start from the fundamentals to answer it. This means ascertaining if there is an unmet desire to collaborate among those who work and volunteer there, and when doing so, including the possibility that this unmet desire may be oriented toward either informal or formal collaborative goals. Here it is worth reiterating how calls for new collaboration often implicitly focus on its formal variety, yet by actively legitimizing and elevating informal collaboration, organizational leaders (a) demonstrate the value of less resource-intensive knowledge exchange and (b) show that they recognize that this form of interaction may be what potential collaborators need and have the capacity for at a given moment.

I am choosing to reiterate this latter point about the less resource-intensive nature of informal collaboration because I recognize that, to some organizational leaders, a focus on policies that support new collaborative relationships in civic life may seem off the mark for truly tackling problems in communities they care about. For some organizational leaders, what they tell me they need above all else is more staff and bigger budgets. While fostering new collaboration can certainly have those effects, the path is typically indirect, and so devoting already-scarce resources to fostering new collaborative relationships can seem like a luxury not a necessity.

Yet one response is that this is precisely the moment to focus on informal collaboration because it is less resource-intensive. And, as we saw at several moments in Chapter 5, even a single conversation can influence strategic decision-making. Making space for new knowledge exchange, especially with people who bring diverse forms of expertise to problems they are facing in their work and that are useful for setting strategy and that they do not typically interact with, can have an outsized benefit.

This point also speaks to a common concern raised by researchers and university administrators. On the one hand, many university-based researchers want their work to influence policy and practice. Yet on the other hand, they are busy and building collaborative relationships (and devoting time to public engagement more generally) is typically not incentivized within their organizations, either for those in teaching or tenure-track roles.

One response is to highlight the need for policies that change promotion and tenure standards. There is a good reason to support changes along those lines.[6] Yet here too it is worth emphasizing how new collaborative relationships need not be very time- or resource-intensive, especially when the goal is knowledge exchange and when a third-party matchmaker takes steps to actively overcome uncertainty about relationality and smooth the initial conversation. For busy researchers, we can frame a new collaborative relationship with practitioners and policymakers who bring diverse forms of expertise to problems they care about as worth the time.

In short, the first policy recommendation is for organizational leaders to communicate the value of both informal and formal collaboration and invest in ways to surface and meet the unmet desire to collaborate among their members, perhaps using an unmet desire survey and follow-up matchmaking (and recognizing the implementation of both as distinct practices that are valued unto themselves). Organizations also need to be clear about the need for matchmaking that crosses expertise-based lines of difference, not only those that cross other lines of difference in civic life such as partisanship (in practice they may overlap, but that need not be the case).[7]

One example of an organization that has chosen to be intentional about surfacing and meeting unmet desire is the Robert Wood Johnson Foundation. Its Evidence for Action (E4A) program "prioritizes research to evaluate specific interventions (e.g., policies, programs, practices) that have the potential to counteract the harms of structural and systemic racism and improve health, well-being, and equity outcomes."[8] There is specific focus on understanding *what works* – they fund research that "should be able to inform a specific course of action and/or establish beneficial practices, not stop at characterizing or documenting the extent of a problem."

---

[6] Elsewhere I have written about the importance of creating new promotion-related incentives for engaging in collaborative relationships with non-researchers (Levine 2022). In the present chapter, I assume that university-based researchers' motivation to engage already exists, which I believe is quite reasonable in many cases. For instance, the data from research4impact 2.0 in Chapter 5 show that there is unmet desire for cross-sector knowledge exchange, which can inform strategic decision-making and also does not take a great deal of time.

[7] A related point is that organizations that wish to foster new collaborative relationships oriented toward formal partnerships in particular should create mechanisms to support them over time. For instance, in Appendix C, I include a step-by-step guide to research partnerships, and one possibility of a mechanism like this would be having people to facilitate each of these steps.

[8] www.rwjf.org/en/library/funding-opportunities/2021/evidence-for-action--innovative-research-to-advance-racial-equity.html (Accessed December 16, 2022).

Early on, E4A leaders observed that there were many organizations implementing promising community-level initiatives, yet they did not always meet the program's criteria for "rigor, actionability, or research team qualifications."[9] At this point, one response could have been to advise these organizations to remedy this shortfall themselves by finding a research partner, yet that approach was unlikely to be successful for many of the reasons explored in this book. Instead, they funded a matching service, in which a third-party organization would match them directly with research partners so that they can work together to conduct systematic evaluations.[10] This matching service is inextricably linked with the overall goals of the program, as it opens the funding opportunity to less well-resourced organizations who do not otherwise have access to the technical capacity that E4A demands of its grantees. Put differently, the matching service can help fulfill E4A's equity goals. It also provides researchers with access to new data and opportunities that they would not otherwise have.

I highlight E4A because in my view, it is a great example of an organization taking the existence of unmet desire, and the need for new infrastructure to meet it, seriously. In contrast to E4A, in my experience, matchmaking is something that individuals may do in the course of their everyday jobs, but it is not often a central aspect of anyone's title, job description, and professional identity, and not necessarily something that they think about in a systematic way. We need organizations to allocate sufficient resources specifically to the activity of matchmaking along with clear standards for who is best suited to the role and how they can expand the range of people in the network. Leadership plays a vital role in achieving this goal. Having explicit support from organizational leaders for matchmaking both legitimizes and elevates the activity.

Policy Recommendation 2: What Shape Science Policy Can Take

The second policy recommendation relates to science policy itself, and in particular the kinds of research that should be supported. The studies in

[9] www.evidenceforaction.org/funding/applicant-technical-assistance (Accessed December 16, 2022).
[10] www.jhsph.edu/research/centers-and-institutes/health-services-outcomes-research/research/accelerating-collaborations-for-evaluation-matching-service.html (Accessed December 16, 2022).

this book are an example of the science of collaboration, and how our understanding of collaboration in civic life should include the recognition that there can be an unmet desire to collaborate among those who seek change. Moreover, the reasons why this desire remains unmet go beyond the most visible constraints – lack of time and/or organizational incentives – to also include people's uncertainty about relating to others they don't know.

This book provides several lines of evidence in support of these arguments. The examples and empirical analyses showcase a wide range of unmet desire in civic life, including interest in new collaborative relationships involving different types of researchers, local policymakers, nonprofit practitioners, teachers, federal government agency staff, and grantees. And the unmet desire survey examples from earlier in this chapter underscore the versatility of that tool for a wide variety of decision-makers.

Future work can deepen our understanding of the full texture of unmet desire in civic life, the reasons why it remains unmet, and how to meet it in a wide variety of civic spaces. We can build on the approach developed here and conduct a wider array of unmet desire surveys, perhaps by defining *a priori* broad categories of collaborative relationships that groups of people may wish to engage in, and then conducting studies to measure what elements of relationality potential collaborators are most uncertain about in those settings. Fiske et al.'s (2006) rich research agenda on competence and warmth, and how people's perceptions of these fundamental attributes of social cognition vary based on occupation, race, ethnicity, age, gender, income, organizational affiliation, and so on, is perhaps a good model for how to construct a research agenda along these lines. One could start with many of the same social groupings and then investigate unmet desire as well as the elements of relationality that people would be uncertain about if they were to be engaged in a collaborative relationship with someone from another group. That research, in turn, could be the basis for new tests of the intervention hypotheses akin to what appears in Chapter 5.

This body of work would set the stage for broadening beyond the empirical analyses in this book in another way as well. Recall from Chapter 2 how status-based stereotypes influence whether one's expertise is socially recognized – in particular, those with salient social group memberships and organizational affiliations accorded lower status are less likely to have their expertise recognized than others. Based on this, we would expect that these attributes would influence the success that different kinds of people have implementing the three actionable strategies for creating new collaborative relationships discussed earlier in this chapter. In particular, we might expect that people with salient attributes associated with lower status may have a more difficult time implementing the self-service strategy and acting as a third-party matchmaker. The empirical analyses in this book vary the ways in which uncertainty about relationality is overcome and also include several examples (especially in Chapter 5) that entail a wide variety of matchmakers, yet future research could systematically vary the attributes of the people involved in order to better understand which matchmakers are most effective and under what conditions.[11]

Relatedly, another useful area of future research entails further expanding how we measure the success of new collaborative relationships. Recall that in Chapter 5, my measure was tied to short-term goal attainment: did the people who requested matchmaking gain knowledge that was useful to their strategic decision-making and, if applicable, did they launch a new research partnership? I argued that this measure was reasonable given the nature of the requests and that this measure had the added advantage of being comparable across new collaborative relationships that entailed very different contextual details.

That said, there are many cases in which we may want measures of impact that capture longer-term outcomes. In new collaborative relationships oriented toward knowledge exchange, we may want to know about the longer-term impact of gaining this new knowledge (what indirect influence on collective action ultimately emerges, and with what consequence?) and we might also want to study the enduring effect of overcoming uncertainty about relationality. When collaborators are interested in knowledge exchange leading to new formal

---

[11] As just one example, research4impact was co-founded by Jake, Don, and I, three men who identify as white, who held permanent faculty positions at well-regarded research universities in the United States, and who aimed to connect researchers with practitioners. One might reasonably pose the counterfactual question: what would happen if an organization like research4impact existed, but was led by non-researchers, researchers at other types of universities, individuals with different social attributes, and so on? How would that influence the types of populations that reached out for matchmaking and the new collaborative relationships that arose?

partnerships, then long-term measures may want to assess the downstream consequences as well.

Last, in this book, my focus has been on individuals collaborating with each other in civic life, and these collaborative relationships have largely entailed two or perhaps a small group of people. They are situations in which back-and-forth interaction, the hallmark of collaborative relationships, is feasible among all parties. For many problems that people are tackling in civic life, this kind of intimate interaction is exactly what is needed. The people involved are able to either indirectly or directly influence collective action because they have leverage – that is, their decisions are able to move many other people (Peter Levine 2022). For instance, the relationships between the researcher and volunteer group leaders in the climate organization described in Chapter 5 "only" entailed two people each, yet the knowledge exchange that happened went on to influence the actions of thousands of volunteers who were members of these groups all across the United States.

All of that said, it's important to acknowledge that tackling some kinds of important civic problems requires interaction among a much broader set of people. The climate volunteers aim to put pressure on elected officials in their districts across the country, yet crafting and passing federal climate policy (and strategizing how to do so effectively) involves more than dyadic collaborative relationships. More generally, some kinds of collective problem-solving may require organizational collaboration at a higher level, with many more people involved, and in which decisions hold authority over a much wider range of people. The collaborative relationships I focus on have their place and can be very impactful,[12] yet they are not the only form of engagement that may be needed. Studying the degree to which the strategies for reducing

---

[12] In addition to the measures of impact used in Chapter 5, there are other studies that have compared the nature of output that occurs in small teams versus large teams (i.e., formal collaboration between groups as small as two people versus larger groups). It turns out there are striking differences. For instance, one study that examined millions of scientific papers, technology patents, and software products found that "small teams disrupt science and technology by exploring and amplifying promising ideas from older and less-popular work ... [whereas] large teams develop recent successes, by solving acknowledged problems and refining common designs" (Wu et al. 2019:381). Both outcomes are potentially important, and so I highlight this difference not to universally argue in favor of one versus the other, but rather only to underscore that in some cases, there may be good reason to actively seek out collaborative relationships with only one or a small handful of others.

uncertainty about relationality can apply with more people, and more complicated group dynamics, would be a fruitful area to investigate in the future.

FINAL WORDS: COLLABORATE NOW!

My hope is that the book inspires readers to think about new ways to "collaborate now!" One immediate step to take along those lines is to reflect upon the possibility of unmet desire for new collaborative relationships in your own civic sphere and among others in your network. Are there collaborative relationships with diverse thinkers that you would value, yet are not currently happening? And what about colleagues? If so, what strategy (or strategies) would be best for trying to surface and meet this unmet desire?

Another immediate next step is to recognize the role of relationality more explicitly in collective action we observe in the world. One way to do this is to change how we talk about it. Here I return to the community garden example in Chapter 2. That example was about how, when people observe a new community garden, they may be likely to describe what happened along the lines of "neighbors came together to build a beautiful new garden that will bring accessible fresh food options." While that characterization is a very reasonable way to describe the substantive goal that was pursued, it omits any mention of vital process-related details. Building a brand-new community garden requires many upstream decisions about where it will be located, who will do what tasks to make it happen, what to grow, and so on. If neighbors are new to this kind of collective action, it is reasonable to expect that they may need collaborative relationships with others they do not know in order to be successful, including people who live down the street that they've never interacted with before, business leaders who will help fund it, agricultural researchers who can help figure out what would grow best in the location, and so on. These are the kinds of strategy-focused collaborative relationships that precede collective action and may be necessary to make the community garden a reality, yet they are not typically part of how we describe collective action that we observe in the world. Thus, another immediate step is to recognize the importance of these collaborative relationships and practice talking about them in an explicit way alongside substantive goals.

In short, being on the lookout for unmet desire in our own networks and changing how we think about the collective action we see in the world are immediate ideas that I hope readers take away from this book. These individual-level changes coupled with the policy recommendations mentioned earlier will provide more opportunities to "collaborate now!"

Appendix A

Qualitative Interviews Protocol

In this appendix, I provide a few more details on the interviews reported in Chapter 3, including the protocol that I used as my starting point for the semi-structured conversations. This part of the research is based on a series of interviews with people who sought change in the communities they were part of and also believed that engaging with new diverse thinkers would be beneficial for that work.

As noted in Chapter 3, I began with theoretical expectations about the importance of perceptions of competence, trustworthiness, and likeability (as key components of relationality). From there, I recruited a diverse sample that focused on achieving theoretical range (Yin 2003, Gerring 2017). I stopped once I had reached a saturation point in which the contextual details varied but the underlying theoretical elements that people were mentioning were largely the same (Small 2009).

Interviewees were not paid. Given that the interview portion of the call typically occurred after inquiries about research4impact (and often a plan for how they could engage research4impact to find new connections for their work), I tried to make the transition as seamless as possible. All interviewees knew that I was asking these questions as part of a book, and that any content that I used in the book would be anonymized. Consent was verbally given. In practice, I used only a very small portion of what any single individual told me in the book itself (though many of the other details were helpful for finding research4impact matches, for example).

Overall, and just to reiterate details that appear in Chapter 3: during spring and into early summer 2020, I interviewed 52 people: 17 were local elected officials (at either the city, county, or town level), 26 worked at nonprofits in which they either had experience interacting with researchers or had given it some thought (the types of nonprofits included museums, schools, and community-based organizations), and nine were researchers (all of whom are in the social sciences). Of the 52, 50 percent were female, 78 percent were Non-Hispanic white, 94 percent were located in the United States, and 23 percent reported that they saw part of their professional identity as a matchmaker. This last attribute indicated significant experience with cross-sector experiences, and these were always people who had been referred by others (rather than reaching out to research4impact themselves). I was particularly interested in whether they would identify elements of uncertainty about relationality that they've observed in their work and how they sought to overcome it.

INTERVIEW GUIDE

I constructed the following template in advance. In practice, all conversations were semi-structured. This guide ensured that all conversations started in the same way, and I tried to at least ask one question from each of the sections marked below. As is common with semi-structured interviews, in each case, respondents wanted to go into more details on some topics rather than others and I was more than happy to have that happen. The specific text of each question, especially later ones, would directly reference content shared earlier as appropriate. I would also substitute references to groups/organizations that made sense for the interviewee. For instance, if I was speaking with a researcher, I would ask about their interactions with "nonprofit practitioners" (or a more specific term that made sense in the context – for instance, when speaking with an education researcher, I would use the term "teacher" or "math teacher"). If I was talking with local policymakers, I would ask about "researchers" or "researchers from [local university x]." If I was talking with informal science educators (for instance, who work at a science museum), I would ask about "STEM researchers." And so on.

I started all interviews by saying a bit about myself and this book, gathering their verbal consent, and asking people how much time they had to talk.

Personal Background

First, please tell me a bit about your work.

What are some of the main problems that you are working on right now in your work? What are your top priorities these days?

Existing Experiences with Collaborative Relationships

So, as you work to address these problems, where do you get the information you need? Who do you rely on?

I know that some people do this and some do not. I'm curious about your experiences. Would you say you interact with [researchers/practitioners/policymakers] in your work, or not really?

[If yes:] What have your experiences been like? What's it been like to work with [them]?

Any examples in which you can say that engaging with [them] was really beneficial and impactful?

Any examples in which engaging with [them] was harmful or just not worth the time? Why is that?

Unmet Desire for (and Barriers to) New Collaborative Relationships

Switching gears a bit, are there ways that you wish you engaged with [them] for some problems you're currently facing, or not really?

Now let me ask about the flip side: do folks from [relevant organization] reach out to you unprompted? I know it might sound weird, but I'm just curious.

[If no:] Why might it not happen? Why do you think [relevant people] don't reach out to you?

[If yes from earlier q:] Coming back to your situation, what makes you hesitate to initiate these new collaborative relationships? Either to reach out to someone yourself, or if someone reaches out to you?

Comparison to Colleagues

What about other colleagues of yours? Do they engage directly with [folks from relevant organization]?

[If yes:] What have their experiences been like? For what kinds of projects? Was the experience smooth and enjoyable, or not really?

[If no:] Why do you think they don't reach out to [relevant people]? Why do you think others might hesitate?

Stereotypes

People often rely on stereotypes when they don't have other personal information. Do you hear your colleagues/staff use stereotypes to refer to [other relevant people]?

Would you agree with these stereotypes, or not really?

How to Meet Unmet Desire (Also: An Indirect Way of Measuring Salient Stereotypes)

If you were going to give advice to [people from other organization] who wanted to reach out to engage, what would you say to them? How should they approach you?

Final Questions

Given what I shared about my research at the very beginning, is there anything I should have asked but didn't?

Is there someone else you know that I should be speaking with?

Appendix B

More Details on Local Policymaker Survey

Chapters 3 and 5 report results from a national survey of local policymakers. This appendix includes more details on the survey itself as well as the results reported in those two chapters. This content is broken down into several sections which are as follows:

- Appendix B1: More details on open-ended responses regarding topics for collaborative relationships with researchers
- Appendix B2: Multivariate models
- Appendix B3: Sample recruitment, consent, and composition
- Appendix B4: Questionnaire (including coding)
- Appendix B5: Survey timing considerations
- Appendix B6: Policymakers' frequency of interaction with other policy-relevant information sources

APPENDIX B1: MORE DETAILS ON OPEN-ENDED RESPONSES REGARDING TOPICS FOR COLLABORATIVE RELATIONSHIPS WITH RESEARCHERS

As noted in the main text, respondents had the opportunity to volunteer an issue (via an open-ended question) on which they would like to collaboratively engage with a researcher. Arguably answering this question requires more effort than the other closed-ended measures of unmet desire, in part because it is open-ended and also because specific collaboration topics with researchers may not be top-of-mind. Thus, it is perhaps not surprising that many respondents ($n = 260$, or 48.1 percent of the sample) skipped this question altogether.

Overall, 182 policymakers wrote about either a specific issue and/or a general desire for more relationships. Table B.1 includes unweighted count data of the full list of topics that were mentioned, along with their frequency. As shown in the table, the diversity of topics mentioned is quite broad, reflecting the wide variety of issues on local political agendas.

TABLE B.1 *Frequency of topics mentioned for new collaborative relationships*

Topic	(Unweighted) Number of mentions
More relationships to inform decision-making	59
Housing	22
Environmental issues	21
Economic development	20
Land use/planning	15
Functioning of local government	13
Jobs/workforce	11
Public health	11
Roads/transportation/traffic	10
Policing/public safety	9
Energy	8
Broadband	8
Equity	7
Education (K-12)	7
Higher education (access/student preparation)	6
Polling/using data	6
Health care	5
Education (adult)	5
Free speech	4
Grant-writing (e.g., so that municipalities can apply for state and federal grants)	4
Higher education (concerns about its curriculum)	4
Regionalization/regional needs	4
Cannabis	3
Local finance	3
Population growth	3
Tax policy	3
Tourism	3
Water	3
Disaster preparedness	2
Economic inequality	2
Election integrity	2
Immigration	2

Topic	(Unweighted) Number of mentions
Intergovernmental cooperation	2
Partnerships with nonprofits	2
Recreation	2
Agriculture	1
Critical race theory	1
Debt	1
Fire	1
Food insecurity	1
Indigenous people	1
Veterans	1
Voter registration	1
Waste management	1

Notes:
"Public health" includes mentions of the Covid-19 pandemic, opioids, substance abuse, and general mentions of public health.
"Environment" includes all mentions of climate change and natural resources.
"Energy" includes any general mention of energy or a form of energy such as wind power.
"Functioning of local government" includes any mentions about wanting to improve the functioning of local government (including transparency or increasing civic involvement in the process of local government).

APPENDIX B2: MULTIVARIATE MODELS

In addition to the descriptive results I also estimated multivariate models using the data in Chapter 5. I present both raw results and average marginal effects for select variables (i.e., the average difference in predicted probability between the listed category and the omitted category).

These models include the political and demographic attributes in the policymaker figures in Chapter 5 (Figures 5.4 and 5.5), along with controls for attributes of the policymaker's town/county. These models also include one demographic factor not included in Figures 5.4 and 5.5, which is education level. While at first blush, we might expect policymakers' education level to influence unmet desire, prior studies find little evidence that level of education matters for research use (as opposed to, for example, the specific nature of their professional training). For that reason, I omitted education from the Chapter 5 figures. That said, I chose to include it in these multivariate models given my own interviews with local policymakers suggesting, at least anecdotally, that those with college degrees may have higher unmet desire than those without.

TABLE B.2 *Multivariate models of local policymakers' prevalence of prior collaborative relationships with local researchers*

	Had prior interaction?	Had unprompted contact?
Democrat	.404	.534*
	(.299)	(.283)
Independent	−.124	.065
	(.307)	(.313)
Female	.107	−.338
	(.274)	(.259)
Age	−.334	−.31
	(.252)	(.256)
College grad	.693**	1.003***
	(.334)	(.359)
White	−.141	.454
	(.278)	(.314)
Prop. college degree	.66*	.666*
	(.385)	(.395)
Total population	.969**	−.149
	(.44)	(.468)
Prop. urban	−.04	.624
	(.469)	(.502)
Prop. Biden vote	.635	1.003**
	(.416)	(.402)
College in county	−.204	−.283
	(.299)	(.295)
County official	1.049**	1.089**
	(.445)	(.481)
Municipal official	.72*	.494
	(.381)	(.41)
Top official	.88***	.645**
	(.272)	(.274)
Constant	−3.495***	−4.151***
	(.658)	(.668)
Observations	465	465
Pseudo R^2	.126	.124

Standard errors are in parentheses
***$p < 0.01$, **$p < 0.05$, *$p < 0.1$ (two-tailed tests)

First, Table B.2 displays logit models explaining policymakers' prevalence of prior collaborative relationships with local researchers (using the two measures of prevalence in Chapter 5). More prior interaction with researchers using both measures is associated with the policymaker having at least a four-year college degree, the policymaker being a county official relative to a township official, and the policymaker being a top elected official as opposed to governing board member.

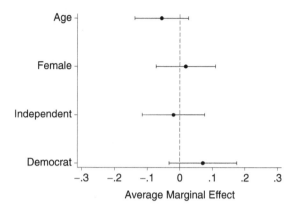

(A) Probability of Having Previously Interacted with Researchers Over the Past Year

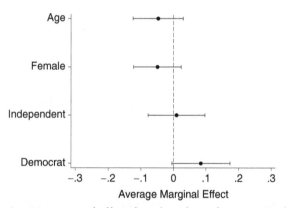

(B) Probability of Having Had Researchers Reach Out Unprompted Over the Past Year

FIGURE B.1 Average marginal effects based on the multivariate models, for several policymaker attributes highlighted in Chapter 5 (the prior interaction figures), along with 95 percent confidence intervals

Second, Table B.3 displays logit models of local policymakers' desire for more collaborative relationships with local researchers than they currently have (using the two measures in Chapter 5). Unmet desire is widespread (as shown in the descriptive results in Chapter 5) and few of these political and demographic attributes are consistently and strongly related to it. The proportion of the county who voted for Biden as President in 2020 is weakly related to both measures of unmet desire (yet whether the policymaker is a Democrat is only related to one of them). The policymaker being a municipal official (as opposed to a township official) is also related to both measures.

TABLE B.3 *Multivariate models of local policymakers' unmet desire for collaborative relationships with local researchers*

	Want more interaction?	Welcome unprompted contact?
Democrat	.915***	.329
	(.311)	(.437)
Independent	−.109	−.041
	(.287)	(.368)
Female	−.057	.562
	(.266)	(.371)
Age	.464**	−.206
	(.235)	(.316)
Prior interaction	−.024	.717*
	(.255)	(.4)
Societal benefit from research	.46*	.441
	(.264)	(.401)
College grad	.191	.426
	(.275)	(.356)
White	.336	.193
	(.307)	(.423)
Prop. college degree	−.596*	−1.193**
	(.359)	(.482)
Total population	.59	1.214**
	(.461)	(.6)
Prop. urban	−.032	−.093
	(.447)	(.531)
Prop. Biden vote	.679*	.966*
	(.391)	(.494)
College in county	.279	.206
	(.287)	(.347)
County official	.252	−.118
	(.418)	(.502)
Municipal official	.754**	.808**
	(.328)	(.376)
Top official	.189	1.152***
	(.262)	(.376)
Constant	−1.766***	−.718
	(.583)	(.683)
Observations	458	458
Pseudo R^2	.11	.163

Standard errors are in parentheses
***$p < 0.01$, **$p < 0.05$, *$p < 0.1$

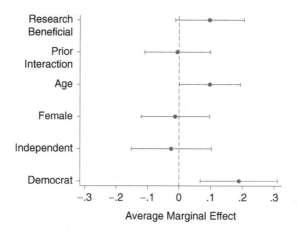

(A) Probability of Wanting More Interaction
with Researchers

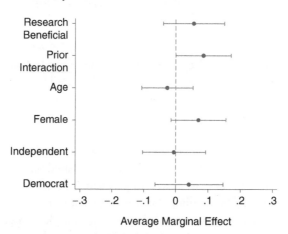

(B) Probability of Welcoming Unprompted
Outreach by Researchers

FIGURE B.2 Average marginal effects based on the multivariate models, for several policymaker attributes highlighted in Chapter 5 (the unmet desire figures), along with 95 percent confidence intervals

APPENDIX B3: SAMPLE RECRUITMENT, CONSENT, AND COMPOSITION

The data come from a national, multi-collaborator online survey panel of local government officials collected through CivicPulse. The sample of respondents was randomly drawn from the population of policymakers in US local

TABLE B.4 *Comparisons between sample and population data*
A: *Township and municipality officials**

	Sample median	Population median
Proportion urban	.96	.72
Proportion college-educated	.27	.22
Population size	5,944	3,324
2020 democratic vote share	.45	.39

B: *County officials*

	Sample median	Population median
Proportion urban	.54	.40
Proportion college-educated	.22	.19
Population size	43,521	25,758
2020 Democratic Vote Share	.37	.30

* *Presidential vote share is estimated at the county level, and so each sub-county government is matched to the relevant county in which it is located.*

governments (i.e., township, municipality, and county governments) with a population over 1,000 residents, and included top elected officials and governing board members. The survey took place from April 8 to May 24, 2021, and included 541 respondents. CivicPulse obtained informed consent at the beginning of the survey electronically, in which respondents were informed about how long it would take, the topics it would cover, and the researchers who developed the content. It also said that responses would be confidential, and also that they would receive a follow-up report based on the survey (thus emphasizing direct benefits to survey respondents). Participants voluntarily agreed to participate after reading this consent document.

Table B.4 provides unweighted data of the sample compared to the population. All analyses in the main text are weighted using probability weights supplied by CivicPulse to increase sample representativeness.

APPENDIX B4: QUESTIONNAIRE (INCLUDING CODING)

Below is the question-wording for all questions used in the policymaker figures in Chapters 3 and 5, and in the multivariate models in Appendix B2. The all-caps labels match variable labels in those multivariate models. My module on the CivicPulse multi-investigator survey included only a couple of questions not listed here.

* * * * *

Next, we are going to ask you a few questions about your interactions with the colleges and universities in your region (which includes two-year community colleges as well as four-year colleges and universities). Some policymakers are in touch with people at these institutions, whereas others are not.

[COLLEGE IN COUNTY] Where is the nearest college or university?

- In the county that I live in
- Adjacent to the county that I live in
- Far away from the county that I live in

Coded as 1 = "in the county that I live in" and 0 otherwise

[PRIOR INTERACTION] Over the past year, on average how often have you interacted with individual researchers who work at the colleges and universities in your region to talk about policy issues?

- More than once a week
- Once a week
- Once or twice a month
- Once or twice a year
- Never

Coded as 0 = "Never" and 1 otherwise

[UNPROMPTED CONTACT] Over the past year, on average how often have individual researchers from colleges and universities in your region reached out unprompted to discuss research related to policy issues (not including survey requests)?

- More than once a week
- Once a week
- Once or twice a month
- Once or twice a year
- Never

Coded as 0 = "Never" and 1 otherwise

[WANT MORE INTERACTION?] Looking ahead, how much would you like to be in touch with researchers who work at colleges and universities in your region to talk about policy issues you are facing?

- A lot more than now
- Somewhat more than now
- The same as now
- Somewhat less than now
- A lot less than now

Coded as 1 = "A lot more than now" or "Somewhat more than now" and 0 otherwise

[WELCOME UNPROMPTED CONTACT] In general, are you open to college and university researchers in your region cold-contacting you to talk about whether research might be helpful for policy issues you are facing?

- No
- Yes

Coded as 1= Yes, 0 = No

[OPEN ENDED QUESTION] Are there any policy issues in which you're not currently in touch with researchers from colleges and universities in your region but would like to be? If yes, which ones and why would it be beneficial to engage with these researchers? Reasons might include: to inform your position on an issue, learn more about existing challenges, explore a new topic, and/or help build coalitions to support a particular course of action. *[open-ended text box]*

[LIST OF HESITANCIES] Below is a list of possible concerns policymakers may have when interacting with university researchers. Which of the following might you have when interacting with university researchers? *Please select all that apply.*

1   They may not have domain-specific expertise.
2   They may not have trustworthy information.
3   They may not have practical information.
4   They may not value my knowledge and experience as a policymaker.
5   They may lecture me.
6   They may use unfamiliar language.
7   They may push a political agenda.
8   They may just criticize everything I do.
9   Other (please specify):
10 None of the above

All of these are coded 1 if the respondent selected it, 0 otherwise.

[SOCIETAL BENEFIT FROM RESEARCH] Thinking about higher education in general, how much do American colleges and universities contribute to research that benefits society?

- A lot
- Some
- Not much
- Nothing

Coded as 1= "A lot" and 0 otherwise. Note that this question appeared in an entirely different part of the multi-collaborator survey.

COLLEGE GRAD: coded as 1 if the respondent received at least a four-year college degree; 0 otherwise

WHITE: coded as 1 if the respondent stated that White best describes their race/ethnicity; 0 otherwise

PROP. COLLEGE DEGREE: proportion of 25-years-or-older residents in given geographic area who have completed a four-year post-secondary degree. Data supplied by CivicPulse in terciles, and coded as 0-1 (with 1 = highest tercile)

TOTAL POPULATION: total number of residents living in a given geographic unit. Data supplied by CivicPulse in terciles, and coded as 0-1 (with 1 = highest tercile)

PROP. URBAN: proportion of residents in given geographic unit who reside in an urban area. Data supplied by CivicPulse in terciles, and coded as 0-1 (with 1 = highest tercile)

PROP. BIDEN VOTE: proportion of the votes, by county, for Joe Biden in the 2020 presidential election (each sub-county government is matched to the relevant county in which it is contained). Data supplied by CivicPulse in terciles, and coded as 0-1 (with 1 = highest tercile)

COUNTY OFFICIAL: government position of policymaker is at the county level (omitted category is township)

MUNICIPAL OFFICIAL: government position of policymaker is at the municipal level (omitted category is township)

TOP OFFICIAL: policymaker is a top elected official (as opposed to a governing board member)

APPENDIX B5: SURVEY TIMING CONSIDERATIONS

Given that the survey took place in spring 2021 in the midst of the Covid-19 pandemic, I also thought it was prudent to include the following question after those that measured the prevalence of prior interaction.

* * * * *

Did the pandemic increase, decrease, or not change the frequency of your policy-related interactions with researchers from colleges and universities in your region (relative to before the pandemic started)?

Results: I do not find evidence that the Covid-19 pandemic influenced the prevalence responses. The large majority of respondents (81.9 percent) said it had no effect. Among this 81.9 percent, the pattern in the results in Chapter 5 is largely the same.

APPENDIX B6: POLICYMAKERS' FREQUENCY OF INTERACTION WITH OTHER POLICY-RELEVANT INFORMATION SOURCES

The survey also included a short battery of questions about the frequency of policymakers' interactions with other people who would share policy-relevant information. I discuss these results briefly in Chapter 5. Below is the question-wording of that battery and a table showing the full distribution of results. The last row of Table B.5 also shows the analogous data for researchers at colleges and universities within the policymaker's region (from Figure 5.4).

* * * * *

Over the past year, on average how often have you interacted with each of the following individuals to talk about policy issues?

Rows [Order Randomly Presented]
1   Other government officials in the county you live in
2   Government officials outside of the county you live in
3   Business leaders
4   Grassroots/community leaders
5   Lobbyists/Interest group leaders
6   Researchers who work at colleges and universities outside your region
7   Staff at national or state-level municipality/town/county organizations (e.g., NACo and NATaT)

TABLE B.5 *Percent of local policymakers in contact with various sources of policy-relevant information*

	More than Once a Week	Once a Week	Once or Twice a Month	Once or Twice Over the Entire Year	Never
Other government officials in your county	32.0	15.8	31.9	16.1	4.2
Grassroots/ community leaders	22.1	16.2	35.6	16.5	9.5
Business leaders	19.8	17.9	36.7	19.7	6.0
Government officials outside county	6.6	5.7	28.7	40.9	18.2
Staff at national/state organizations	6.4	8.1	21.7	29.4	34.5
Lobbyists/interest group leaders	2.0	3.4	18.4	27.2	49.0
Researchers at colleges/ universities outside your region	.1	.6	5.5	24.0	69.7
Researchers at colleges/ universities within region	.3	.7	3.6	21.9	73.5

Numbers in each row may not equal 100 due to rounding.
All results are weighted to increase sample representativeness.

Response Options
- More than once a week
- Once a week
- Once or twice a month
- Once or twice over the entire year
- Never

Appendix C

Step-by-Step Guide for Conducting One Type of Formal Collaboration: A New Research Partnership

As discussed throughout the main text, the goal of new collaborative relationships between those who seek change in society may be to influence collective action either indirectly or directly. Both routes entail knowledge exchange – that is, back-and-forth interaction between people who bring diverse, task-relevant expertise to issues affecting communities they care about, and who often begin as strangers to each other. When collaborative relationships are oriented toward influencing collective action *indirectly*, it means that the content of their interaction concerns strategy but that they intend to remain independent decision-makers. When collaborative relationships are oriented toward influencing collective action *directly*, it means that they intend to become interdependent in some way, and that the content of their interaction concerns strategy related to a new project over which they will have shared ownership and decision-making authority, and agree to be held accountable to each other. In this latter case, there is quite a bit of knowledge exchange that occurs in advance of "officially" deciding to partner (and after that decision is made as well).

Because knowledge exchange is always the primary activity of any new collaborative relationship (regardless of whether the goal is to influence collective action indirectly or directly), a good deal of the main text of this book examines the conditions under which diverse thinkers want to engage in new knowledge exchange with each other.

However, once we focus specifically on formal projects, a wide variety of activities is possible. This is because the range of possible projects in civic life is vast – partners could jointly organize an event such as tabling or a fundraiser, or they could form a coalition to lobby together, or they could conduct a new research project together, or some combination of all or none of the above. The point is that, because the range of new projects is extremely broad, it is hard in one book to examine all possible types in detail.

What is possible, and what I do in this appendix, is examine one type of project in detail that I expect will be of interest to many readers. This is a *research partnership*. Research partnerships are formal collaborations between researchers and practitioners (people in the nonprofit, government, and/or for-profit sectors) in which the goal is to conduct a research project over which the parties involved share ownership of the data, share decision-making authority associated with the design and implementation of the research study, and agree to take on roles and responsibilities that entail being held accountable to each other.

INTRODUCTORY CONSIDERATIONS RELATED TO RESEARCH PARTNERSHIPS

In recent years, these kinds of research partnerships have become more common (for instance, see Butler (2019) for data on this point in political science). In part, this trend reflects the fact that people from these diverse sectors share many of the same fundamental goals and concerns about the communities they are part of. These goals may be intensely local in nature (e.g., the desire to reduce traffic and pollution on local streets and promote bike-riding as an alternative mode of transportation) or they may apply to a much larger geographic scale (e.g., the need to address climate change, make health care more affordable across the country, increase voter engagement, improve governance, etc.). On top of that, both often have intrinsic reasons for wanting to partner – they are intensely curious and the possibility of generating new research findings can be fun and exciting.

The format of the research project itself may vary tremendously, such as conducting a new field experiment, engaging in new interviews, conducting a new program evaluation, analyzing administrative data, engaging in participant observation, and so on. For instance, one research partnership that arose through research4impact involved a communications researcher and practitioner whose work focused on visual storytelling. They worked together to design experiments that studied the impact of visually presenting information about pressing social issues such as climate change, and then measured how these different presentations influenced respondents' issue-relevant attitudes and behavior (as compared with non-visual forms of information). Another partnership involved an elections researcher and a practitioner who worked at a nonprofit organization that advocates for election reform in the United States. In this case, the nonprofit organization had access to a wealth of administrative data on this topic, yet did not have the capacity to analyze it at that time. Instead, the practitioner shared it with the researcher, who then analyzed it on his own and wrote up the results in academic papers. The organization could cite the papers when engaging with policymakers and the outside public. And the researcher could submit them for peer review, as they spoke to key theoretical questions about the impact of election reform on candidate extremity, polarization, and voting behavior.

Importantly, research partnerships are not fee-for-service consulting arrangements. Rather, these partnerships offer a distinct benefit exchange, and both parties typically have specific professional reasons for wanting to be involved. For researchers, partnering to conduct a project with a practitioner can offer a unique opportunity to answer a research question that is both theoretically interesting and has practical significance. Indeed, arguably the best way to ensure that decision-makers find research findings useful is to have them be involved with formulating the question and conducting the study. In addition, practitioners have context-based expertise that enables broader understanding and data collection opportunities that researchers do not have on their own. For practitioners, participating in a research partnership offers the opportunity to gain access to research-based skills that they may not be trained in. Research partnerships can also produce new knowledge that deepens understanding of what works, and is thus directly relevant to their goals. Last, another professional reason why practitioners may value research partnerships is tied to funding opportunities. Private foundations and government initiatives often offer funding to evaluate the effectiveness of a program or policy, and so partnering with a researcher who brings research-based expertise can lead to new funding opportunities. For this very reason, these funders may even offer innovative matching services to pair practitioners and researchers (e.g., the Robert Wood Johnson Foundation example discussed in Chapter 6).

STEP-BY-STEP GUIDE FOR CONDUCTING
A RESEARCH PARTNERSHIP

In what follows, I provide a step-by-step guide for conducting research partnerships.[1] The eight steps described herein are an adapted version of what appears in a book chapter I published in 2021 entitled "How to Form Organizational Partnerships to Run Experiments" (and which appears in the *Advances in Experimental Political Science* volume; Levine 2021). That book chapter includes a very detailed discussion of why and how to partner to conduct research and also includes a very lengthy example of the process from start to finish. That said, there are two main reasons why I have decided to include a separate appendix here rather than just refer readers to that book chapter.

First, nowadays when engaging with people interested in research partnerships (typically via my work with research4impact), I have frequently run into hesitation about whether that book chapter is right for them. The chapter was written for an edited volume targeting political scientists, and in particular political scientists interested in research projects that entail experiments. When I interact with practitioners, researchers who are not political scientists, and researchers who want to partner with practitioners to conduct work that is not experimental, they often raise questions about how the content in the book chapter applies to them. My answer is always that most of it does apply, but I also acknowledge that some of the language in the chapter is specific to experiments. The fit is not perfect.

The second reason to include this appendix is that I expect that a good deal of the readership interested in the content of this book's main text will also be interested in pursuing research partnerships. As a result, having this appendix means that everything is in one place. All readers can learn about the formation of new collaborative relationships (Chapters 1 to 6), and those specifically interested in collaborative relationships oriented toward a new research partnership have easy access to relevant step-by-step information as well. My hope is that this is especially useful given that journal articles and other publicly available writing that report the results of research partnerships

---

[1] I should acknowledge from the outset that this is not the only possible model of how to conduct a research partnership. For an overview of several other models, please see Cooper et al.'s (2021:1387) discussion of community science, which includes "community-based participatory research (CBPR), community-engaged research, community-owned and managed research (COMR), street science, and other participatory methods."

do not typically include details about how those partnerships arose. This is even the case in situations where the partners are named in print.[2]

That said, there are two important considerations related to research partnerships that I do not cover in this appendix. First, I omit a detailed discussion of ethical issues associated with research partnerships and considerations that speak to whether researchers and practitioners should partner or not. Second, I omit discussion of specifics that may apply only to particular types of practitioners. In this appendix, I use the general term "practitioner" to refer to those who conduct paid work in either the nonprofit or government sector as well as those who may volunteer as part of civic organizations, advocacy groups, and so on. While the steps described herein apply broadly to people in all of these positions and who are members of all of these types of organizations, it is possible that partnerships with certain types of practitioners may involve extra steps (e.g., contracting regulations associated with government agencies). A detailed discussion of ethical considerations and a brief discussion of specifics related to different types of practitioners appear in the first half of the book chapter referenced earlier (especially the content on pages 199–205).

Overall, the primary audience for this appendix includes researchers and practitioners who have already decided that they are interested in a research partnership. For readers who are political scientists interested in a research partnership to conduct an experiment, then this discussion will be complete yet they may also wish to read the book chapter for even more details about some of the individual steps. For all others, this appendix offers a complete and thorough discussion of the required steps without weighing the text down with information that may not be applicable.

Table C.1 contains an overview of the eight steps involved with a research partnership. A more in-depth discussion of what each step entails is as follows.

---

[2] For one example of this, consider a highly influential paper that helped justify the use of face masks in the fight against Covid-19 (Abaluck et al. 2021). This research resulted from a very elaborate partnership, with the partners listed on page 6 of the NBER online working paper. Yet the paper does not say anything about how the partnership came about, why the partners chose to participate, why other potential partners chose not to participate, what hesitations they had about each other and the work at the beginning and during the process, and so on. The fact that this information is not discussed is not unique to this paper.

TABLE C.1 *Steps in a research partnership*

---

1. Initiate new collaborative relationship
2. The "dating phase" (ascertain partner's willingness and capacity, and discuss what the research study would entail)
3. Put plans in writing
4. Secure institutional review board (IRB) approval
5. Acquire funding (if necessary)
6. Collect data, including possibly a pilot study
7. Analyze data and present results
8. Follow-up and possibly do another study together

Note: Some steps may occur concurrently, as noted in text

STEP 1: INITIATE NEW COLLABORATIVE RELATIONSHIP

This initial step mirrors the content of Chapters 1 to 6 of this book. It entails people with diverse forms of expertise, who may not already know each other, choosing to engage in a back-and-forth interaction to learn about each other's work and come to a broader understanding of a problem facing a community they care about. The three strategies described in Chapter 6 – third-party individuals, self-service, and third-party organizations – are common ways in which these new collaborative relationships can arise. They can help collaborators successfully relate to each other right from the beginning.

How should a collaborative relationship oriented toward a new research partnership proceed? The primary purpose of these initial conversations is to learn about each other's goals and values, and then decide whether to continue with future conversations that delve into more detail about what a research project might look like.

The content of the initial conversations tends to be at a relatively high level, in which collaborators share their goals, strategic priorities, research-related needs and interests, timing, and past experiences engaging in these kinds of partnerships. Spending time learning about these attributes and also identifying shared values – why this work matters to the people involved – are helpful for guiding and grounding later conversations. During these initial conversations, collaborators also seek to identify a shared understanding of the problem, and to talk about the broad outlines of what a research project might look like and the reasons why they might be interested in being part of it. A good habit for partners to get into, even during these initial high-level conversations, is to take detailed written notes. These notes serve as an important memory heuristic later on, and are useful in case of turnover and/or any discrepancies that arise down the line. Last, two other points to keep in mind right from the beginning are to ensure that all parties are involved with creating the agenda, and that translators are present in case collaborators speak different languages. Third parties can work to ensure both of these (e.g., the RITM matchmaking method described in Chapter 5 involves scope calls and other one-on-one interaction prior to facilitating a match in order to ensure that the agenda is clear and agreeable to all involved), but both of these points are important to keep in mind for new collaborative relationships not initiated by third parties as well as for all future interactions beyond Step 1.

Overall, these initial conversations rarely delve into the details of what a research project may look like. Instead, collaborators should ascertain if there is shared understanding of the problem that needs to be addressed and a mutual desire to conduct a research project together over an agreeable timeframe. If the answer is yes, then parties may decide to continue the conversation to talk about the details of what that research project may look like. That is Step 2.

STEP 2: "THE DATING PHASE"

If initial conversations from Step 1 seem promising, then follow-up conversations begin to delve more deeply into details about what the research project might look like. Step 2, like Step 1, is primarily about knowledge exchange, yet the primary purpose of these conversations is different. During Step 2, the main goal is for partners to decide whether to move forward with putting everything into writing (which is Step 3).

To do that, conversations during the "dating phase" aim to assess both the *willingness* and *ability* of your partner (and yourself) to conduct a research project together. Willingness refers to whether everyone involved genuinely wants to learn something new. This may sound like an obvious point in conversations about conducting new research, yet it is non-trivial precisely because the research study may not produce results that collaborators would like. All parties involved have the potential to be disappointed by the results (for example, when an experimental intervention shows a null result, yet both parties expected, and perhaps hoped for, a statistically significant and substantively meaningful difference). Thus, ascertaining willingness to learn something new upfront is critical. This is also a good opportunity to discuss the possibility of doing a pilot study (if that is feasible given the nature of the research) and doing more than one research study. Discussing this latter possibility early on helps to avoid seeing the results of any single research study as the "final word" on the topic.

As part of these conversations about willingness, researchers will need to be advocates for good research design (e.g., sharing technical details about data collection, data analysis, experimental design, participant observation, etc.), and practitioners will need to explain what kind of study is feasible and important given the context, history, and organizational priorities.

In addition to ascertaining willingness, both parties need to ascertain ability, which is the capacity to conduct the research study on a mutually agreed-upon timeline. One thing to be mindful of is that research partnerships typically entail asking people to engage in new tasks, including ones that are outside their usual types of activities and/or their job description. For instance, researchers may be asked to provide a new overview of a research literature or the fundamentals of a research method. Practitioners may be asked to collect new data or manage staff and volunteers who are helping implement a new intervention. In addition, conversations about ability often include initial conversations about funding, a topic I will return to later.

Note that all of the conversations in Steps 1 and 2 take place prior to any official agreement about partnering. This point underscores how these partnerships have the potential to provide a wealth of new benefits (as noted earlier in the appendix), yet successfully realizing them takes time due to the relationship-building that's needed in Steps 1 and 2. Overall, a good indication that conversations are progressing is that collaborators promptly respond to emails/phone calls and indicate a willingness to talk about specific details – what the research will consist of, what responsibilities each partner will have, what timing is preferable, what outcomes will be measured, and so on.

STEP 3: PUT PLANS IN WRITING

Steps 3 to 5 (and possibly Step 6 if the partnership includes a pilot study) often occur simultaneously, not sequentially. If conversations in Steps 1 and 2 reveal a research question and design that are mutually beneficial, then the next step is to codify plans in writing. Putting plans in writing can be a make-or-break moment for research partnerships, and doing so is critical to ensure that partners are on the same page and feel mutually accountable.

The following type of information should be put into writing: each partner's goals, roles, and responsibilities, details on study funding and timing, data ownership considerations, plan for how the data and findings will be disseminated and written-up, overall timeline and process for ending the partnership, and any conflicts of interest. Although there are several pieces of information that should be put into writing, any written document will never cover every single eventuality and decision. It is thus an opportunity to put the broad outlines of the project into writing, yet with the understanding that partners will still face many decision points to come. All parties must acquire the necessary approvals for the written document, which also provides a moment to ensure that any organizational buy-in that is needed is obtained. That is especially important in case of staff turnover.

A key part of any written document covers data ownership and dissemination. With regard to data ownership, partners will frequently want to put into writing that data collected are jointly owned. This ensures that researchers have the right to publish data and findings (one of the main benefits they receive for engaging in research partnerships) and also ensures that practitioners have the right to analyze and use data as they see fit as well. Dissemination plans should also be discussed and put into writing upfront, especially to talk about the form that write-ups will take and also whether or not any parties wish to be anonymous in print. Questions about anonymity are especially likely to arise with practitioners (and their organizational affiliations) who may not want their name in print for a variety of reasons, such as if there are political sensitivities associated with the research.

Last, the written document can take several forms. It may be relatively informal and take the form of an email that all have reviewed and responded to. Or it may include more formal documentation, such as a memorandum of understanding (which carries a degree of mutual accountability and seriousness, yet is not legally binding) or a legally binding contract. Parties need to decide what is best for them and consult others in their organization as needed.

STEP 4: SECURE INSTITUTIONAL REVIEW BOARD (IRB) APPROVAL

Step 4 is primarily the responsibility of researchers, and they should already be aware of how that process works at their university. In the course of IRB review, it is possible that questions may arise about the practitioner partners and their organizations (and thus require something separate in writing to be submitted to the IRB), though for the most part, this step is likely to be conducted by researchers on their own.

In addition, IRBs typically require quite a bit of detail about the proposed study (as do funding bodies; see Step 5 later). This point underscores how, even once the broad outlines of a study are put in writing in Step 3, further conversations will be needed to finalize aspects of the study procedure (e.g., the precise process for recruiting participants, the final details of study protocols and interventions, the precise list of outcomes to be measured, etc.).

STEP 5: ACQUIRE FUNDING (IF NECESSARY)

Initial conversations about funding should take place early on, well before putting plans in writing as part of Step 3. That said, if new funding must be acquired for the study, then those applications tend to be finalized and submitted only after the partners have officially put their plans in writing.

When I have conversations with people about the possibility of conducting new research partnerships, a common misperception is that they have to be very costly and thus require large new grants (and/or the parties involved need to have deep pockets). While that may sometimes be the case, it need not be. In fact, I have been part of several research partnerships that cost $0 in out-of-pocket research expenses for me, and required a minimal time commitment for my partner and their staff. Typically this situation arose if the study entailed a small change in organizational procedure, such as randomizing communication that was not already being randomized. In addition, I should underscore that Step 5 focuses on acquiring *new* funding, yet it is possible that either the researcher and/or practitioner will already have a grant to cover study costs.

Last, it is important to acknowledge that lack of funding (perhaps due to unsuccessful funding applications, or previously promised funding that falls through, or some other reason) can certainly be a barrier to new research partnerships. This possibility should be acknowledged when putting plans into writing in Step 3 (i.e., this possibility can be discussed in the section that covers the process for ending the partnership).

STEP 6: COLLECT DATA, INCLUDING
POSSIBLY A PILOT STUDY

Some research partnerships entail new data collection, whereas others do not (for instance, this latter case may involve analyzing existing administrative datasets). During Step 6 collaborators will need to finalize several details – who's involved with any new data collection, how and when will it be conducted, what specific types of data will be collected and used, when data collection will end, and any details relevant for pre-analysis plans.

In addition, there are a few other considerations to keep in mind at this point. One is that, if at all possible, parties should plan to spend time at the data collection sites themselves and also conduct a pilot study in advance of full-study implementation. Second, even if all parties involved in the partnership are not actively involved with the data collection, they should be in regular communication throughout the entire process. A wide variety of errors can arise during implementation (see Karlan and Appel (2016) Chapters 4 and 5 for an overview), and so all parties want to be in active communication to ensure that implementation and data collection are proceeding as planned. If an experiment is involved, this includes making sure that randomization has occurred correctly. Last, it is important to make sure that data collection proceeds until the pre-arranged stopping rule, unless some extenuating circumstance arises.

STEP 7: ANALYZE DATA AND PRESENT RESULTS

The process for analyzing data and writing up results is something that partners should talk about when they put plans into writing during Step 3. While researchers may be accustomed to taking the lead on tasks like these, many practitioners want to be actively involved as well. In addition, those earlier conversations should have discussed the form that write-ups will take. While researchers are often used to writing papers or book manuscripts that go through peer review, practitioners may highly value a memo, policy brief, and/or short presentation.

In addition, echoing the point mentioned in Step 2, all parties involved should be prepared for the possibility that the findings are not what they would have hoped for – the evidence does not show program effectiveness, or does not provide support for a key hypothesis, and so on. This is why it is useful, early on, to talk about the possibility of doing more than one study, which brings me to Step 8.

STEP 8: FOLLOW-UP AND POSSIBLY DO ANOTHER STUDY TOGETHER

Conducting research partnerships is not only about the research itself – it also entails continual collaborative relationship-building. Interaction throughout the process is critical, including during and after the data analysis process to collectively make sense of the results and what they mean for the problem at hand. What new theoretical understanding have we reached? What evidence have we learned that a program or intervention works or does not work? How might the results apply in a different context? In addition, given that partners have already built a new collaborative relationship, and given that any individual research study is never the final word on a topic, partners may wish to discuss the possibility of doing another study together as well.

References

Abaluck, Jason, Laura H. Kwong, Ashley Styczynski, et al. 2021. "Normalizing Community Mask-Wearing: A Cluster Randomized Trial in Bangladesh." NBER Working Paper 28734: www.nber.org/system/files/working_papers/w28734/w28734.pdf

Ahlquist, John and Margaret Levi. 2014. *In the Interest of Others: Organizations and Social Activism.* Princeton University Press.

Albertson, Bethany and Shana Kushner Gadarian. 2015. *Anxious Politics: Democratic Citizenship in a Threatening World.* Cambridge University Press.

Alexander, Jennifer. 2000. "Adaptive Strategies of Nonprofit Human Service Organizations in an Era of Devolution and New Public Management." *Nonprofit Management and Leadership* 10: 287–303.

Allen, Danielle. 2003. *Talking to Strangers.* University of Chicago Press.

Allen, Danielle. 2013. "A Connected Society." *Soundings: A Journal of Politics and Culture* 53: 103–113.

Allen, Danielle. 2016. "Toward a Connected Society." In Earl Lewis and Nancy Cantor (Eds.) *Our Compelling Interests* (pp. 71–105). Princeton University Press.

Allen, Danielle. 2023. *Justice by Means of Democracy.* University of Chicago Press.

American Academy of Arts and Sciences (AAAS). 2020. *Our Common Purpose: Reinventing American Democracy for the 21st Century.* American Academy of Arts and Sciences (AAAS)

Anderson, Elizabeth. 2006. "The Epistemology of Democracy." *Episteme* 3: 8–22.

Andrews, Kenneth T., Marshall Ganz, Matthew Baggetta, Hahrie Han, and Chaeyoon Lim. 2010. "Leadership, Membership, and Voice: Civic Associations That Work." *American Journal of Sociology* 115: 1191–1242.

Anzia, Sarah F. 2021. "Party and Ideology in American Local Government: An Appraisal." *Annual Review of Political Science* 24: 133–150.

Baggetta, Matthew, Hahrie Han, and Kenneth T. Andrews. 2013. "Leading Associations: How Individual Characteristics and Team Dynamics Generate Committed Leaders." *American Sociological Review* 78: 544–573.

Balliet, Daniel. 2010. "Communication and Cooperation in Social Dilemmas: A Meta-Analytic Review." *Journal of Conflict Resolution* 54: 39–57.

Bartunek, Jean M. 2007. "Academic-Practitioner Collaboration Need Not Require Joint or Relevant Research: Toward a Relational Scholarship of Integration." *Academy of Management Journal* 50: 1323–1333.

Baumgartner, Frank and Beth Leech. 1998. *Basic Interests*. Princeton University Press.

Bednarek, Angela T., Carina Wyborn, Chris Cvitanovic, et al. 2018. "Boundary Spanning at the Science-Policy Interface: The Practitioners' Perspectives." *Sustainability Science* 13: 1175–1183.

Bednarek, Angela and Vivian Tseng. 2022. "A Global Movement for Engaged Research." *Issues in Science and Technology* 38: 53–56.

Berry, Jeffrey M. 1999. *The New Liberalism: The Rising Power of Citizen Groups*. Brookings Institution Press.

Bogenschneider, Karen and Tom J. Corbett. 2010. *Evidence-Based Policymaking: Insights from Policy-Minded Researchers and Research-Minded Policymakers*. Taylor & Francis.

Bogenschneider, Karen, Elizabeth Day, and Emily Parrott. 2019. Revisiting Theory on Research Use: Turning to Policymakers for Fresh Insights. *American Psychologist* 74: 778–793.

Bowers, Jake and Paul F. Testa. 2019. "Better Government, Better Science: The Promise of and Challenges Facing the Evidence-Informed Policy Movement." *Annual Review of Political Science* 22: 521–542.

Boyer, Ernest L. 2016 [1990]. *Scholarship Reconsidered*. Jossey-Bass.

Brady, Henry E., Kay Lehman Schlozman, and Sidney Verba. 1999. "Prospecting for Participants: Rational Expectations and the Recruitment of Political Activists." *American Political Science Review* 93: 153–168.

Broockman, David E. and Joshua Kalla. 2016. "Durably Reducing Transphobia: A Field Experiment on Door-to-Door Canvassing." *Science* 352: 220–224.

Brossard, Dominique and Bruce V. Lewenstein. 2009. "A Critical Appraisal of Models of Public Understanding of Science: Using Practice to Inform Theory." In LeeAnn Kahlor and Patricia A. Stout (Eds.) *Communicating Science: New Agendas in Communication* (pp. 11–39). Routledge.

Brownson, Ross C., Charles Royer, Reid Ewing, and Timothy D. McBride. 2006. "Researchers and Policymakers: Travelers in Parallel Universes." *American Journal of Preventive Medicine* 30: 164–172.

Busby, Ethan. 2021. *Should You Stay Away from Strangers?* Cambridge University Press.

Bush, Vannevar. 1945. *Science: The Endless Frontier*. United States Government Printing Office.

Butler, Daniel M. 2019. "Facilitating Field Experiments at the Subnational Level." *Journal of Politics* 81: 371–376.

Butler, Daniel M., Craig Volden, Adam M. Dynes, and Boris Shor. 2017. "Ideology, Learning, and Policy Diffusion: Experimental Evidence." *American Journal of Political Science* 61: 37–49.

Cairney, Paul. 2016. *The Politics of Evidence-Based Policy Making*. Palgrave.

Cartwright, Nancy and Jeremy Hardie. 2012. *Evidence-Based Policy: A Practical Guide to Doing It Better*. Oxford University Press.

Casciaro, Tiziana and Miguel Sousa Lobo. 2008. "When Competence Is Irrelevant: The Role of Interpersonal Affect in Task-Related Ties." *Administrative Science Quarterly* 53: 655–684.

Chen, Serena, David Shechter, and Shelly Chaiken. 1996. "Getting at the Truth or Getting Along: Accuracy- Versus Impression-Motivated Heuristic and Systematic Processing." *Journal of Personality and Social Psychology* 71: 262–275.

Christopherson, Elizabeth Good, Dietram A. Scheufele, and Brooke Smith. 2018. "The Civic Science Imperative." *Stanford Social Innovation Review*. Spring.

Coburn, Cynthia E. and William R. Penuel. 2016. "Research-Practice Partnerships in Education: Outcomes, Dynamics, and Open Questions." *Educational Researcher* 45: 48–54.

Cohen, Wesley M. and Daniel A. Levinthal. 1990. "Absorptive Capacity: A New Perspective on Learning and Innovation." *Administrative Science Quarterly* 35: 128–152.

Cook, Fay Lomax, Michael X. Delli Carpini, and Lawrence R. Jacobs. 2007. "Who Deliberates? Discursive Participation in America." Institute for Policy Research Working Paper.

Cooper, Caren B., Chris L. Hawn, Lincoln R. Larson, et al. 2021. "Inclusion in Citizen Science: The Conundrum of Rebranding." *Science* 372: 1386–1388.

Cramer, Katherine. 2016. *The Politics of Resentment: Rural Consciousness in Wisconsin and the Rise of Scott Walker*. University of Chicago Press.

Cramer, Katherine J. and Benjamin Toff. 2017. "The Fact of Experience: Rethinking Political Knowledge and Civic Competence." *Perspectives on Politics* 15: 754–770.

Cramer Walsh, Katherine. 2004. *Talking about Politics: Informal Groups and Social Identity in American Life*. University of Chicago Press.

Crowley, D. Max, J. Taylor Scott, Elizabeth C. Long, et al. 2021. "Lawmakers' Use of Scientific Evidence Can Be Improved." *Proceedings of the National Academy of Sciences* 118.

Delli Carpini, Michael X. and Scott Keeter. 1996. *What Americans Know about Politics and Why It Matters*. Yale University Press.

Dietz, Thomas. 2013. "Bringing Values and Deliberation to Science Communication." *PNAS* 110: 14081–14087.

Dobbins, Maureen, Steven E. Hanna, Donna Ciliska, et al. 2009. "A Randomized Controlled Trial Evaluating the Impact of Knowledge Translation and Exchange Strategies." *Implementation Science* 4.

Douglas, Heather E. 2009. *Science, Policy, and the Value-Free Ideal*. University of Pittsburgh Press.

Druckman, James N. 2015. "Communicating Policy-Relevant Science." *PS: Political Science and Politics* 48: 58–69.

Druckman, James N. and Donald P. Green. 2021. "A New Era of Experimental Political Science." In James N. Druckman and Donald P. Green (Eds.) *Advances in Experimental Political Science* (pp. 1–15). Cambridge University Press.

Eagly, Alice H. and Steven J. Karau. 2002. "Role Congruity Theory of Prejudice toward Female Leaders." *Psychological Review* 109: 573–598.

Einstein, Katherine Levine, David M. Glick, and Maxwell Palmer. 2019. "City Learning: Evidence of Policy Information Diffusion from a Survey of U.S. Mayors." *Political Research Quarterly* 72: 243–258.

Ely, Robin J. and David A. Thomas. 2001. "Cultural Diversity at Work: The Effects of Diversity Perspectives on Work Group Processes and Outcomes." *Administrative Science Quarterly* 46: 229–273.

Epley, Nicholas and Juliana Schroeder. 2014. "Mistakenly Seeking Solitude." *Journal of Experimental Psychology General* 143: 1980–1999.

Epstein, Steven. 1995. "The Construction of Lay Expertise: AIDS Activism and the Forging of Credibility in the Reform of Clinical Trials." *Science, Technology, & Human Values* 20: 408–437.

Eveland, William P., Alyssa C. Morey, and Myiah J. Hutchens. 2011. "Beyond Deliberation: New Directions for the Study of Informal Political Conversation from a Communication Perspective." *Journal of Communication* 61: 1082–1103.

Farrell, Caitlin C., Cynthia E. Coburn, and Seenae Chong. 2019. "Under What Conditions Do School Districts Learn from External Partners? The Role of Absorptive Capacity." *American Educational Research Journal* 56: 955–994.

Farrell, Henry and Cosma Rohilla Shalizi. 2015. "Pursuing Cognitive Democracy." In Danielle Allen and Jennifer S. Light (Eds.) *From Voice to Influence* (pp. 211–231). University of Chicago Press.

Fishkin, James S. 2011. *When the People Speak: Deliberative Democracy and Public Consultation.* Oxford University Press.

Fiske, Susan T., Amy J. C. Cuddy, and Peter Glick. 2007. Universal Dimensions of Social Cognition: Warmth and Competence." *TRENDS in Cognitive Science* 11: 77–83.

Fiske, Susan T., Amy J. C. Cuddy, Peter Glick, and Jun Xu. 2002. "A Model of (Often Mixed) Stereotype Content: Competence and Warmth Respectively Follow from Perceived Status and Competition." *Journal of Personality and Social Psychology* 82: 878–902.

Fiske, Susan T. and Cydney Dupree. 2014. "Gaining Trust as well as Respect in Communicating to Motivated Audiences about Science Topics." *PNAS* 111: 13593–13597.

Frohlich, Norman and Joe A. Oppenheimer. 1992. *Choosing Justice: An Experimental Approach to Ethical Theory.* University of California Press.

Frohlich, Norman, Joe A. Oppenheimer, and Oran R. Young. 1971. *Political Leadership and Collective Goods.* Princeton University Press.

Fung, Archon. 2003. "Associations and Democracy: Between Theories, Hopes, and Realities." *Annual Review of Sociology* 29: 515–539.

Galinsky, Adam D., Andrew R. Todd, Astrid C. Homan, et al. 2015. "Maximizing the Gains and Minimizing the Pains of Diversity: A Policy Perspective." *Perspectives on Psychological Science* 10: 742–748.

Gamoran, Adam. 2018. "Evidence-Based Policy in the Real World: A Cautionary View." *Annals of the American Association of Political and Social Science* 678: 180–191.

Ganz, Marshall. 2000. "Resources and Resourcefulness: Strategic Capacity in the Unionization of California Agriculture, 1959–1966." *American Journal of Sociology* 105: 1003–1062.

Ganz, Marshall. 2009. *Why David Sometimes Wins*. Oxford University Press.

García Bedolla, Lisa and Melissa R. Michelson. 2012. *Mobilizing Inclusion: Transforming the Electorate through Get-Out-the-Vote Campaigns*. Yale University Press.

Gastil, John and Peter Levine (Eds.). 2005. *The Deliberative Democracy Handbook: Strategies for Effective Civic Engagement in the Twenty-First Century*. Jossey-Boss.

Gazley, Beth. 2017. "The Current State of Interorganizational Collaboration: Lessons for Human Service Research and Management." *Human Service Organizations: Management, Leadership, and Governance* 41: 1–5.

Gerring, John. 2017. *Case Study Research: Principles and Practices*. Cambridge University Press.

Goldman, Alvin. 2001. "Experts: Which Ones Should You Trust?" *Philosophy and Phenomenological Research* 63: 85–110.

Goss, Kristin A. 2006. *Disarmed: The Missing Movement for Gun Control in America*. University of Chicago Press.

Green, Donald P. and Alan S. Gerber. 2010. "Introduction to Social Pressure and Voting: New Experimental Evidence." *Political Behavior* 32: 331–336.

Green, Donald P. and Alan S. Gerber. 2019. *Get Out the Vote: How to Increase Voter Turnout*. Brookings Institution Press.

Habermas, Jurgen. 1989. *The Structural Transformation of the Public Sphere*. MIT Press.

Hall, Kara L., Amanda L. Vogel, Grace C. Huang, et al. 2018. "The Science of Team Science: A Review of the Empirical Evidence and Research Gaps on Collaboration in Science." *American Psychologist* 73: 532–548.

Hall, Nina. 2022. *Transnational Advocacy in the Digital Era: Think Global, Act Local*. Oxford University Press.

Han, Hahrie. 2009. *Moved to Action: Motivation, Participation, and Inequality in American Politics*. Stanford University Press.

Han, Hahrie. 2014. *How Organizations Develop Activists*. Oxford University Press.

Han, Hahrie and Carina Barnett-Loro. 2018. "To Support a Stronger Climate Movement, Focus Research on Building Collective Power." *Frontiers in Communication* 3.

Han, Hahrie, Elizabeth McKenna, and Michelle Oyakawa. 2021. *Prisms of the People: Power & Organizing in Twenty-First-Century America*. University of Chicago Press.

Hayes, Danny and Jennifer L. Lawless. 2021. *News Hole: The Demise of Local Journalism and Political Engagement*. Cambridge University Press.

Haynes, Abby S., James A. Gillespie, Gemma E. Derrick, et al. 2011. "Galvanizers, Guides, Champions, and Shields: The Many Ways That Policymakers Use Public Health Researchers." *The Milbank Quarterly* 89: 564–598.

Hersh, Eitan. 2020. *Politics Is for Power*. Scribner.

Hilgartner, Stephen, J. Benjamin Hurlbut, and Sheila Jasanoff. 2021. "Was 'Science' on the Ballot?" *Science* 371: 893–894.

Hird, John A. 2005. *Power, Knowledge, and Politics: Policy Analysis in the States.* Cambridge University Press.

Hofstadter, Richard. 1966. *Anti-intellectualism in American Life.* Knopf.

Huckfeldt, Robert, Paul E. Johnson, and John Sprague. 2004. *Political Disagreement: The Survival of Diverse Opinions within Communication Networks.* Cambridge University Press.

Insel, Thomas. 2022. "What American Health Care Is Missing." *The Atlantic,* February 13.

Jacobs, Lawrence R., Fay Lomax Cook, and Michael X. Delli Carpini. 2009. *Talking Together: Public Deliberation and Political Participation in America.* University of Chicago Press.

Kalla, Joshua L., Adam Seth Levine, and David E. Broockman. 2022. "Personalizing Moral Reframing in Interpersonal Conversation: A Field Experiment." *Journal of Politics* 84: 1239–1243.

Karpowitz, Christopher F., Tali Mendelberg, and Lee Shaker. 2012. "Gender Inequality in Deliberative Participation." *American Political Science Review* 106: 533–547.

Karlan, Dean and Jacob Appel. 2016. *Failing in the Field.* Princeton University Press.

Klar, Samara and Yanna Krupnikov. 2016. *Independent Politics: How American Disdain for Parties Leads to Political Inaction.* Cambridge University Press.

Kuklinski, James H. and Paul J. Quirk. 2001. "Conceptual Foundations of Citizen Competence." *Political Behavior* 23: 285–311.

Kumar, Amit and Nicholas Epley. 2018. "Undervaluing Gratitude: Expressers Misunderstand the Consequences of Showing Appreciation." *Psychological Science* 29: 1423–1435.

Lacombe, Matthew J. 2021. *Firepower: How the NRA Turned Gun Owners into a Political Force.* Princeton University Press.

Leary, Mark R. 2010. "Affiliation, Acceptance, and Belonging: The Pursuit of Interpersonal Connection." In Susan T. Fiske, Daniel T. Gilbert, and Gardner Lindzey (Eds.) *Handbook of Social Psychology* (pp. 864–897). John Wiley & Sons, Inc.

Levendusky, Matthew S. and Dominik A. Stecula. 2021. *We Need to Talk: How Cross-Party Dialogue Reduces Affective Polarization.* Cambridge University Press.

Levine, Adam Seth. 2015. *American Insecurity: Why Our Economic Fears Lead to Political Inaction.* Princeton University Press.

Levine, Adam Seth. 2019. "Why Social Science? Because It Tells Us How to Create More Engaged Citizens." *Why Social Science?* Blog.

Levine, Adam Seth. 2020a. "Research Impact Through Matchmaking (RITM): Why and How to Connect Researchers and Practitioners." *PS: Political Science & Politics* 53: 265–269.

Levine, Adam Seth. 2020b. "Why Do Practitioners Want to Connect with Researchers? Evidence from a Field Experiment." *PS: Political Science & Politics* 53: 712–717.

Levine, Adam Seth. 2021a. "How to Form Organizational Partnerships." In James N. Druckman and Donald P. Green (Eds.) *Advances in Experimental Political Science* (pp. 199–216). Cambridge University Press.

Levine, Adam Seth. 2021b. "Single Conversations Expand Practitioners' Use of Research: Evidence from a Field Experiment." *PS: Political Science & Politics* 54: 432–437.

Levine, Adam Seth. 2022. "Unmet Desire." *Issues in Science and Technology.* Spring.

Levine, Adam Seth and Elizabeth Day. 2023. "Practitioners' Demand for Research." Working Paper.

Levine, Adam Seth and J. Nathan Matias. 2021. "How to Generate Research Ideas That Impact Society." *Inside Higher Ed.* April 22.

Levine, Adam Seth and Danielle Mulligan. 2020. "Chapter Matchmaking." research4impact and Scholars Strategy Network Technical Paper.

Levine, Peter. 2022. *What Should We Do? A Theory of Civic Life.* Oxford University Press.

Long, Janet C., Frances C. Cunningham, Peter Carswell, and Jeffrey Braithwaite. 2014. "Patterns of Collaboration in Complex Networks: The Example of a Translational Research Network." *BMC Health Services Research* 14: 225.

Loyd, Denise Lewin, Cynthia S. Wang, Katherine W. Phillips, and Robert B. Lount, Jr. 2013. "Social Category Diversity Promotes Premeeting Elaboration: The Role of Relationship Focus." *Organization Science* 24: 757–772.

Lungeanu, Alina, Yun Huang, and Noshir S. Contractor. 2014. "Understanding the Assembly of Interdisciplinary Teams and Its Impact on Performance." *Journal of Informetrics* 8: 59–70.

Lupia, Arthur. 2006. "How Elitism Undermines the Study of Voter Competence." *Critical Review: A Journal of Politics and Society* 18: 217–232.

Lupia, Arthur. 2013. "Communicating Science in Politicized Environments." *Proceedings of the National Academy of Sciences* 110: 14048–14054.

Lupia, Arthur. 2016. *Uninformed: Why People Know So Little about Politics and What We Can Do about It.* Oxford University Press.

Lupia, Arthur, Yanna Krupnikov, and Adam Seth Levine. 2013. "Beyond Facts and Norms: How Psychological Transparency Threatens and Restores Deliberation's Legitimating Potential." *Southern California Law Review* 86: 459–493.

Lupia, Arthur and Mathew D. McCubbins. 1998. *The Democratic Dilemma: Can Citizens Learn What They Need to Know?* Cambridge University Press.

Mansbridge, Jane J. 1983. *Beyond Adversary Democracy.* University of Chicago Press.

Maruyama, Geoffrey and Lara Westerhof. 2018. "Education: Building Trusted Partnerships with Schools." In Linda R. Tropp (Ed.) *Making Research Matter* (pp. 123–140). American Psychological Association.

McGinty, Emma E., Sameer Siddiqi, Sarah Linden, Joshua Horwitz, and Shannon Frattaroli. 2019. "Improving the Use of Evidence in Public Health Policy Development, Enactment, and Implementation: A Multiple-Case Study." *Health Education Research* 34: 129–144.

McKenna, Elizabeth and Hahrie Han. 2014. *Groundbreakers: How Obama's 2.2 Million Volunteers Transformed Campaigning in America*. Oxford University Press.

Michener, Jamila. 2018. *Fragmented Democracy: Medicaid, Federalism, and Unequal Politics*. Cambridge University Press.

Mill, John Stuart. 1956. *On Liberty*. Bobbs-Merrill. (Original published 1859).

Miller, Graham N. S., Freda B. Lynn, and Laila I. McCloud. 2021. "By Lack of Reciprocity: Positioning Historically Black Colleges and Universities in the Organizational Field of Higher Education." *The Journal of Higher Education* 92: 194–226.

Mooney, Chris and Sheril Kirshenbaum. 2009. *Unscientific America: How Scientific Illiteracy Threatens Our Future*. Basic Books.

Munson, Ziad. 2009. *The Making of Pro-life Activists: How Social Movement Mobilization Works*. University of Chicago Press.

Murray, Vic. 1998. "Interorganizational Collaborations in the Nonprofit Sector." In J. M. Shafirtz (Ed.) *International Encyclopedia of Public Policy and Administration, Vol. 2* (pp. 1192–1196). Westview.

Mutz, Diana. 2006. *Hearing the Other Side: Deliberative Versus Participatory Democracy*. Cambridge University Press.

Neblo, Michael A., Kevin M. Esterling, Ryan P. Kennedy, David M. J. Lazer, and Anand Sokhey. 2010. "Who Wants to Deliberate – And Why?" *American Political Science Review* 104: 566–583.

Neblo, Michael A., Kevin M. Esterling, and David M. J. Lazer. 2019. *Politics with the People: Building A Directly Representative Democracy*. Cambridge University Press.

Nichols, Tom. 2017. *The Death of Expertise*. Oxford University Press.

Nutley, Sandra M., Isabel Walter, and Huw T. O. Davies. 2007. *Using Evidence: How Research Can Inform Public Services*. The Policy Press.

Nyhan, Brendan, John Sides, and Joshua Tucker. 2015. "APSA as Amplifier: How to Encourage and Promote Public Voices within Political Science." *PS: Political Science & Politics*, 48: 90–93.

Ober, Josiah. 2008. *Democracy and Knowledge*. Princeton University Press.

Oliver, Kathryn, Simon Innvar, Theo Lorenc, Jenny Woodman, and James Thomas. 2014. "A Systematic Review of Barriers to and Facilitators of the Use of Research Evidence by Policymakers." *BMC Health Services Research* 14: 1–12.

Olson, Mancur. 1965. *The Logic of Collective Action*. Harvard University Press.

Oreskes, Naomi. 2019. *Why Trust Science?* Princeton University Press.

Ostrom, Elinor. 1990. *Governing the Commons: The Evolution of Institutions for Collective Action*. Cambridge University Press.

Ostrom, Elinor. 2010. "Beyond Markets and States: Polycentric Governance of Complex Economic Systems." *American Economic Review* 100: 641–672.

Page, Scott E. 2017. *The Diversity Bonus*. Princeton University Press.

Palinkas, Lawrence A. and Haluk Soydan. 2011. *Translation and Implementation of Evidence-Based Practice*. Oxford University Press.

Pamuk, Zeynep. 2021. *Politics and Expertise: How to Use Science in a Democratic Society*. Princeton University Press.

Pauli, Benjamin J. 2019. *Flint Fights Back: Environmental Justice and Democracy in the Flint Water Crisis.* MIT Press.

Penuel, William R. and Daniel J. Gallagher. 2017. *Creating Research-Practice Partnerships in Education.* Harvard Education Press.

Peterson, Mark. A. 2018. "In the Shadow of Politics: The Pathways of Research Evidence to Health Policy Making." *Journal of Health Politics, Policy and Law,* 43: 341–376.

Phillips, Katherine W. 2017. "What Is the Real Value of Diversity in Organizations? Questioning Our Assumptions." In Scott E. Page (Ed.) *The Diversity Bonus* (pp. 223–245). Princeton University Press.

Pielke Jr., Roger A. 2007. *The Honest Broker: Making Sense of Science in Policy and Politics.* Cambridge University Press.

Public Health on Call Podcast. 2021. "A Vaccine with That Haircut? Barber Shops and the Fight Against Covid-19." July 28.

Putnam, Robert D. 2001. *Bowling Alone: The Collapse and Revival of American Democracy.* Simon and Schuster.

Putnam, Robert D. and Lewis M. Feldstein. 2003. *Better Together.* Simon & Schuster.

Ridgeway, Cecilia L. 2001. "Social Status and Group Structure." In Michael A. Hogg and R. Scott Tindale (Eds.) *Blackwell Handbook of Social Psychology: Group Processes* (pp. 352–375). Blackwell Publishers.

Ridgeway, Cecilia L., Elizabeth Heger Boyle, Kathy J. Kuipers, and Dawn T. Robinson. 1998. "How Do Status Beliefs Develop? The Role of Resources and Interactional Experience." *American Sociological Review* 63: 331–350.

Rosenstone, Steven J. and John Mark Hansen. 1993. *Mobilization, Participation, and Democracy in America.* Macmillan Publishing Company.

Rothenberg, Lawrence S. 1992. *Linking Citizens to Government: Interest Group Politics at Common Cause.* Cambridge University Press.

Russell, Jill, Trisha Greenhalgh, Petra Boynton, and Marcia Rigby. 2004. "Soft Networks for Bridging the Gap between Research and Practice: Illuminative Evaluation of CHAIN." *BMJ* 328: 1174.

Salisbury, Robert H. 1969. "An Exchange Theory of Interest Groups." *Midwest Journal of Political Science* 13: 1–32.

Sanders, Lynn. 1997. "Against Deliberation." *Political Theory* 25: 347–376.

Sandstrom, Gillian M. and Erica J. Boothby. 2020. "Why Do People Avoid Talking to Strangers? A Mini Meta-Analysis of Predicted Fears and Actual Experiences Talking to a Stranger." *Self and Identity* 20: 47–71.

Sarewitz, Daniel. 2016. "Saving Science." *The New Atlantis.* Spring/Summer: 5–40.

Scheufele, Dietram A. 2014. "Science Communication as Political Communication." *PNAS* 111: 13585–13592.

Sides, John. 2011. "The Political Scientist as a Blogger." *PS: Political Science and Politics* 44: 267–271.

Sinclair, Betsy. 2012. *The Social Citizen: Peer Networks and Political Behavior.* University of Chicago Press.

Skocpol, Theda. 2003. *Diminished Democracy.* University of Oklahoma Press.

Skocpol, Theda. 2014. "How the Scholars Strategy Network Helps Academics Gain Public Influence." *Perspectives on Politics* 12:695–703.

Small, Mario. 2009. "How Many Cases Do I Need? On Science and the Logic of Case Selection in Field-Based Research." *Ethnography* 10: 5–38.

Stasser, Garold, Dennis D. Stewart, and Gwen M. Wittenbaum. 1995. "Expert Roles and Information Exchange during Discussion: The Importance of Knowing Who Knows What." *Journal of Experimental Social Psychology* 31: 244-265.

Stasser, Garold, and William Titus. 2003. "Hidden Profiles: A Brief History." *Psychological Inquiry* 14: 304–313.

Stokes, Donald E. 1997. *Pasteur's Quadrant: Basic Science and Technological Innovation*. Brookings Institution Press.

Strolovitch, Dara. 2007. *Affirmative Advocacy: Race, Class, and Gender in Interest Group Politics*. University of Chicago Press.

Sunstein, Cass R. and Reid Hastie. 2015. *Wiser*. Harvard Business Review Press.

Teles, Steven and Mark Schmitt. 2011. "The Elusive Craft of Evaluating Advocacy." *Stanford Social Innovation Review*.

Tropp, Linda R. (Ed.). 2018. *Making Research Matter: A Psychologist's Guide to Public Engagement*. American Psychological Association.

Vacca, Raffaele, Christopher McCarty, Michael Conlon, and David R. Nelson. 2015. "Designing a CSTA-Based Social Network Intervention to Foster Cross-Disciplinary Team Science." *Clinical and Translational Science* 8: 281–289.

Van Dijk, Hans, Bertolt Meyer, Marloes van Engen, and Denise Lewin Loyd. 2017. "Microdynamics in Diverse Teams: A Review and Integration of the Diversity and Stereotyping Literatures." *Academy of Management Annals* 11: 517–557.

Van Dyke, Nella and Bryan Amos. 2017. "Social Movement Coalitions: Formation, Longevity, and Success." *Sociology Compass* 11: e12489.

Verba, Sidney, Kay Lehman Schlozman, and Henry Brady. 1995. *Voice and Equality*. Harvard University Press.

Vorauer, Jacquie D., Annette Gagnon, and Stacey J. Sasaki. 2009. "Salient Intergroup Ideology and Intergroup Interaction." *Psychological Science* 20: 838–845.

Wagner, Richard. 1966. "Pressure Groups and Political Entrepreneurs." *Papers on Non-Market Decision Making* 1: 161–170.

Walker, Jack L., Jr. 1991. *Mobilizing Interest Groups in America: Patrons, Professions, and Social Movements*. University of Michigan Press.

Wang, Dan J. and Sarah A. Soule. 2012. "Social Movement Organizational Collaboration: Networks of Learning and the Diffusion of Protest Tactics, 1960–1995." *American Journal of Sociology* 117: 1674–1722.

Wang, Dan J. and Sarah A. Soule. 2016. "Tactical Innovation in Social Movements: The Effects of Peripheral and Multi-Issue Protest." *American Sociological Review* 81: 517–548.

Warren, Mark R. 2001. *Dry Bones Rattling: Community Building to Revitalize American Democracy*. Princeton University Press.

Warren, Rueben C., Lachlan Forrow, David Augustin Hodge, Sr., and Robert D. Truog. 2020. "Trustworthiness before Trust – Covid-19 Vaccine Trials and the Black Community." *The New England Journal of Medicine* 383: e121.

Weiss, Carol H. 1989. "Congressional Committees as Users of Analysis." *Journal of Policy Analysis and Management* 8: 411–431.

Weiss, Carol H. and Bucuvalas, Michael J. 1980. *Social Science Research and Decision-Making.* Columbia University Press.

Wilson, James Q. 1973. *Political Organizations.* Basic Books.

Wojciszke, Bodgan. 1994. "Multiple Meanings of Behavior: Construing Actions in Terms of Competence or Morality." *Journal of Personality and Social Psychology* 67: 222–232.

Wu, Lingfei, Dashun Wang, and James A. Evans. 2019. "Large Teams Develop and Small Teams Disrupt Science and Technology." *Nature* 566: 378–382.

Wyatt, Robert O., Elihu Katz, and Joohan Kim. 2000. "Bridging the Spheres: Political and Personal Conversation in Public and Private Spaces." *Journal of Communication* 50: 71–92.

Yin, Robert K. 2003. *Case Study Research: Design and Methods.* Sage Publications.

Index